Kerry Downes

English Baroque
Architecture

A. ZWEMMER LTD

London 1966

TO MY WIFE

CONTENTS

LIST OF PLATES

LIST OF TEXT ILLUSTRATIONS

Note: plans are approximate. Wherever possible a scale of 100 ft is given and North is indicated.

ACKNOWLEDGEMENTS

The following plates are reproduced by gracious permission of Her Majesty the Queen: 3, 5, 260 (Royal Library photos), 109 (Ministry of Public Building and Works photo), 4, 6, 7, 9, 73, Fig. 19a.

Drawings and other objects are reproduced by permission of the following: the Warden and Fellows and Librarian of All Souls College, Oxford, Pls 74–82, 549, Figs 4, 10, 16, 19b, 20, 31; the Trustees of the Barber Institute of Fine Arts, University of Birmingham, Pl. 303; Bodleian Library, Oxford, Pl. 217; the Trustees of the Bristol Municipal Charities, Fig. 39b; the Trustees of the British Museum, Pls 130, 133, 147, 171, 298, 301, 368, 497, 514, Figs 9, 17, 24, 58; Guildhall Library, London, Pl. 406, Fig. 7; the Archbishop of Canterbury and the Trustees of Lambeth Palace Library, Fig. 49; the Provost and Fellows of the Queen's College, Oxford, Fig. 64; Royal Institute of British Architects, Pls 145–6, 553, Fig. 15; the Trustees of Sir John Soane's Museum, Figs 12, 13; Victoria and Albert Museum, Pls 214, 268, Fig. 40; the Provost and Fellows of Worcester College, Oxford, Pl. 545, Figs 30, 60–2, 65; Mr Sidney F. Sabin, Pl. 383.

The following credits are also due: Bath Corporation (Mowbray Green negatives), Pl. 318; G. Bell and Sons Ltd, Fig. 14; Country Life Ltd, Pls 118, 121 and 124 (from *Decorative Painting in England*, Vol. I, by Edward Croft-Murray), Fig. 2 (from St John Hope's *Windsor Castle*) and Pls 139, 230, 292, 389, 569, 573; Courtauld Institute of Art, Pls 25, 127, 145–6, 214, 361–2, 490, 537; Greater London Council, Pls 432–4; A. F. Kersting, Pls 122, 297, 412, 544; National Buildings Record, Pls 22, 107, 126, 223, 243, 316, 317, 382, 416, 450, 456, 502, 509, 511, 513, 516–17, Fig. 54; Oxford University Press, Pl. 299; Royal Commission on Historical Monuments, by permission of the Controller of Her Majesty's Stationery Office, Pls 526, 528–9, 531; Thomas Photos, Oxford, Pl. 105; Warburg Institute, Pls 94, 280–2, 430, 575.

Most of the other illustrations are the author's. Figs 2, 7–9, 14, 17, 28, 45–6, 52, 54–6, 60 were re-drawn by Mr John Bancroft.

PREFACE

The study of a style is not easy to write; it necessitates broad generalizations and invites rash ones, and only in illustrations is it possible to see the sum of the varied formal and inconographical tendencies that make up English Baroque. Although the material has grown dramatically during its preparation, this is still meant to be a book of plates with commentary. I have accordingly left largely unexplored both philosophical considerations and the teleology of certain Baroque motifs and traits.

I have tried in an uneven field to keep the balance between great and little masters; to illustrate as much as possible that is unfamiliar without mere eccentricity, and in the text to formulate and perhaps answer questions I have not found answered – and some I have not found asked – elsewhere. In certain cases a tentative hypothesis has seemed preferable to silence; in one case confirmation arrived at the galley-proof stage.

Certain deliberate limitations seemed defensible. The subject is restricted geographically to England. Of gardens and urban layout I have said very little, because those subjects, however neglected, demand a greater amount of description and reconstruction than could be afforded. The book is of its nature based on monuments and not on archive material and divided by topics and types of building rather than by artists or by a rigid chronology; one function of an index should be to trace certain items which have obstinately refused to settle otherwise than in arbitrary positions.

I make no pretence of completeness: over the past fifteen years I have seen almost without exception all the buildings mentioned and many others which are not. My greatest debt is to the owners of houses and the custodians of churches and other buildings, so numerous that it is only practicable to thank them collectively. To those who have granted me exceptional facilities for access or photography I am especially grateful. The keepers of documents and drawings also have invariably been helpful. In the great age of tourism, when many of the great houses are again, as they were in the eighteenth century, show-places open to the public, it should be made clear that some of the buildings mentioned or illustrated are not ordinarily accessible. It is also easy for all but those who bear it to forget how much the upkeep of historic buildings costs, and while St Paul's, Blenheim and Oxford now seem safe for this century many other monuments need urgent rehabilitation or long-term endowment. Two minor but sizable houses have been demolished while this book was being set, because no grounds could be found for their economic preservation; on a higher level, Sutton Scarsdale remains as a shell and as a warning of the fate from which two of the Hawksmoor churches are not yet secure.

A book necessarily depends on the help and encouragement of many people. My thanks are due to all of them, but space allows the details only of special debts. Without the discreet and continued support of Professor Ellis Waterhouse I should not have been able to write the book. If those who have shared with me in the wisdom, example and encouragement of Professor Johannes Wilde fail to recognize their effect here the fault is entirely mine. Dr Margaret Whinney has given me constant encouragement, and on reading the book in manuscript not only suggested many minor ameliorations but also showed me how its shape, balance and clarity could be greatly improved. Miss Joan Smith resolved a collection of Delphic palimpsests into clean typescript. But inasmuch as an author is helpless without a publisher my greatest thanks are due to Mr Desmond Zwemmer, who has with equanimity allowed a small short project to grow into a large and seemingly endless one. Among those who have given me the benefit of their researches in other fields I must name Mr Geoffrey Beard, Dr Lindsay Boynton, Mr Howard Colvin, Dr Katharine Fremantle, Mr John Harris, Mr Oliver Millar and Professor Theo Lunsingh Scheurleer. Of those brave persons who shared with me circuitous and sometimes fruitless excursions to remote monuments, and long and sometimes fruitful ruminations on old problems, my most constant, tireless and invariably cheerful companion has not only tolerated most of the machinery of authorship and illustration but also confirmed her acceptance of the dedication.

BIBLIOGRAPHY

These notes include (1) most of the books on which I have more constantly relied and (2) the full titles of certain works referred to in shortened form in footnotes. As a rule, mis-statements and errors which have come to my notice in sources have been tacitly corrected. The place of publication is London unless otherwise stated.

General historical sources. Relevant documentary series include the printed *Calendars* of State Papers, Domestic (CAL. S. P. DOM.) and Treasury Papers (T.P.) and Books in the Public Record Office, and the appendixes to the Reports of the Historical Manuscripts Commission (H.M.C.). *Local histories* of the eighteenth and nineteenth centuries and guide-books often show a bias against buildings of the period. Of the Victoria County Histories (V.C.H.) the earlier volumes are in general less useful, and some counties are not yet covered. The standard edition of the valuable *Diary* of John EVELYN is now that by E. S. de Beer (Oxford, 1955). Narcissus LUTTRELL, *A brief relation of historical and state affairs* (Oxford, 1857) remains an important source in diary form. Other diarists such as PEPYS are of incidental importance, as are the accounts of contemporary travellers; these include Celia FIENNES, *Journeys* (ed. C. Morris, 1949), J. MACKY, *A journey through England and Wales* (1722) and Daniel DEFOE, *Tour through . . .Great Britain* (1724–7).

General architectural sources. The Royal Commission on Historical Monuments (R.C.H.M.) is slowly inventorizing the whole country, while the SURVEY OF LONDON is recording in greater detail the former County of London area; the early volumes of the R.C.H.M. stop at 1700 or 1714. *The Buildings of England*, by Nikolaus PEVSNER, is invaluable for the half of England so far covered; although not free from errors and omissions it provides the most accessible account. The unique twenty-volume series of the WREN SOCIETY (1924–43) contains many documents (including the building accounts of St Paul's) and drawings relating to Wren and his school. Several important publications appear in the annual volumes of the WALPOLE SOCIETY, including the complete note-books of George VERTUE, a nearly contemporary source. The study of English architecture has been revolutionized by H. M. COLVIN's *Biographical dictionary of English architects, 1660–1840* (1954). The standard histories for the period are now M. D. WHINNEY and O. MILLAR, *English art, 1625–1714* (Oxford, 1957) and Sir John SUMMERSON, *Architecture in Britain, 1530–1830* (1953, 4th revised edn 1963). G. F. WEBB, *Baroque art* (*Proceedings of the British Academy*, XXXIII, 1947), a lecture, is still fundamental.

Visual documents of the period. Colin Campbell's VITRUVIUS BRITANNICUS (3 vol., 1715, 1717, 1725) is described on pp. 10–11; executed and projected work are not always distinguished. The three volumes of L. KNYFF and J. KIP (*Britannia* or *Nouveau théâtre de la Grande-Bretagne* (1708–15) are especially useful for bird's-eye views of buildings in their original setting. W. WILLIAMS, *Oxonia depicta* (1731) is important for Oxford but requires the same caution as Campbell's work. The libraries of All Souls and Worcester Colleges, Oxford, the Gough Collections in the Bodleian, the Print Room of the Victoria and Albert Museum and the King's Topographical Collection in the British Museum (B.M.K.) contain particularly important collections of original drawings and rare prints; there is also the Crace Collection, relating to London, divided between the Map and Print Rooms of the British Museum. H. M. COLVIN's *Catalogue of architectural drawings of the 18th and 19th centuries in the Library of Worcester College* (Oxford, 1964) [COLVIN, WORCESTER COLLEGE] illustrates many drawings.

Houses. The weekly articles in COUNTRY LIFE amount to a series of short illustrated monographs on country houses of all periods. Earlier articles were collected in the ENGLISH HOMES volumes, of which Period IV, Vols. 1 and 2 and Period V, published in the 1920's, are relevant. They are complemented rather than superseded by C. HUSSEY, *English country houses, early Georgian* (1955). The Georgian house as a phenomenon both artistic and social is the subject of Sir John Summerson's Cantor lectures (*Journal of the Royal Society of Arts*, CVII, 1959). A. S. OSWALD's books on country houses of Kent (1933) and Dorset (2nd edn 1959) are important for those counties.

Churches. London is discussed by J. SUMMERSON, *Georgian London* (1945), G. COBB, *The old churches of London* (1942 and later edns) and E. and W. YOUNG, *Old London churches* (1956). Outside London M. WHIFFEN, *Stuart and Georgian churches* (1948) is supplemented by *Collins's guide to English parish churches* (1958) and B. F. L. CLARKE, *The building of the eighteenth century church* (1963).

Individual buildings. Many buildings in state custody, country houses open to the public and some churches have guide-books. Not all remain in print and there are naturally variations in quality. Major monographs are few, but the following should be noted. E. LAW, *A history of Hampton Court Palace*, III (1891). W. H. ST. J. HOPE, *Windsor Castle* (1913). F. THOMPSON, *A history of Chatsworth* (1949). D. GREEN, *Blenheim Palace* (1951). For Cannons and its builder, C. H. COLLINS BAKER and M. I. BAKER, *The life and circumstances of James Brydges, Duke of Chandos* (Oxford, 1949). For St Paul's, besides the *Wren Society*, Arthur F. E. Poley's volume of measured drawings (1932) is essential. J. LANG, *Rebuilding St Paul's* (1956) is based on all published sources. G. F. WEBB, *The letters and drawings of Nicholas Hawksmoor concerning the Mausoleum at Castle Howard*, in *Walpole Society*, XIX (1931) covers that building.

Patronage. The literature is sparse, but F. JENKINS, *Architect and patron* (1961) is useful.

Decoration and decorators. F. LENYGON, *Decoration in England, 1640–1760* (2nd edn 1927). R. GUNNIS, *A dictionary of British sculptors, 1660–1851* (1953). E. CROFT-MURRAY, *Decorative painting in England*, 1 (1962) extends as far as Thornhill but not to the Venetians, who will be covered by a second volume. M. D. WHINNEY, *Sculpture in Britain, 1530–1830* (1964).

Monographs on architects. The best guide is Colvin's *Dictionary*, described above under 'General architectural sources'. The following require mention. W. G. HISCOCK, *Henry Aldrich* (Oxford, 1960) and the relevant parts of his *Christ Church miscellany* (Oxford, 1946), both somewhat speculative as well as documentary. M. WHIFFEN, *Thomas Archer* (1950). B. LITTLE, *The life and work of James Gibbs* (1955), largely biographical. S. LANG, "Gibbs . . . his architectural sources", *Architectural Review*, CXVI (1954), pp. 20–6. J. FIELD, "Unknown early Gibbs", *ibid.*, CXXXI (1962), pp. 315–19. K. DOWNES, *Hawksmoor* (1959). S. LANG, "By Hawksmoor out of Gibbs", *Architectural Review*, CV (1949), pp. 183–90. M. D. OZINGA, *Daniel Marot* (Amsterdam, 1938) is inadequate on Marot in England. C. H. COLLINS BAKER, *Lely and the Stuart portrait painters* (1912) contains otherwise inaccessible material on Hugh May. R. T. GUNTHER, *The architecture of Sir Roger Pratt* (Oxford, 1928) is compiled from Pratt's notebooks and gives a valuable insight into seventeenth-century practice. M. D. WHINNEY, "William Talman", *Journal of the Warburg and Courtauld Institutes*, XVIII (1955), pp. 123–39. VANBRUGH, LETTERS, ed. G. F. Webb (*Works*, Nonesuch Edition, 1928, IV). L. WHISTLER, *Sir John Vanbrugh* (1938) and *The imagination of Vanbrugh* (1954). STEPHEN WREN, *Parentalia or memoirs of the Family of the Wrens* (1750) was largely compiled by Christopher, son of the architect and father of Stephen. The part relating to Sir Christopher was reprinted by E. J. Enthoven (1903) and a facsimile of the original edition is in preparation. The best modern studies of Wren are by G. F. WEBB (1937), J. SUMMERSON (1953) and E. F. SEKLER, *Wren and his place in European architecture* (1956).

I

English Baroque in general

THE SETTING

The idea of Baroque as an architectural term was conceived and developed in Germany, Austria and Italy. It was formed by scholars born and trained in those countries, and with reference to the art of those countries. Sir Christopher Wren observed that "our English Artists are dull enough at Inventions but when once a foreigne patterne is sett, they imitate soe well that commonly they exceed the originall". He was thinking of technique and craftsmanship, but with the partial exception of himself and the two younger geniuses of English Baroque architecture, Vanbrugh and Hawksmoor, his remark is a fair comment on the state, if not on the quality, of architecture during his lifetime. If "abroad" begins at Dover and Harwich, so too both the art and the thought of the Continent undergo a sea-change on the way to Great Britain. The idea of English Baroque involves modifying a Continental term, in order to fit a style which is likewise a modification of a Continental style.

This book is based on the assumption (now generally admitted) that there was an English Baroque style, and the plates are intended to do what words cannot, both to justify and to illustrate this assumption. Parallels can constantly be found between England and Europe, but only a Procrustean would dare to expect English art to behave in the same way as, say, French or Italian art. The ninety-one years of Wren's life saw changes in English architecture comparable to three whole centuries in Italy; more than that, the period began with Inigo Jones and ended with Palladianism, or more accurately the Inigo Jones revival. Baroque in Italy lasted from about 1600 to about 1740; in Central Europe it ran from the middle of the seventeenth century into the 1760's. In France and the Low Countries its life was shorter and its sway less complete, but even there, though limited in form, it fits into an historical succession that may reasonably be termed a development.

Politically, England had two revolutions during the seventeenth century. In the first she abolished the King, only to bring back his eldest son as monarch eleven years later. The second was bloodless; the martyr-king's younger son was allowed to flee, and in his place the Dutchman, William III, and Mary Stuart accepted a throne circumscribed by a constitution empirically achieved but generally practical. A parallel should not be imagined with the arts, but the fact remains that there is nothing elsewhere like either the would-be absolutist interlude of Charles II and James II between the Commonwealth and the Whig constitution, or the Baroque interlude between Jones's classicism and that of the Palladians.

Architecturally the situation is further complicated, because there was a considerable time-lag between court or capital and the provinces. Jones was the first truly literate user in England of the Italian Renaissance grammar and vocabulary, and his style, introduced through the court, took time to be assimilated. When in 1622 the scaffolding was struck on the front of his Whitehall Banqueting House (Pl. 29), a façade that would hardly be notable in Vicenza or Rome, London saw a building of a quite unprecedented classical purity and restraint. Fifty years later, when Edward Jerman rebuilt the Royal Exchange after the Great Fire, his façade showed far less classical feeling; it is a medley of disparate shapes and members, with fussy little balconies (Pl. 490). Admittedly Jerman was not a designer of genius or even of great imagination, and City taste was conservative, but there are comparable examples in the 1660's and '70's. Yet by the turn of the century Vanbrugh was designing his first great palace-house, Castle Howard, remote in Yorkshire, and English Baroque was already ripe (Pl. 227). At the same time in London Wren was dreaming of a new Whitehall in which the Banqueting House was to be dwarfed (Pl. 76).

By 1715 the time-lag had practically disappeared. The local builder or architect, though less sensitive and less learned, could usually manage the kind of detail and the relative disposition of voids and solids that Jones had introduced. The field was ready for a national style. The launching of Palladianism could not have been better timed to conquer the whole country. While many minor Baroque buildings were designed after 1715, most of the great vital works were already at least begun. Men like Benson, Campbell, Burlington and Kent took up English architecture where Jones had left it at the end of the Civil War (he died in 1652). With their insistence on Palladio and Jones, the English Baroque interlude might as well, historically speaking, never have existed.

THE GENESIS OF BAROQUE

In Italy, the source of the Renaissance, and to a lesser extent in other countries, there is a recognizable sequence from Renaissance to Mannerism and Baroque. In the pure, orderly, classical style of Alberti and Bramante there are clearly implicit rules of design, and visual and structural logic are parallel, one expressing the other. During the sixteenth century we find on the one hand the beginnings of academic classicism and the formula-designs of Palladio, Scamozzi and Giacomo della Porta, on the other hand the partial or complete disregard (though not ignorance) of logic. Examples are the dropped keystones of Giulio Romano and the columns in the vestibule of Michelangelo's Laurenziana which, instead of supporting (or appearing to support) the interior, are embedded in the walls and therefore do not even appear to carry weight.

Early seventeenth-century Rome saw the establishment of a style at once simpler and richer than that of the preceding half-century. In Italian Baroque architecture the close relation between decorative and structural elements, disrupted by the Mannerists, is re-established. Yet Baroque architecture is not infrequently logical only on its own terms; Borromini, for example, will base a design on the premise that walls are curved, not plane, surfaces.

Baroque art is less esoteric and more direct than the art of Mannerism. It is dramatic, often to the point of theatricality, and its appeal is often directly to the senses and the emotions. Its language is one of contrasts, of rhetoric, of unexpected size, position and lighting, of movement and change. Baroque detail has all the variety of invention, all the formal freedom and punning wit of Mannerism; it has also a new visual logic and a new robustness and confidence.

In England there was no comparable development. Jones and his followers such as Sir Roger Pratt exemplify a period of classicism which lasted through the Civil War and the Commonwealth. But from Jones onwards English architects could draw on the whole range of Italian, French and Netherlandish building from the early Renaissance to the Baroque of their own day; their choice was limited only by preferences due to their personalities and training, and by what they were able to see, either at first hand by travelling or through the large number of engravings (and even drawings) imported into the country. The progress of English architecture in the seventeenth century is, as Wren's remark suggests, largely progress in learning, not in sheer invention. In effect, Wren and the English Baroque architects were ready to look at anything, from Greek to Gothic, while Jones and his later worshippers narrowed their vision drastically.

The three greatest masters of English Baroque were Wren, Nicholas Hawksmoor and Sir John Vanbrugh; Hawksmoor was Wren's pupil and personal assistant, Vanbrugh was from 1702 second only to Wren, holding the Comptrollership in the Royal Works. Wren is a Baroque artist only in certain aspects of his mature and later works; the other two belong wholly to the style. To see how much England depended on the Continent we need not look beyond Wren.[1] He went abroad only once, in 1665-6, at the beginning of his career (and then to France, not to Italy), and later advised his son to weigh "the seeing of fine buildings" against the "expence and hazard" of travelling. But he brought back with him "almost all France in paper", that is, in engravings, and his library included most of the important architectural books of his time. The diary of Robert Hooke (1635–1703), his colleague in the Royal Society and in the rebuilding of the London churches, is full of references to books and engravings seen, borrowed or bought. Hawksmoor also had a good library, and there is evidence to confirm the substance of the statement in his obituary that he "was perfectly skill'd in the History of Architecture, and could give an exact Account of all the famous Buildings, both Antient and Modern, in every Part of the World". Hawksmoor seems never to have been abroad, and his omnivorous eclecticism therefore relied entirely on prints and drawings. Even Thomas Archer, who travelled from 1691 to 1695 in Holland, Italy and almost certainly Germany and Switzerland or Austria,[2] used engravings, sometimes slavishly, for his detail. Although (especially during the political troubles of the mid-century) there were numerous Englishmen abroad, and some of them (like the diarist Evelyn) were interested in buildings, English architectural dependence on the Continent was largely by way of prints until well into the eighteenth century. The growth of book- and print-publishing during the seventeenth century and a corresponding increase of architectural engravers are undoubtedly one of the factors that made the English Baroque style possible.

WREN'S CLASSICISM

There are, arguably, very limited Baroque features even in Inigo Jones. The ceiling of the Banqueting House is the work of the greatest of Baroque painters, Rubens, and its façade breaks forward in the centre but not at the ends, unlike a Renaissance palace. And one of the best known of his scenic designs, now at Chatsworth, shows a sense of light comparable to Elsheimer or even Claude Lorrain. But to include Jones in English Baroque on such indications is to take all meaning from the style.

There is nothing properly to be called Baroque before the King Charles building at Greenwich (1663-9) by his pupil and nephew by marriage, John Webb (Pl. 86). The giant order rising from ground level and embracing two storeys gives the building a scale of few, large, units. The order is used decoratively, and used at the points at which its effect is greatest. Moreover, the monumental effect does not depend solely on the order; the building is composed of large, simple, bold parts, and the particular feeling of this block is due to the absence of a basement storey, which gives it a stumpy appearance, and to the heavy end attics. These appear rather too emphatic, since Webb intended the block to be one of a pair on the east and west sides of the court, leading up to a south range with a domed hall in the

---

[1] *Cf.* SEKLER, *Wren.*
[2] *Architectural Review*, CXXII, 1957, pp. 88, 344.

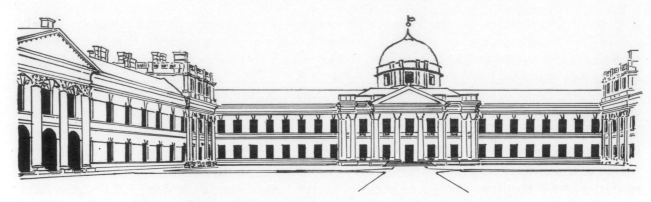

Fig. 1.   Greenwich Palace. Reconstruction of John Webb's project.

centre (Fig. 1); this was never built. The dramatic massive style of King Charles Block is quite unlike the Banqueting House, though the detail is still Jones's.[3] It is foreshadowed in Webb's unexecuted project for Durham House (1649) and he might have taken it further if he had not died in 1672.

Upon Sir John Denham's death in 1669 Charles II appointed Wren to succeed him as Surveyor-General, over the heads of Webb and Hugh May. At the age of 37 Wren thus became, in name at once and within a few years in practice as well, the most important official architect in the country. Since there was no prejudice against private commissions, his prestige was even greater. That same year saw the opening of his Sheldonian Theatre in Oxford, a building which is a curious mixture of old and new, of dullness and ingenuity. The main south end elevation is a flat and uninspired Serlian exercise; the wall treatment in general, however, shows the effect of Wren's visit to France, made after building had started. There is something of archaeology in the adoption of the D-shaped ancient Roman theatre-form (and its name) for the University's ceremonial hall. Yet the timber construction which roofs the hall in a single-span ceiling, without any internal supports, is an example of seventeenth-century mechanical ingenuity, and as such it attracted enthusiastic comment at the time. Moreover this span is used inside for a major work of Baroque illusionism. Robert Streeter's ceiling shows the canvas roof of an ancient theatre drawn back over its supporting ropes so that we look up into the blue sky at allegorical figures riding the clouds (Pl. 105). The combination of architectural academicism, eclectic borrowing, science and archaeology and a real feeling for Baroque art-forms is characteristic of Wren.

During the 1670's Wren was in charge of the rebuilding of the London City churches destroyed or damaged in the Great Fire of 1666. This was the first major church-building programme since before the Reformation, and it provided the patterns for the Baroque churches of the next generation. Of a total of fifty-two churches, twenty were begun in the years 1670–2, and by 1678 another fifteen were building. Wren's control of such a large scheme was necessarily loose, and at least one church, St Edmund the King, Lombard Street, if not more, appears to have been designed by Robert Hooke.[4] The work for which Wren was personally and solely responsible at this time shows a classicism nearer to that of High Renaissance Italy than anything of Jones, yet distilled from wider sources. The Great Model design for St Paul's Cathedral, constructed in 1673–4, has a geometrical simplicity of general shape, a purity of detail, a subordination of ornament to form, and a homogeneity of style which recall both Bramante's monumental design for St Peter's in Rome and Alberti's

[3] Jones's giant portico at Old St Paul's is hardly a precedent for Webb, since it was not over-large in relation to the cathedral front.

[4] COLVIN, *Dictionary*, p. 710, n. 1; see below, p. 24. Hooke also shared the responsibility for the Monument to the Fire, erected 1671–6 on Fish Street Hill (Pl. 576).

concept of beauty as a harmony of parts incapable of improvement or alteration (Pl. 25).

The Great Model design came to nothing beyond the wooden model, eighteen feet long, from which it is named; the final design underwent very considerable modification and improvement in the course of building. The classicism of this period is beautifully evident in the Library of Trinity College, Cambridge, begun in 1676. The court front (Pl. 30) of two arcaded storeys bears a general resemblance to Sansovino's Library of St Mark in Venice, and this type of façade was certainly known to Wren from Italian examples; more significantly, Trinity Library is more closely Italianate in detail (Pl. 49) than any other by Wren. But its classicism is not only in details but in the perfect proportions of the two storeys on both main fronts, the regularity of their design and the quietness of the deviations in centres and ends, and the clarity of their articulation – which effectively disguises the structural ingenuity (itself a piece of Baroque illusionism) whereby the upper storey floor lies behind the tympana of the lower arches.

OTHER TRENDS IN RESTORATION ARCHITECTURE

The sophisticated balance of Trinity Library, and its Italianate detail, are largely personal to Wren and not typical of the 1670's. The interest in French models, to which he returned in the next decade, is already quite evident in Hooke's Bedlam (Bethlehem Hospital) of 1674–6, in which the alternation of long two-storey blocks and taller pavilions is certainly French in origin. Hooke was also familiar with illustrations of Dutch buildings (a drawing survives which he appears to have copied from an elevation of the New Church in The Hague) and Holland is the direct source for the elevations of his pavilions, built of brick with stone dressings, with pilasters on the upper storey only and high-pitched roofs (Pl. 130).

Nevertheless the crown of Hooke's pavilion-roof is a flat platform surrounded by a balustrade, and in the middle is a small cupola. The balustraded platform roof and the cupola giving access to it from a spiral staircase go back to a type of house conceived by Jones in the 1630's but of which the earliest certainly executed example was Pratt's Colcshill, begun in 1649. The type became very popular after the Restoration; one of the most famous examples was Pratt's short-lived Clarendon House in Piccadilly (built 1664–7, demolished 1683), one of the latest is Belton, Lincs, 1685–8 (Pls 127, 129). The typical elevation is long in relation to its height – Coleshill had nine bays, Clarendon House had fifteen – but Ashdown, Berks (built as a hunting-box c.1664) is tall and square like the Bedlam pavilions (Pl. 128). The houses are astylar, with quoined corners, and the use of pilasters at Bedlam is Dutch. A pilastered building of a similar type, however, occurs in Wren's circle. The Town House at Abingdon, completed in 1680, was built and probably designed by Christopher Kempster, an Oxfordshire mason (Pl. 489). It is a logical adaptation of the Coleshill type to a traditional form of civic or market building, and its most remarkable feature is the giant pilaster order all round. This may have been suggested by Wren, who knew and elsewhere employed Kempster. Grand though it is, however, the simplicity of the Town House is the result of natural taste as against the cerebration of Trinity Library, and Wren cannot possibly have sanctioned the stair tower stuck asymmetrically on the back of the Abingdon building.

The same type was used again by Henry Bell of King's Lynn for the Customs House there (1683),[5] but with superimposed instead of giant pilasters, and fenestration similar to Jerman's Royal Exchange (Pl. 488). East Anglian links with Holland have always been strong, and Bell may have thought of the Dutch weigh-houses which are basically similar structures. The possibility of alternative sources is typical of the period.

[5] It was designed as an Exchange, but was sold to the Customs in 1718. The features shown on the roof and lantern in Bell's own engraved view were probably not all executed.

Dutch influence certainly reached England at the Restoration, through the returning English exiles. Among them was Hugh May, who has been briefly mentioned already and was an architect of great significance although much of his work has been destroyed. He was born in 1622 and was the Duke of Buckingham's "servant for twenty years together, in all his wants and dangers", as he told Pepys. He must have spent a considerable time in Holland with Buckingham, and in 1656 he returned there to join the exiled court with the painter Lely. At the Restoration he was appointed Paymaster of the Works, the first evidence we have of a connection with architecture; in 1668 he was promoted to Comptroller. Though Wren was made Surveyor over his head in the following year he was not neglected, and royal favours culminated, in 1673, in his succeeding to the Comptrollership of Works at Windsor Castle. In the next ten years – the last decade of his life – May remodelled the Upper Ward of Windsor into a remarkable series of Baroque interiors. This work was quite independent of Wren; had it not been virtually destroyed after 150 years, in the Gothic Revival, May would be more generally known as a Baroque architect. He may initially have been a painter and in Lely's studio, but a remark of Aubrey's implies that he understood the technical side of architecture. He was a member both of the pre-Fire committee on St Paul's and of that appointed after the Fire to supervise the rebuilding of London. The nature of his services to the exiled court after 1656 is unknown, but they must partly account for his preferment.

May used his eyes in the Netherlands; at Eltham Lodge, Woolwich (1664) he introduced the Dutch red-brick classicism (loosely called Palladianism) which appears a decade later in Hooke's Bedlam. Stone is restricted to the applied portico on the entrance front – pilasters so flat as to be diagrammatic – and the entablature (Pl. 132). May's Berkeley House, Piccadilly, built in 1665 and almost as short-lived as its neighbour, Clarendon House (Berkeley House was burnt in 1733), was a brick building of the same type as Eltham with the addition of quadrant wings. Pratt and May, perhaps largely through these two well-placed London houses, were the joint originators of the so-called "Wren" house of the late seventeenth century, which persisted, in larger and smaller versions, until its displacement by the low-pitched roofs of Baroque and Palladian pretention. Indeed, small examples may be found in the 1720's.

ENGLISH BAROQUE

The range of styles visible in the 1620's (p. 1) was the result of a time-lag in the spread of Italianate taste, which had then only reached the metropolitan court style of Inigo Jones. A century later the pattern of taste remained almost as wide and complex, but it was no longer due to the time-lag, which had gradually been resolved, except in the most provincial work. The grammar and vocabulary of Renaissance art were now common property, and the range from traditional simplicity to Baroque freedom on one side and Palladian restraint on the other was a matter of choice for client and even, as far as knowledge was concerned, for the designer. The period of Wren's Surveyorship was the court style's Indian summer – and an exceptionally brilliant one. Shaftesbury, writing in 1712, condemned the fact that "thro' several Reigns we have patiently seen the noblest publick Buildings perish (if I may say so) under the Hand of one single Court-Architect".[6] This was the enlightened Whig view of artistic absolutism, and it mattered little to Shaftesbury that Wren, self-taught, had rebuilt the Office of Works as a highly organized though loosely controlled artistic machine. It was a base for himself, for May, Talman, Hawksmoor and Vanbrugh, and to some extent

---

[6] *A letter concerning design.*

for Archer. Moreover, Wren ensured as far as possible that there were no sinecures and that each man did the job for which he was most suited. There is some confirmation of this in a memorial from the officers of the Works to the Treasury in 1717, which states that "whatever the clerks may have been formerly, they are now required to be well skilled in all kinds of admeasurement, in drawing, making plans of the palaces, and taking elevations, and completely versed in all parts of architecture . . . likewise knowing in the goodness, choice and value of all sorts of materials".[7]

In the years after 1715 this achievement was undone. Wren's Surveyorship was made almost nominal "by appointing other worthy gentlemen with me in Commission, which was under such regulations and restrictions, as that altho' I had the honour to be first nam'd with the old title of Surveyor, yet in acting, I had no power to override, or give a casting vote".[8] This did no more than hamper him, but in 1718 greater changes were made in the Office. His son had been deprived as Chief Clerk the previous year; now William Benson, an elusive figure but the author of a Whig pamphlet and an amateur architect, "under specious pretences of saving money to his Majesty in the works and repairs of his palaces . . . got Sr Chr. Wren turned out, and himself put into his place; his brother, lately come from a merchant in Ireland, Clerk of the Works, in the room of Mr. Hawksmoor, to the palaces . . . and his agent, Colin Campbell, chief clerk".[9] Benson proved singularly incompetent and was replaced after a year by Sir Thomas Hewett, who promptly put in a deputy. The office became the province of nonentities with political influence and their protégés in the Palladian camp. The early Georges were not interested in building – they were hardly interested in living in England – and the Whig government was not interested in royal building for them. The court style did not turn Palladian; instead it disappeared, because architecture virtually ceased to be a court activity.

The reaction against Baroque in England must presently be discussed, for the light it throws on the style. In this reaction, as in Baroque itself, Vanbrugh has a central and rather paradoxical position. He was (albeit with the help of Hawksmoor) the architect of Blenheim, the most notorious house in England and the focus of anti-Baroque criticism, and for us the building which may most usefully be considered in *European* stylistic terms. He is the best known English Baroque architect and the one in whose work, in the present century, the style was first examined. At the same time, he was a firm Whig, and though he took little active part in politics his patrons and Kit-Cat Club friends were prominent Whig politicians. And his use of Palladio after about 1715 was considerable, if entirely personal.

It is instructive to compare the exterior of Blenheim with a much praised and imitated early Palladian mansion such as Colin Campbell's Wanstead, Essex. Wanstead was, until its demolition in 1824, easily accessible from London, and Campbell published three successive designs in *Vitruvius Britannicus*. It was largely completed by 1715 (when Blenheim was not yet roofed) according to Campbell's second design (Pl. 221) with the exception of the cupola. This feature was probably a retort to Vanbrugh's Castle Howard (Pl. 215) but was never built; in his final design (1720) Campbell omitted the cupola but planned corner towers at the ends of the façade.

Both houses consist basically of a central block with a portico on the main front and with lower side wings. In both, the portico stands before a large hall on the central axis, leading to a large saloon and flanked by a staircase on either side. There the likeness ceases, and in discussing the differences there is no need to dwell on the fact that the whole plan of Wanstead is contained in a single long rectangle whereas that of Blenheim encloses three sides of

[7] Cal. T.P., 1714–19, p. 309.
[8] *Ibid.*, pp. 448–9.
[9] *Ibid.*, p. 416.

a court. In Wanstead both the plan and the outline of the elevation are as simple as possible. The centre block is defined from the lower wings by very slight, almost linear, projections, and all outlines are uncompromisingly rectangular. The cupola is an ornamental addition and as such is far smaller in proportion than that at Castle Howard which is an essential part of the whole main block. The elevation is clearly divided horizontally, by mouldings and a change of texture, into a high basement and a main storey. In the centre block there is an attic, which we see as an upwards extension rather than a separate part, since it is tied to the main storey by the portico columns. Only three types of window are used in the building, one for each floor, and as there are no columns or pilasters except in the portico the articulation of the exterior depends mainly on the regular rhythm of the windows. The portico is in Campbell's words (*Vitruvius Britannicus* (1), p. 5) "a just Hexastyle, the first yet practised in this manner in the Kingdom". Its ridge-roof was continued visibly over the hall and saloon and above the main roof, as if a Roman temple were indeed set into the house.

At Blenheim (Pl. 228) the hall is embedded in the centre block and sticks out in a clerestory, like a tall church nearly half as high again as the rest and distinct from the portico. Its roof-line, like the whole Blenheim skyline, is complex and angular. The two storeys of the main block are nearly equal in height, and below the giant order which ties them together the basement is almost unnoticed. There are twenty steps up to the entrance but it remains recognizably on the ground floor. The wall breaks back for one bay between the two end bays of the main block and the portico section, and the windows in this bay are wider than the others, so that the change of plane and roofline goes with a change of rhythm across the façade. The rhythm of the portico is also complex, for it consists of two columns standing between close pairs of square piers. The wings have the same baseline and their main entablature is continued at first floor level through the centre block. The orders are used right across the elevation, and there are several kinds of window. Finally, whereas the analysis of Wanstead would apply almost equally to the garden front, the two main fronts of Blenheim are totally different in rhythm, texture, plane variation and bay design. (A comparable discrepancy occurs at Castle Howard, and was justified by Hawksmoor on the grounds that it was effective.) Wanstead must have been imposing; its effect came from exact order almost to the point of dullness. Blenheim has a quality of excitement derived from constant variations of order; it is a rule proved by an infinity of exceptions.

Our comparison may be taken further in respect of details, of formal qualities, and of what we may call propriety. To take the last first, Jones had already at the beginning of his career formulated a distinction very like the literary idea of the "kinds":

> And to saie trew all thes composed ornaments the wch Proceed out of ye aboundance of dessigners and wear brought in by Michill Angell and his followers in my oppignion do not well in sollid Architecture and ye fasciati of houses, but in gardens loggis stucco or ornaments of chimnies peeces or in the inner parts of houses thos compositiones are of necessety to be yoused. For as outwarly every wyse man carrieth a graviti in Publicke Places, whear ther is nothing els looked for, yet inwardly hath his immaginacy set on fire, and sumtimes licenciously flying out, as nature hir sealf doeth often tymes stravagantly, to dellight, amase us sumtimes moufe us to laughter, sumtimes to contemplation and horror, so in architecture ye outward ornaments oft to be sollid, proporsionable according to the rulles, masculine and unaffected.[10]

Jones was writing with Michelangelesque Italy fresh in his mind, but this remark justifies in advance the elaboration of his double cube room at Wilton, and also (though they probably did not know his words) the "double standard" of Campbell, Burlington and Kent,

---

[10] J. A. GOTCH, *Inigo Jones*, London, 1928, pp. 81–2.

by which the interiors of Chiswick and the gallery at Mereworth (Pl. 297) are brilliantly ornate with gilt decoration and strong colours which the coldly simple exteriors would never suggest. At the opposite pole, the inside of the arcade-lined hall at Blenheim, which contemporaries thought more like a church, appears cold in the extreme after the fire of the outside approach.

Jones's own attitude to detail is clear from his statement and consistent in his work, and it was taken over by the eighteenth-century Palladians. Their vocabulary derives from the academic branch of the High Renaissance stem; it is conservative and limited. The transformation and irrationalization of detail "brought in by Michill Angell" and the Mannerists was the source of Baroque experiment and invention, and it persists in the details of Blenheim (Pl. 247).

In respect of formal qualities: a house like Wanstead could not change much in appearance from differing viewpoints. From any distance and direction it was a simple composition of blocks decorated on the surface with very little depth. At Blenheim the aspect varies dramatically with distance and direction, and the wall surfaces are developed in three dimensions. In contrast to the inert walls of a Palladian house, those of Blenheim are alive. This is architecture of change, of movement, of surprise; the same principle underlies the great Baroque palaces of Europe.

ANTI-BAROQUE

There are several reasons for the relative failure and the short life of English Baroque. Continental Baroque arose, and was associated, with the Catholic Counter-Reformation and with absolutist monarchy. Where the former gained no hold and the latter became outlawed the style could only be considered tainted; it could not long flourish, and there would later be historians prepared to hold that in England it never existed. It cannot have been difficult for a Whig mind to see "law and order" threatened alike by Stuart claims to the monarchy and by Baroque disregard for imposed rules of taste. Moreover, Jones's remark about interiors and exteriors epitomizes – and applies to architecture – traditional English reserve.

Yet in the diversity and relative freedom of English thought of the time, associations with Catholicism, with Stuart and French monarchism and with a loose upper lip were merely negative factors; at most they could (and did) build up a climate of opinion in which other forces had their effect. These forces were the personalities of the leading Baroque architects themselves, the very good publicity of the opposition, and the lines on which its attack was directed.

English Baroque failed to become a coherent style in the first place; there was no *esprit de corps*. In architecture at least, freedom was paramount. Wren's aesthetic was largely built on two basic ideas of seventeenth-century scientific thought, the existence of an inner universal harmony (as a result of which certain regular, mathematical shapes were more beautiful than other, irregular ones), and the importance of experimental investigation. But Wren believed in both "natural" (geometrical) beauty and "customary" or associative beauty, which "familiar or particular inclination breeds" in "things not in themselves lovely". By admitting other than absolute canons of beauty, he was free to choose and modify his forms to produce the visual effect he wanted. The designing and building of St Paul's Cathedral was a prolonged experiment, and Wren's concern for the visual effect he wanted is itself a Baroque symptom. He was not alone in this concern; it was frequently stated by Vanbrugh and Hawksmoor and is implicit in the work of May and Archer. These men did not share Wren's insistence on mathematical regularity. They were not, as he was, "jealous of Novelties, in which Fancy blinds the Judgment" and Vanbrugh and Hawksmoor did not apologize, as he did, for making use of Gothic forms. The "Wren School" was a school of individualists, and their works were extremely personal statements; as such they could be corporately attacked, but not corporately defended. As such, too, their common qualities are less precise and harder to define than those of Palladian conformity.

The publicity of the attack was above all that of Colin Campbell, who has already been mentioned as the architect of Wanstead. This enterprising Scot settled in the south about 1712 and published in 1715 the first volume of *Vitruvius Britannicus, or the British architect*, a collection of 100 engraved plates with a dedication to George I. This was followed in 1717 by a second volume of 100 plates, and shortly afterwards a re-issue of the first with a revised list of subscribers; a third volume appeared in 1725.[11] Campbell's plates are surprisingly representative. They include works by Jones and Wren, houses such as Belton and Stoke Edith, and a large number of the Baroque school (for which they are an important historical source) as well as buildings and projects of his own and other Palladians. Houses far outnumber churches and other buildings; Campbell must have known that battles of taste are won in house-building, and accordingly took care that his work should appeal to the house-building class. The only major – and complete – omission is the work of his compatriot, James Gibbs, whom, from other evidence, he seems to have tried deliberately to discredit.

The burden of Campbell's book is clear from its title, which was probably not entirely his invention. Inigo Jones had been described in print as "the Vitruvius of his age" and "the English Vitruvius" in the 1660's.[12] But a mere neo-Palladian manifesto would not have had the success at which he aimed. By producing a set of prints with something of every taste, on a lavish scale and obtainable by subscription, Campbell reached the greater part of the art-conscious public. In the preface to the first volume he condemned the British Quality's enthusiasm for things that are foreign, and attacked by name the Italians: the "affected and licentious" works of Bernini and Fontana and the "wildly extravagant" designs of Borromini, "who has endeavoured to debauch Mankind with his odd and chimerical Beauties". Against the *modern* Italians he placed with approval "those Restorers of Architecture which the Fifteenth and Sixteenth Centurys produced in Italy": above all, Palladio, who "seems to have arrived to a Ne plus ultra of his art". And as proof that "in most we equal, and in Some Things we surpass, our Neighbours" he produced the name of Jones, "this great Master" whom any impartial judge would consider "to have outdone all that went before".

Jones and Palladio were being praised in preference to the Baroque before 1715. This is implied by the fact that Giacomo Leoni's first activity after reaching this country in 1713 – and perhaps the proximate reason for his coming – was the preparation of the first English version of Palladio's *Quattro Libri dell'Architettura*; the first volume appeared in 1716 (with the date 1715) and promised – prematurely in the event, as the owner withheld his permission – the text of Jones's annotations to his copy of Palladio. But there were already explicit signs of a Jones revival. In the first volume of *Vitruvius* Campbell illustrated Wilbury House, Wilts, begun about 1710, according to a design close enough to Jones to be called a copy, by William Benson. Benson, whose effective and sinister official part in the architectural revolution has already been mentioned, was then 28 and politically active. His homage to Jones was perhaps brief, for when finished about 1725 the house differed considerably from the first design.

Then in 1711 John James, who was already in the Office of Works, wrote to ask the Duke of Buckingham's help to obtain an additional post, so "that I may once in my Life have an Opportunity of shewing that the Beautys of Architecture may consist with ye

[11] WOOLFE and GANDON produced a continuation, Vols IV–V, 1767–71.

[12] By JOHN WEBB in *Stone-Heng restored* and WALTER CHARLETON in *Chorea gigantum* respectively.

Greatest plainness of the Structure". This demonstration, he added, "has scarce ever been hit by the Tramontani [those north of the Alps] unless by our famous Mr. Inigo Jones". Too little is known about James, who was an extremely capable architect if not an inspired one. There is evidence that he was greatly respected by many, and he built a number of rather plain churches and private houses, but he received little preferment in the Office of Works under either Wren or the new régime. He had previously published translations of Perrault's *Ordonnance* (1708), the anti-doctrinaire treatise on the orders, and Pozzo's *Perspectiva* (1707), the leading Baroque painter's manual. His heralding enthusiasm for Jones is all the more remarkable because it did not lift him on to the bandwagon in the years after 1715. It was, to judge from his later works, quite sincere but sprang rather from antipathy to the Baroque than from any particular Palladian conviction. In the same letter he complains to Buckingham that the exact estimating of cost "is so little understood by us that no small number of noble as well as private persons have been led into an expence that has proved ye ruine of their Estates and Familys". The whole passage might well have been written by Shaftesbury.

The 3rd Earl of Shaftesbury's *Letter concerning design*, written in Italy early in 1712, was addressed to Lord Somers and immediately became known in England though it was not published until 1731. It sets out the Whig aesthetic in general terms, and prophesies its acceptance in the society of the Whig supremacy. Shaftesbury specifically attacked French taste and influence in the arts, and went so far, in the passage quoted above (p. 6), as to class Wren as an architectural tyrant. Among the resulting disasters he named Hampton Court and St Paul's, and he all but named more advanced Baroque buildings as yet in embryo, the newly proposed Fifty New Churches. "Since a Zeal of this sort [church building] has been newly kindled amongst us, 'tis like we shall see from afar the many Spires arising in our great City, with such hasty and sudden growth, as may be the occasion perhaps that our immediate Relish shall be hereafter censur'd." And there cannot be much doubt that Blenheim and Castle Howard were in his mind and his readers' when he wrote:

> The ordinary Man may build his Cottage, or the plain Gentleman his Country-house according as he fansys: but when a great Man builds, he will find little Quarter from the Publick, if instead of a beautiful Pile, he raises, at a vast expence, such a false and counterfeit Piece of Magnificence, as can be justly arraign'd for its Deformity, by so many knowing Men in Art, and by the whole People, who, in such a Conjuncture, readily follow their Opinion.

Shaftesbury gave no positive indication of the style he expected from the "national taste", from a "united Britain the principal Seat of Arts". To this question Campbell's book suggested the answer. It is significant that Campbell's patron, John, 2nd Duke of Argyll, was, like Shaftesbury and Somers, a prominent Whig. It is also significant that Campbell was described in 1718 as Benson's agent, and became his deputy in the Works, though we do not know when they first met. There was nothing intrinsically Whiggish in Jones's style or in a revival of it, but when the Whig notion of a national style had been conceived (as it clearly was by Shaftesbury at least) Campbell adroitly provided the ideal. He also fired the young Earl of Burlington with a zeal for Palladio and Jones, and before Burlington made his second trip to Italy in 1719 (specifically to see the works of Palladio) Campbell had replaced Gibbs as architect of Burlington House.

THE DIFFUSION OF ENGLISH BAROQUE; PATRONS AND ARCHITECTS

In an age of flat- and office-building, and in the face of the later destruction or remodelling of half the houses built between 1680 and 1730, it is difficult to realize the extent of the country-house building boom. Its economic history has been little studied, but the material awaits the student and certain facts are evident. Building was expensive. At a time when a bricklayer's labourer earned 1s 6d a day, Castle Howard cost about £35,000, the grounds and outworks about £24,000 and the Mausoleum nearly £19,000. The house took fourteen years to build, and was then incomplete on the west side. This length of time was by no means unusual. The rebuilding of Chatsworth, for the 1st Duke of Devonshire, went on, one side at a time, for twenty years. A documented case is Burley-on-the-Hill, built for Daniel Finch, 2nd Earl of Nottingham, between 1696 and 1704 (Pl. 148). In that period he spent about £19,000 on building; amounts varied each year, but were under £3,000 except for two years in each of which he spent over £4,000. The total cost was about £30,000, and work went on till 1710. This sum was twice Nottingham's original estimate, but the difference was largely spent on the gardens and outbuildings and the decoration of the house. It has been shown that most of the expenditure was met from current income, but even so Nottingham did not avoid short-term loans.[13] Like some of the German princes, the less prudent Britons built more on credit, with the consequences described above by James; the matter needs further investigation.

The two houses which received most contemporary comment, Blenheim and Cannons, are special cases. The carcase of Blenheim was mostly completed between 1705 and 1710; the house cost nearly £300,000, the greater part of which was paid for by the Treasury, as a state gift to Marlborough. Payment was so much and so long in arrears that in 1713–14 some of the artificers prepared to sue the Duke for their money. Slow payment was usual in the Office of Works, and the builders of Greenwich Hospital and the Fifty New Churches were affected. These buildings were contracted for a part at a time, so that when money was short building stopped. St Alfege, Greenwich, was structurally complete in two years, but some of the other churches took ten years. "Princely" Chandos made his fortune, which a contemporary speaking well of him put at £600,000, by speculating with public money as Paymaster to the Forces. He rebuilt Cannons (Pl. 299) and lived there with the style of the self-made speculator that he was, and it was style, rather than size, pretention rather than architectural invention, that attracted comment. Pope's general criticisms of ostentation and lack of taste in the *Epistle to Lord Burlington* were rapidly assumed to refer to Chandos, an assumption which the poet rightly denied but which has persisted.

Prestige did not affect church-building, with the exception of town churches like St Philip, Birmingham, St George, Yarmouth, and St Martin-in-the-Fields, and propaganda churches such as those built in London under the Tory government's Fifty New Churches Act of 1711. The appearance of churches depended more on the needs of individual cases, the taste of patrons or councils, and the money available, than on fashion. The designer was very often a local man (this was the case even with Archer in Birmingham); many churches of the period are excessively plain, but the more ambitious ones frequently have unusual detail.

The great new house commissions after 1714 are mostly Whig ones, and mostly Palladian. Chatsworth, the first great Whig house, begun in 1687, the year before the Revolution, is a Baroque palace. Its "continental grandeur . . . was a challenge not merely to the Belton style of house-building but to the Court style itself . . . Chatsworth was the first flaunting symbol in architecture of territorial Whiggery."[14] Not only Whigs began to build palaces. Burley-on-the-Hill may certainly be called a prestige house although it does not rival Chatsworth in either grandeur or cost, and Nottingham was a Tory. But it was initially Campbell's achievement to provide for the Whig builders a more acceptable and identifiable stylistic ideal.

[13] H. J. HABAKKUK, "Daniel Finch, 2nd Earl of Nottingham, his house and estate", in J. H. PLUMB, *Studies in social history*, London, 1955.

[14] SIR J. SUMMERSON, in *Journal of the Royal Society of Arts*, July 1959, CVII, p. 541.

Vanbrugh clearly believed that his own Baroque style *was* acceptable. Writing to Brigadier Watkins in 1721 in praise of Hawksmoor, he exclaimed, "What wou'd Monsr: Colbert in France have given for Such a Man? I don't Speak as to his Architecture alone, but the Aids he cou'd have given him, in almost all his brave designs for the Police."[15] His admiration for Louis XIV's minister is undisguised. "To the mind of Vanbrugh . . . Greenwich Hospital was the rival of the Invalides in splendour, but built by freemen, and all the resources of Baroque eloquence were only fitting to celebrate at Blenheim the victory of their faith that freedom is as consistent with an effective state as any absolutism, however imposing."[16] This explains the apparent paradox that he and most of his patrons were as staunchly Whig as the Palladians. Edward Southwell, for whom he built King's Weston (Pl. 262), was also an early patron of Campbell. Vanbrugh's position as a member, like several of his patrons, of the inner club of Whiggism, the Kit-Cat, accounts for the strong Baroque element within it.

Vanbrugh's entry into architecture was through the agency of the 3rd Earl of Carlisle, who allowed a patent beginner to design his palace (Castle Howard) and a few years later, on the accession of Queen Anne, obtained for him the Comptrollership of Works in place of William Talman, whom he had already ousted at Castle Howard. He was offered the Surveyorship in 1716, and refused it "out of Tenderness to Sir Chr. Wren", a refusal which he later regretted when, in 1718, Benson was appointed over his head. Personally he fired and sustained the enthusiasm and held the trust and friendship of his patrons; he apparently talked Carlisle into Castle Howard and Marlborough into Blenheim. His natural gifts were remarkable, but for the first work he can have had few qualifications to show beyond charm and enthusiasm; the second, even vaster, undertaking, was begun before the success of the first can have been fully evident. In the light that modern research has shed on Hawksmoor's importance for the early Vanbrugh style, it is easy to underrate Vanbrugh, but it is wrong to do so. He was the one man of undoubted genius whom the Whigs introduced into the Office of Works. With Carlisle, Newcastle and Manchester, and Cobham among his friends, he was well protected. The Tories revoked his patent as Comptroller in 1713, but he was reinstated by the new Whig government the next year. The same personal qualities that eased his rapid preferment at the turn of the century helped him to ride out the storm of 1718 in which Wren and Hawksmoor fell.

Vanbrugh could save himself, but he could not save either the Office of Works or the Baroque style. Seaton Delaval was projected that same year, 1718, and it is as fine and as wild as anything he built (Pl. 275). But at Kensington Benson, and then Kent, took control, and at Greenwich Hospital the Queen Mary Block was completed with discreet buildings which neither openly disagree with the wild glories (probably Hawksmoor's) of King William Block, nor do anything to complement them. Vanbrugh died in 1726; his invention outlived him in the hands of Hawksmoor, who effaced himself to carry out the Temple on the hill at Castle Howard (Pl. 562). When Hawksmoor died ten years later there was nobody, and although Carlisle had supported him without fail to the end, his Mausoleum on the next hill (Pl. 565) was finished by alien hands. Archer is not known to have designed anything after 1722. Gibbs's Radcliffe Camera (Pl. 539) was not completed until 1749 and is in some respects a Baroque building, but Oxford was conservative and Gibbs varied his style to suit his patron. In this case also he borrowed considerably from Hawksmoor's earlier designs for the building.

Provincial Baroque continued into the 1730's with the work of the Smiths in the Midlands and the Bastards in and around Blandford. It is creditable and sturdy, but it is not the work of genius. A rather similar watered-down or vernacular Baroque can be found in parts of

---

[15] *Police* means management of the state and its amenities, and the "brave designs" were probably Colbert's.
[16] WEBB, *Baroque art.*

Europe in the early eighteenth century. The massive Protestant churches of Schleswig-Holstein, for example, have ground plans based on multiple polygons, with thick walls carrying single-span roofs. In general shape they are thus similar to the basically oval south German Baroque churches, but they are almost undecorated inside, and the exterior brickwork, unplastered, is bare except for giant pilasters and pilaster-strips.

The Smiths and the Bastards, and others like Thomas White of Worcester, the Ettys of York, the Townesends of Oxford, the Strongs who moved from Oxford to London, and the London Tufnells, were masons; firms descended from father to son. They would carry out faithfully an architect's designs, or they would be capable of providing designs themselves if required. Often they had either worked on one of the great Baroque buildings or at least were in proximity to one. Thus Francis Smith built Heythrop for Archer and Ditchley for Gibbs, but at Sutton Scarsdale (Pl. 389) he was "gentleman architect"; thus the younger Edward Strong (1676–1741) worked for Wren and Hawksmoor in London, but himself designed the north gate of St Bartholomew's Hospital (Pl. 495). An unknown mason built the house at the corner of the Hensington road in Woodstock, near Blenheim (Pl. 348). Near Blandford are Chettle, possibly by Archer, and the remains of Vanbrugh's enormous Eastbury. These men come at the end of the long medieval tradition of mason-architects. They stand apart alike from those who, like Wren, Vanbrugh or Dean Aldrich, came to architecture by way of something else, and from the first of the professional architects, John Webb, Hawksmoor and Gibbs.

ARCHITECTURAL DRAWINGS

Wren recommended that "the Architect ought, above all Things, to be well Skilled in Perspective; for, every thing that appears well in the Orthography [elevation], may not be good in the Model; especially when there are many Angles and Projectures; and every thing that is good in Model, may not be so when built." One would expect to find many perspectives among the surviving drawings of his school; there are in fact very few, though they include a sketch for Whitehall Palace which is probably from his own hand (Pl. 74) and a beautiful pencil and wash drawing by Hawksmoor for Warwick church (Pl. 549). It is most likely that Wren meant "perspective" in the sense not only of drawing but of visualizing his works in depth and from particular distances and angles. This is in keeping with Wölfflin's concept of "malerisch" in Baroque art as a whole, with the pictorial and scenic aspects of Baroque architecture and the capacity of Baroque buildings to look quite different from different points, and with those picturesque qualities which, for instance, the Adam brothers saw in the work of Vanbrugh.

It may be significant too that architectural drawing reached a peak in the Baroque era to which it has never returned. Sixteenth-century architectural drawing, whether in England or in Renaissance Italy, remains to a considerable extent conceptual, like that of Villard de Honnecourt or the modern blueprint. This is not true of an all-round artist of the calibre of Michelangelo, but it is true of Palladio, and the bold wood-blocks of Serlio are only credible to us – and can only have been intelligible to his contemporaries who used them so liberally – as schematic images. In England architectural drawing first becomes something more expressive in the hand of Inigo Jones, who began as a painter, not as a mason. In France, Le Vau and François Mansart tended to draw like painters, the buildings growing out of the paper into reality through sensitive line and hatched shading.

Wren drew as a boy, and evidently liked drawing. The pre-Fire drawings for the crossing of St Paul's are beautifully wash-shaded over pen-work of a miniaturist's precision. His hand can be traced through later drawings, but it becomes looser and more idiomatic. There is a gain in vividness without any loss of accuracy, and affinities with French drawings of the last third of the century suggest that part of his time in France in 1665–6 was spent in the study of architectural drawing. The result is quite different from the equally skilled drawings of John Webb for Whitehall and Greenwich, or from those made by Edward Woodroffe for the Great Model for St Paul's.[17] Woodroffe seems to have worked initially for Webb, and to have been one of the first professional draughtsmen.

Hooke's drawings aim more frankly and coarsely for realism, by the use of coloured washes, such as pink for brickwork, rather as Vanbrugh (who never drew either neatly or professionally) brushed in dark blobs for windows and drew smoke curling from his chimneys. But the apogee was reached in Hawksmoor, who drew with ease, with precision, and often with a sparkle that any painter might have envied. Except when gout hindered him, he could express every form, the shape of every moulding, the contour of any statue, in short vigorous twirls and strokes of the pen. To his penwork he frequently added a soft grey wash, with the result that the building stands before us as vividly as if a painter like Claude had drawn it, yet with all the underlying accuracy of a draughtsman thoroughly versed in his subject. Small wonder that he drew not only for himself but often for Wren and Vanbrugh!

It would be dangerous and unfair to suggest that later architects could not draw thus. Some of them did. The change in architectural drawing was a result of increased professionalism. It appears in the office of Hardouin-Mansart in France and under Carlo Fontana in Rome; drawing becomes more a skill that can be acquired and less a natural talent that can be developed. Gibbs, who studied under Fontana, drew beautifully, but his drawings are not pictures, as many of Hawksmoor's are; they are no longer works of art in themselves. They no longer intend anything to be left to the imagination, as it was when Hawksmoor wrote to a client, of a drawing, that "it is but a Scizza".[18]

---

[17] *Wren Soc.* I, pls XVI–XVIII.
[18] I.e. a sketch.

II

Baroque in the court
style and the Surveyorship of Wren

THE WINDSOR OF CHARLES II

The first great Baroque ensemble in England was May's remodelling of Windsor Castle for Charles II between 1674 and 1684; it was not only the first but also the largest. Its nearest rivals, Hampton Court and Greenwich Hospital, are more truly architecture and less interior decoration, and they have the advantage of having survived; the only comparable ranges of interiors, Chatsworth and Burghley, have neither the extent nor the overall brilliance of Windsor, and their dependence on Windsor emphasizes the latter's importance.

Charles spent £200,000 on Windsor, a sum worth ten or fifteen times as much today; this alone is spectacular for a king chronically short of money. Hugh May reconstructed the north side of the Upper Ward, inside and out, inventing a new external wall treatment and creating, with a team of artists and craftsmen, the score of state rooms, in which architecture, carving and painting were united as grandly and luxuriantly – and with as much skill and conviction – as in any of the Baroque palaces of Europe. With the exception of three of the less important rooms, the Queen's Presence and Audience Chambers and the King's Dining Room, and some of the carving which was re-used in new positions, the whole decorative fabric, interior and exterior, was swept away between 1800 and about 1830, and its appearance and importance can only be judged from old descriptions and such illustrations as those in Pyne's *Royal Residences* (1819).

May's exterior refacing covered the whole court of the Upper Ward and also the north and east outer fronts of the Castle. It was very bare, almost to the point of seeming primitive. This is unlikely to have been due to economy, in view of the lavishness of the interiors and their iconographic insistence on the King's greatness. Charles's choice of Windsor must have been influenced by the attraction of its being away from the Metropolis, like Versailles, and away from the eye of Parliament. But there were other considerations. The antiquity of the Castle and the wealth of its historical associations with the monarchy were symbolically very valuable in the support of a throne only recently restored after a bloody revolution. He must also have appreciated that its situation on a long hill-top ridge – a situation originally chosen for ease of defence – offered scenic possibilities beyond those of any other English royal palace, and beyond those open to his rival, Louis XIV.

Although to Augustan and Gothic Revival tastes alike May's treatment seemed too bare, it had by then been an admired prototype for English Baroque, and the drawings of Paul Sandby (Pls. 3, 5) show how effective it was. It depended on the massing of blocks and towers and on the deep recessing of the windows, with heavy incurving architraves rather like simplified Gothic casement moulds. Those in Henry III's Tower survive, though they have suffered from the insertion of tracery bars and plate glass, and Sandby's drawings should be considered with them in mind (Pl. 6).

May's work included the complete rebuilding of one block on the north side, in brick with stone quoins. This was known as the Star Building, from the large Garter star on the outer front, and contained most of the new state rooms. This block and the towers had four

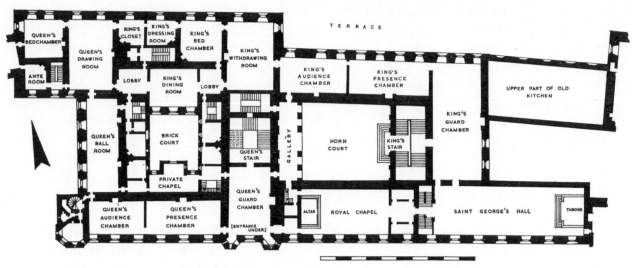

Fig. 2. Windsor Castle. Plan of Upper Ward, north side, as in 1790.

storeys; the rest of the Upper Ward, including the rooms on the court range of the Star Building, had only three storeys. On the south and east sides of the court the round-headed windows spanned the upper two storeys, the glazed portions being separated by a band of balustrading like that surviving in Henry III's Tower. Elsewhere the round-headed windows lit only one floor, while the Royal Chapel and St George's Hall (on the right of Pl. 5) were higher inside and took in the top row of square windows.[19]

The design of the windows gave, if not a Gothic effect, at least a medieval one; the effect of antiquity, ideal for the King's purpose, was enhanced by the use of string courses at the main levels and the absence of more positive ornament. Vanbrugh employed the same elements, though not this particular form of window, at Kimbolton in 1707 (Pl. 254), and in a letter to the Earl of Manchester at that time he made the association perfectly clear:

As to the Outside [he wrote] I thought 'twas absolutely best, to give it Something of the Castle Air, tho' at the Same time to make it regular . . . This method was practic'd at Windsor in King Charles's time, And has been universally Approv'd, So I hope your Ldship won't be discouraged, if any Italians you may Shew it to, shou'd find fault that 'tis not Roman, for to have built a Front with Pillasters, and what the Orders require cou'd never have been born with the Rest of the Castle: I'm sure this will make a very Noble and Masculine Shew; and is of as Warrantable a kind of building as Any.

Hawksmoor confirmed, in both practice and description, the picturesqueness of the deep-set windows. He copied May's windows (even to the inclusion of two storeys in one) in a Gothic design for All Souls (Pl. 545), and he recommended the window because of "the beauty it gives the Overture by Receding". In his churches he took the dramatic exploration of the wall thickness a stage further, punching the windows out and dispensing with mouldings (Pl. 400).

HUGH MAY'S INTERIORS

May's exteriors are a particular case of a general Baroque concern with the wall as a live and plastic medium. The "castle air", however, is exceptional, and seems to have been his

[19] Wyattville's drawings reproduced in HOPE, *Windsor Castle*, I, pls XLIV ff., were made after certain alterations had already been effected, and are a less reliable guide than the freer Sandby drawings.

invention. The Windsor interiors were no less of an innovation for England, but they fit easily into the tradition of European state decoration. The structure May produced for the new state apartments amounted to a series of boxes for decoration, under his supervision, by the painter Verrio, the gilder Cousin, the carver Gibbons and others. By 1671, when Verrio, who was born in Lecce about 1639, reached Paris by way of Naples, Florence (probably also Rome and Genoa), and Toulouse, he was already familiar with full-scale Baroque illusionist decoration. The *Grands Appartements* at Versailles, which acted as a spur to Charles II and his architect, were only begun in 1671, and though Verrio's style was influenced by French academism he can have learned little from Versailles, since he was brought to England the next year (1672) by Charles's ambassador, Ralph Montagu, later 1st Duke of Montagu. Hugh May certainly had early intelligence of the Escalier des Ambassadeurs at Versailles, designed by Le Vau before (though not begun until) 1670, for he imitated it in the King's Staircase at Windsor, while the overhead lantern of the Queen's Staircase (p. 20) suggests that he knew the Château of Blois. It is tempting to think that he had been to France and therefore knew at first hand the kind of team of artists and craftsmen organized initially by Le Vau and taken over at Versailles by Le Brun. However, the spatial organization of the two great staircases at Windsor is proof that May was much more than an *entrepreneur*. His long stay in Holland made him familiar not only with Dutch Palladianism but also with more advanced Baroque aspects of Dutch art. At Cassiobury, a house now destroyed, of which our knowledge is imperfect,[20] he directed a pediment with relief figures in the tympanum of Diana hunting with "the Country Nymphs". The carver was "a stranger", possibly therefore a foreigner, and the tympanum relief was the first English example of a Dutch Baroque form, of which May knew those on the Mauritshuis in The Hague (begun *c.*1633) and the Town Hall (now the Royal Palace) in Amsterdam. The latter was begun in 1648 and quickly became the most famous building in Holland. Quellin's marble reliefs inside the Town Hall were probably May's first introduction to that extremely naturalistic style which in England is popularly synonymous with the wood-carving of Grinling Gibbons, and it was under May at Cassiobury and Windsor that Gibbons became established as a decorator. Moreover, the Town Hall was conceived, iconographically, as a symbol of the glory of Amsterdam, and of the Peace of Munster of 1648 on which the city's new greatness partly depended.[21] Although the correspondence cannot be taken very far, and the illusionism of Windsor goes far beyond anything planned by Van Campen in Amsterdam, links can be found between the two programmes: for example, the tribute of the four continents to Amsterdam on the west pediment of the Town Hall and to Britannia on the ceiling of the Queen's Guard Chamber at Windsor. May would also have been familiar with the grandest painted decorative scheme in Holland, the Oranjezaal of the new Huis ten Bosch (begun 1648) which glorifies in Rubensian programme, forms, scale and illusionism, the achievements of Prince Frederik Hendrik. In both the Town Hall and the Oranjezaal the decoration, carved or painted, embraces whole rooms rather than isolated surfaces, and the spectator moves within it; in this spatial respect Windsor looks to them rather than to the Whitehall Banqueting House with its compartmented Rubens ceiling based on Venetian Cinquecento models.

Of the twenty-one rooms which Verrio decorated (together with the open-air walls of Horn Court between the great staircases) at least fourteen were painted between 1675 and 1678. In these rooms the walls were covered with tapestries or brocades or, like the Queen's Presence Chamber (Pl. 7), panelled; the ceiling was painted to suggest an upward extension of the room space. In some cases (Pl. 4) the cove translated into illusionism the solid carved or stucco frameworks of the Versailles ceilings and those painted in the 1640's by

[20] WHINNEY and MILLAR, pp. 207–8; EVELYN, 18 April 1680; COLLINS BAKER, *Lely*, II, p. 133.
[21] K. FREMANTLE, *The Baroque Town Hall of Amsterdam*, Utrecht, 1959.

Pietro da Cortona in the Pitti Palace in Florence. The flying figures, sky and clouds in the central field are closer to Italian examples than to Versailles, where there is hardly any illusionism. In the Queen's Guard Chamber (Pl. 10), painted 1678–80, the illusionist play was taken further in the framing of the central oval by a snake biting its own tail. In the Queen's Drawing Room (Pl. 2) the framework is more architectural and appears to rise above and outside a balustrade; this leads to the second type (Pl. 9) in which the cove was treated as a parapet and the whole room opened to the sky. The only ceiling of this sort at Versailles, by Houasse in the Salon d'Abondance, is too late to be a prototype,[22] though earlier illusionist decoration can be found in France. In general, therefore, while Windsor rivalled the opulence and symbolism of Versailles, though without the latter's extensive use of marble as a wall decoration, formally the Baroque of Windsor was much more full-blooded.

Iconographically the Stuart state apartments were as demonstrative and as direct, and must have been as oppressive, as the Bourbon ones. Charles II and his Queen constantly appeared in the midst of the pantheon. In the King's Drawing Room the restored monarch trampled on Envy and Ignorance; in the Presence Chamber Mercury showed his portrait to the four quarters of the world; in the State Bedroom he sat enthroned with France kneeling at his feet (he was receiving a secret subsidy from Louis!); in the Audience Chamber Britannia presided at the restoration of the Church of England. He dined (Pl. 4) under a gods' banquet; on the other hand the symbolism of the King's Dressing Room and Closet was limited to Danae and Leda. In the Queen's rooms Catharine of Braganza was shown, usually as Britannia, attended by virtues and goddesses and honoured by the four continents. The royal prerogative was inescapable.

MAY'S STAIRCASES

Accounts of Verrio's two staircases at Windsor (before 1680) are confused but enough can be deduced, with the help of a survey plan made about 1790, to make a schematic reconstruction (Fig. 3). The Queen's Great Staircase was entered from the court through a low vestibule supported by four pairs of Ionic columns and flanked by three niches each side containing antique (or pseudo-antique) busts. At the foot of the stairs was a small landing-place also flanked by niches containing "A Brass Busto of a Roman Vestal" and a bronze of the *Spinario*, and opening through three arches to the stair cage around which three flights of twelve steps each led up to the level of the state rooms; the rail was of wrought iron. The walls from first floor level to cornice level were treated architecturally, with feigned Corinthian pilasters making three bays on each side.[23] In the side bays were feigned bronze statues in niches, heightened with gold, of arts and sciences. The middle bays were treated differently. The door into the Guard Chamber was surmounted by a black marble bust of Venus, apparently real, and painted figures of Time and other personifications. The walls to left and right had "square niches" with Ovidian scenes, the transformation of Phaeton's sisters into trees and of Cygnus into a swan. The arrangement of statues and square histories can be imagined from a similar scheme at Burley-on-the-Hill (Pl. 124), but in the centre of the wall facing the door was the first of the Windsor stair's unusual features, an oval opening into the King's Privy Stair behind, where was visible a fictive relief of the hunt of Meleager. This introduced into a fictive scheme a real spatial experience and one which was only taken up again by Vanbrugh in the arches between stairs and hall at Castle Howard (Pl. 126),

[22] J. GUIFFREY, *Comptes des Bâtiments du Roi sous le règne de Louis XIV*, II, Paris, 1887, p. 317.

[23] G. BICKHAM, *Deliciæ Britannicæ*, 1742, p. 145, gives twelve pilasters as the total, but from his description it is clear that there were four on each side, as at Burley-on-the-Hill. If he was strictly accurate (which other parts of his account make doubtful) there must have been no pilasters on the doorway wall.

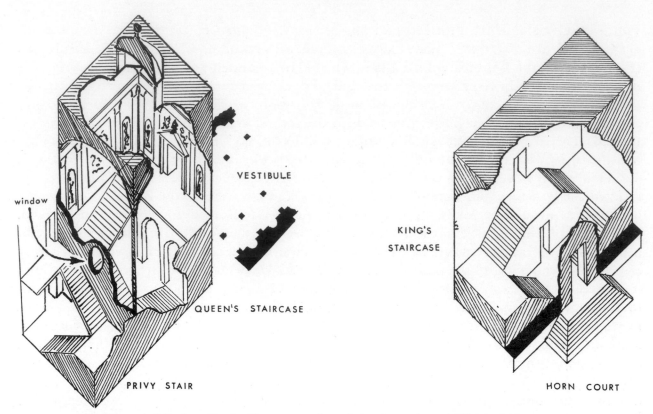

Fig. 3.   Windsor Castle. Reconstruction of the Queen's and King's Staircases.

a building which has other links, both formal and iconographical, with the Windsor stair (p. 76). Normally a staircase is lit by windows on one side; at Windsor the stair was surrounded by other buildings, and its second unusual feature, anticipating more modestly the dome of Castle Howard, was a lantern, probably polygonal like that on the King's Guard Chamber and certainly of wooden construction, rising from the centre of the coved and probably domical ceiling and providing the only source of daylight. The early guides are loose in terminology, but it is certain from careful reading and from examination of early exterior views that such a structure existed. In its roof was a painting of Apollo permitting Phaeton to drive the Chariot of the Sun; in the ceiling below were the winds and the signs of the Zodiac, with the Four Elements in the corners or pendentives.

The King's Staircase was, like Le Vau's Escalier des Ambassadeurs of only a few years before, a wide shallow hall with flights rising to left and right and then returning to meet at the upper landing. The guides describe its roof, painted with the Battle of the Giants, as a dome; it was presumably deeply coved, but had no lantern, the light coming from windows on the entrance wall. The theme of heroic strength was continued on the walls in paintings of the story of Achilles, and battles of Greeks and Trojans. At the base of the stair was a feigned bronze statue of Hercules, conceivably added for William III. These staircases, like much else at Windsor, were never surpassed, and the Queen's Stair's combination of dramatic lighting, illusionism and real spatial complexity has no later parallel.

THE STUART APOTHEOSIS

The most impressive rooms of all must have been the two largest and latest, the redecorated Royal Chapel (1680–4) and St George's Hall (1682–4); each was some 30 feet wide and high, and the chapel was 75 feet and the hall about 108 feet long. They were situated end to end, and each was paved in black and white marble and lit by two tiers of windows along the south side (Pls 1, 8). The painting covered not merely the ceilings but also all but the bottom of the walls, and made a complete fictive framework. On entering the hall from the King's Guard Chamber at the west end of the north side, the visitor turned left to face up the hall towards the dais of five steps, and, originally, the throne at the east end.[24] This had been carved in wood by Louis van Opstal[25] and John Van der Stein with six large figures of slaves, "a Lying figure Called Prudence", another of Justice, three Fames, "two greate Potts" and "three pieces of Trophies". At the lower end of the hall, over the steps leading to the royal pew in the chapel, was a gallery supported by four ten-foot wooden slaves, perhaps an echo of the caryatid figures in the Vierschaar of the Amsterdam Town Hall. In the central plaster-framed oval of the ceiling appeared King Charles in Garter robes attended by England, Scotland and Ireland and being crowned by Religion and Plenty; below him the four Cardinal Virtues beat down Rebellion and Faction. These figures faced the spectator in a direct line above the throne, and when the king himself sat in it the programme was completed. Above the throne was a feigned tapestry of St George on horseback. The throne did not long survive the Glorious Revolution, and was replaced by a more personal – and presumably less offensive – symbol, an illusionist state portrait of William III by Kneller. By the time of Pyne's view, our only visual record (Pl. 1), the end wall had been quite altered and the paintings removed.

The theme of the rest of the hall was the Order of the Garter. The south wall was painted with coupled columns between the windows; the upper windows were framed with Garter mottoes. The north wall had a painted colonnade behind which, as if in an extension of the hall, moved the triumphal parade of the Black Prince. In the cove were putti holding Garter cloaks. The octagons in the end compartments of the ceiling, also plaster-framed, contained allegorical figures supporting the star and collar of the Order. The colouring was light and gay and was dominated by gilt, white and grey and the blue of the Garter cloaks.

The chapel was even more elaborate. The royal gallery was decorated by Gibbons with "Six Vasses with Thistles Roses and two Boyes Laurel and Palmes and other Ornaments in the Front and upon the Topp of the Kings scate with Drapery, Fruit, Flowers, Crootesses, Starres, Roses". He also carved the twenty-eight stall-backs lining the lower walls, with "Fruit, Flowers, Palmes, Laurells, Pelicans, Pigeons". Above, the spiral Corinthian columns which were a favourite Baroque motif (though a much older one) separated the windows on the south and, on the north, paintings of the healing of Lazarus and of the palsied man and other miracles of Christ (Pl. 8). Over the altar Verrio depicted the Last Supper in a feigned niche, whose semi-dome was pierced to emit the sound of a hidden organ – a theatrical though acoustically ruinous contrivance much admired at the time by Evelyn. The entire ceiling was a single picture of the Ascension, in which the clouds of heaven poured in between and below the feigned coffering round the edge.

The prominence given to painting in this account underlines the fact that in May's Baroque rooms painting is not only inseparable from architecture and sculpture but even, through illusionism, interchangeable with them. This was probably true of Verrio's lost redecoration of what is now the Albert Memorial Chapel in St George's Chapel, Windsor; not even the subjects are known, but Verrio received £1,000 for painting the walls and ceiling in 1682–4, and on James II's accession he repainted the ceiling with the glorification of that king.

The Windsor apartments set a new decorative ideal in England, but the scale and splendour of May's hall and chapel were never achieved again and the only room that approaches them is the Painted Hall at Greenwich (Pl. 103). Windsor was quite independent of Wren,

[24] Bickham wrongly puts the dais at the west end.
[25] The son of the famous Gérard van Opstal; fl. 1652, died 1683, worked at Versailles and Marly from 1681

but the latter was in charge of the only Baroque ensemble produced for James II, the Roman Catholic chapel at Whitehall Palace. Its life was shorter even than James's reign; it was inaugurated on Christmas Eve, 1686 and opened to the public five days later, when Evelyn attended Mass there. Its use ceased on James's downfall less than two years later, the carved altar-piece was removed, and the structure perished in the Whitehall fire of 1698. Parts of the altar-piece survive at Burnham-on-Sea and elsewhere (Pls 11–12). The plan, the only visual record (Fig. 4), suggests that it had an oval dome in the roof. The mixture of fascination and pious horror in Evelyn's description of what he saw perhaps explains why other writers, less avid and acute, have left no record:

I was to heare the Musique of the Italians in the new Chapel, now first of all opned at White-hall publiquely for the Popish Service: Nothing can be finer than the magnificent Marble work & Architecture at the End, where are 4 statues representing st. Joh: st Petre, st. Paule, & the Church, statues in white marble, the works of Mr. Gibbons, with all the carving & Pillars of exquisite art & greate cost: The history or Altar piece is the Salutation, The Volto, in *fresca*, the Assumption of the blessed Virgin according to their Traditions with our B: Saviour, and a world of figures, painted by *Verrio*. The Thrones where the K. & Q: sits is very glorious in a Closet above just opposite to the Altar . . . & so I came away: not believing I should ever have lived to see such things in the K. of Englands palace, after it had pleas'd God to enlighten this nation.

THE ANGLICAN CHURCH AND BAROQUE

While May's Windsor was taking shape, Wren was occupied with the rebuilding of London, of St Paul's Cathedral and the City churches, destroyed or damaged in the Great Fire of 1666. St Paul's is in many respects a Baroque building and merits a separate section (p. 26); moreover, while Wren's control of the churches was loose and often only supervisory and did not extend as far as their interior fittings, responsibility for the design of the Cathedral was fully and personally his. Though we correctly speak of the Wren churches, they are a corporate creation of uneven level. And though they provided patterns for Hawksmoor and Gibbs, they themselves have few Baroque features.

The immediate problems in 1670 were the practical ones of speed and planning. Work had already begun on houses and business premises, but the churches were also part of the city's life, and though temporary "tabernacles" were at first set up speed was essential in providing new permanent buildings. Land was valuable; sites were often small, usually circumscribed and irregular and offering only one (sometimes no) front to the street. Those façades which were visible but not quite plain were fields for inventive patterning rather than elaborate decoration; the east end of St Mary-at-Hill is an example of a bold freedom, perhaps knowledgeable enough to be termed Baroque, with the accepted repertory of façade elements (Fig. 5). Sometimes an open site could be exploited, as at St Lawrence Jewry (Pl. 27). The east front, facing the approach to the Guildhall, and contemporary with and resembling one of the Great Model designs for St Paul's, is given a grandeur and plasticity unusual among the churches and dramatically different from the other walls. But it is characteristic both that the outer face of this wall is not parallel to the inside and therefore much thicker at the south end, and that Wren used false perspective arches inside the east windows to compensate for the irregularity.

The planning problem was that of setting a form of worship that had so far adapted to its use, in the main, existing medieval buildings. "It is enough", wrote Wren in 1711 to the Fifty Churches Commission, "if they [the Romanists] hear the Murmur of the Mass, and see

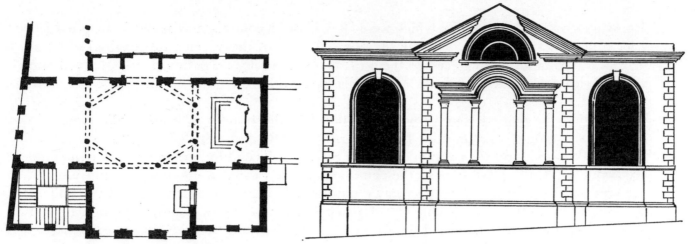

Fig. 4. Whitehall Palace. Plan of James II's chapel (destroyed).

Fig. 5.   St Mary-at-Hill. East end.

the Elevation of the Host, but ours are to be fitted for Auditories." Emphasis on audibility and visibility and a tendency towards spatial unification of interiors were general in seventeenth-century Europe, and the Jesuits as well as the Protestants introduced galleries; Wren's observation curiously seems to take no account of such developments (which were not unknown to him) in the Catholic countries. His antithesis could be made as clearly and as validly between the average English Gothic church, an aggregate of spatially distinct compartments, and his own chapel at Whitehall for James II. The seventeenth century discovered (somewhat as the twentieth is rediscovering with churches and theatres "in the round") the potentialities of presenting the ceremonies, as well as the doctrines, of religion with a theatre-like directness that was deliberately shunned when another kind of spectacle replaced it in the dimly lit surpliced-choir chancels of the Victorian Gothic Revival. In the Catholic church the officially favoured plan since the Counter-Reformation had been a broad Latin cross, and it was thus almost inevitable that in St Peter's itself the perfectly centralized plan, the High Renaissance symbol of the perfection of God, was transformed by the addition of a nave and its original Christian symbolism, no longer understood, was lost. But in the smaller churches of Rome (Borromini), in Piedmont, in France (Mansart's S. Marie de la Visitation), in central Europe, as long as architectural invention flourished the fascination of the centrally-planned interior was immense.

The Wren "auditories" give, as they were intended to give, almost the whole congregation the feeling, visually, aurally and spatially, of direct relation to and participation in the services in a single enclosure. This is true of both small simple interiors and larger churches with aisles and galleries; of St Mary Abchurch (Pl. 20) which, with its plaster dome, painted after 1708, since Hatton does not mention it, by the younger Isaac Fuller or William Snow, rising on cantilever arches from a square plan, is the nearest to a surviving Baroque interior. It is also true of St James, Piccadilly (Fig. 6), not a City church but of a pattern designed by Wren for the City and recommended by him as both "beautiful and convenient, and as such, the cheapest of any Form I could invent". This pattern is indeed little distinguished from the Protestant churches of Holland and France from which it mainly derives, except in its richer decoration (which a less austere form of Protestantism allowed and civic pride demanded) and in the emphasis given decoratively and in the plan to the communion table. In a Catholic church the altar is theoretically the single point of interest and is accordingly emphasized. In a moderate Anglican church of the late seventeenth century this emphasis is neither so marked, because there is no element of miracle in the ritual, nor so exclusive, because of the great liturgical (as opposed to pastoral) importance, in a sermon-conscious age, of the pulpit and lectern. This plurality has an important bearing in particular on

Hawksmoor's churches (p. 100), which were High Church commissions in which the provision of a chancel was specified where the site allowed. Few of the Wren churches had more at the east end than a shallow recess in the wall; many had only a wooden reredos, carved and painted with the Commandments and Lord's Prayer and often with figures of Moses and Aaron.

The fittings in general were provided for not, like the buildings, from public money (a tax on coal coming into London) but from private gifts and parish funds; the reredos of St Mary Abchurch and the carving on that of St James, Piccadilly, are the only documented woodwork by Grinling Gibbons in the churches. In a few cases, none of which survives, the east end was also enriched by decorative painting. St Benet, Gracechurch Street and St Michael, Queenhythe had architectural perspectives, the latter Gothic. At St Michael Bassishaw and St Mildred, Bread Street, St Mary-le-Bow and St Bride, cherubs, clouds or curtains and a "glory" of gold rays were painted. The original appearance of St Bride, which was much altered in the nineteenth century and has recently been restored in pastiche with a totally different floor plan, is recorded in a line drawing (Fig. 7) and in a description in Hatton's *New view of London*, 1708. Besides Moses and Aaron, three columns were painted on either side of the east window; "over the Window 'tis painted *Nebulous*, and above the Clouds appears (from within a large Crimson Velvet Festoon painted Curtain) a Celestial Choir, or a Representation of the Church Triumphant, in the Vision and Presence of a Glory in the shape of a Dove".

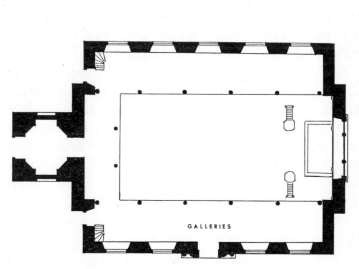

Fig. 6.   St James, Piccadilly. Plan.

Fig. 7.   St Bride, Fleet Street. Original interior.

Much of Wren's invention went into the plans of the churches, which have many variations within half a dozen main types. The larger buildings were aisled (and usually galleried) "auditories", but on small sites necessity encouraged greater freedom. Besides near-square plans such as St Anne and St Agnes, Gresham Street and St Mary-at-Hill, which have intersecting barrel vaults forming a Greek cross, with flat-ceiled corners filling in the square, there are a number of churches which are directed from west to east but have a secondary, but definite, cross axis (e.g. St James, Garlickhythe, Pl. 21); the effect is a compromise between traditional longitudinal and seventeenth-century centralized planning. Two churches destroyed in the nineteenth century, which may well owe more to Hooke than to Wren,[26] were polygonal in plan. St Antholin (Pl. 22) was basically octagonal with the east

[26] Compare for example the (destroyed) polygonal theatre Hooke designed for the College of Physicians (*Walpole Soc.* xxv, pl. xxxvii).

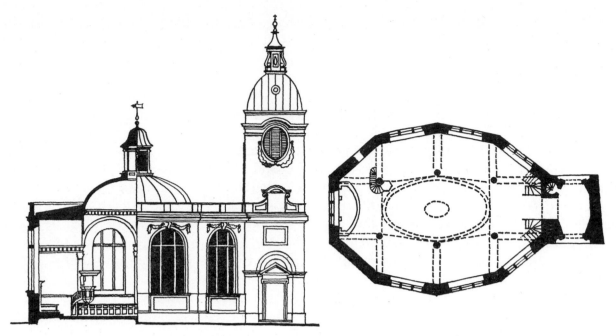

Fig. 8.   St Benet Fink (destroyed). Plan, section and elevation.

end filled out into a rectangle; St Benet Fink (Fig. 8) was a decagon. Both were longer than they were wide; they were thus in effect ovals and had oval domes carried on interior columns. In them, as more clearly and more grandly in the oval churches of Borromini and Bernini, we can trace the Baroque synthesis of directional movement – by lengthening one axis – with the static circular plan of the Renaissance.

The greatest variety and ingenuity occur in the towers and steeples, in which Wren re-created in his own terms the medieval city sky-line of pre-Fire London. Some churches merely had Portland stone towers; others (not always the larger ones) had timber and lead, or stone, steeples above the towers. Some steeples differ little from their Gothic counterparts, others derive from sixteenth- and seventeenth-century Dutch lead spires. The stone spire of St Mary-le-Bow (Pl. 23) is one of the most elaborate and one of the earliest (finished 1680) and it is probably fair to say that Wren never surpassed it either in invention or in construction. In a number of steeples, especially those finished after their churches, the Baroque atmosphere of the spire-city is complemented by Baroque formal qualities, in spite of Wren's expressed preference for straight lines. Edward Strong II built three lanterns concurrently after 1708.[26a] The column-clustered octagon of St Michael Royal (Pl. 55) is obviously, if rectilineally, Borrominesque. At St Stephen, Walbrook (Pl. 18) each face is cut back in layers. The diagonal plan and concave faceted finial of St James, Garlickhythe (Pl. 19) suggest Hawksmoor's hand (cf. Blenheim, Pl. 237). The most remarkable are the barrel-like lead steeple of St Michael, Crooked Lane (1684–98, destroyed, Fig. 9) and the truly Borrominesque concave and convex stone spire of St Vedast (1694–7, Pl. 24). One of the last of the simple towers, at St Andrew, Holborn (finished 1703, Pl. 26) has scrolled pinnacles, and belfry windows whose relief cutting and complication of curves retain the crispness of Wren's Trinity Library (Pl. 49) but are Roman Baroque in feeling. In the light of St Paul's Cathedral it is not necessary to suppose that Wren had been superseded in these works.

In spite of loosely stated claims the City churches as a series are not Baroque architecture. They contain, within a restricting brief, much experiment and variety in planning and structure and much fine craftsmanship, but their language is basically the classicism of Wren's early and middle period, frequently modified to a robust and less refined, and sometimes

[26a] HATTON's silence (*New view of London*, 1708) confirms Edward Strong I's memoir (CLUTTERBUCK,' *Herts*, I, p.168).

cosy, local vernacular. Nevertheless they reflect, through their guiding architect, the changes in English architecture between the Restoration and 1700, and the spread of Baroque ideas and forms.

ST PAUL'S CATHEDRAL

St Paul's is the largest building of our period to be completed as its designer intended; he was 43 when it was begun in 1675 and lived beyond its completion in 1710. This is more than can be said for Vanbrugh's palaces, which withered at the extremities, or for Hampton Court and Greenwich, and it is sufficient, for a start, to put the Cathedral in a special position. Moreover, the evolution of its design, without some knowledge of which it cannot be understood, is well enough documented to show how, and how far, it approaches Wren's ideal for a great church, and how remote – except at the very beginning – that ideal was from the City churches.

The formation of Wren's style and vocabulary continued throughout his career; yet he was never as whole-heartedly Baroque as Vanbrugh and Hawksmoor were. He was wary, as he himself said an architect should be, of "fancy", that element which "blinds the Judgment", while Hawksmoor expressly and Vanbrugh by implication welcomed it. Nevertheless Wren's theoretical writings reflect both sides of the main architectural dispute of seventeenth-century France – absolute versus associative beauty. Wren's rationalistic mind and mathematical training inclined him to the view that beauty conformed to certain fixed, ultimately numerical laws (p. 9). Yet the seventeenth-century post-Baconian part of his training impressed on him the value of experimental solutions in matters of both science and art. If the former view accounted for the basic geometry of St Paul's and its structural ingenuity, the fact that it is a great as well as a large building is as much and perhaps more due to its designer's readiness to make visual experiments on the way to the final effect. It is to this end that he insists that "The Architect ought, above all Things, to be well Skilled in Perspective" so that he can judge the effect of distance and viewpoint on a building.[27]

Wren produced a number of quite different preliminary designs in sequence between 1666 and 1675. Already before the Great Fire, and shortly after his return from France, he made drawings in May 1666 for a new crossing for Old St Paul's with above it a tall dome, that form which, as yet unknown in England, had fascinated him in Paris and was to be the consistent thread of all the later St Paul's designs. Among the post-Fire projects three stand out, known as the First (1670) and Great (1673–4) Model Designs, and the Warrant Design (1675). The First Model partially survives in the Cathedral Library and is also known from one drawing and from descriptions; the Great Model is also in the Cathedral Library. The Warrant Design exists in the drawings at All Souls, Oxford, to which is still attached the Royal Warrant of 14 May 1675 authorizing construction. It was, in terms of development, a throwback, and draws on earlier material such as Inigo Jones's additions to the old cathedral. Wren produced it – having perhaps made it several years earlier – after the rejection of the Great Model scheme and when the latter had already been marked out on the site. The Cathedral was, however, begun in the later summer of 1675 not to the Warrant Design but to a development of it on different dimensions.

The problems of designing the churches stimulated Wren to formulate and overcome them. The problems of designing a cathedral likewise stimulated him, but they were of a different order. There are "iconographical" differences between cathedral and churches: for example, the higher standards of decorative skill Wren was able to command for the

---

[27] See J. SUMMERSON, *Heavenly mansions*, London, 1949, ch. III; SUMMERSON, *Wren*; DOWNES, *Hawksmoor*, ch. II–III.

Fig. 9.　St Michael, Crooked Lane. Steeple (destroyed).

Fig. 10.　St Paul's Cathedral. The Warrant Design. South elevation.

cathedral from the 1680's onwards, and the use there of masonry vaulting instead of plaster. There are also basic formal reasons why a cathedral should not be conceived like a parish church, though Wren may not have appreciated them at the outset. The First Model design for St Paul's was little more than a parish church of the type of the later St James, Piccadilly, though instead of aisles under the galleries opening into the church it had loggias opening outwards, and was glorified by a huge domed vestibule at the west end. The mere confrontation of these two ideas, "auditory" and dome, was perhaps a necessary step for the architect's mind, but that it was an imperfect one he must have begun to realize before, as his son says in *Parentalia*, "observing the Generality were for Grandeur, he endeavour'd to gratify the Taste of the Connoiseurs and Criticks, with something coloss and beautiful, with a Design antique and well studied".[28] In the Great Model (Pl. 25) he showed his ability to offer grandeur in the European manner. The King approved, but the clergy, anxious to preserve and to assert, in a building so much more conspicuous than the parish churches, a formal and thereby a spiritual continuity with the cathedrals of the pre-Reformation Church, wanted a "cathedral form", that is a Latin cross plan. The Great Model was Wren's favourite design, and it is an "ideal" plan such as architects love to make and hope to carry out. It is the very opposite of the practical but ugly and insensitive Warrant Design that followed it (Fig. 10), practical even in "that it might be built and finished by parts" (as the Warrant says), a procedure impossible in the Great Model whose whole core consists of eight equal load-bearing piers carrying the dome.

At least by 1675 the requirements for the building were clear. A choir was needed for the daily services of the Chapter, while for national and other special occasions a much larger space was needed, with adequate room for processions to form and to move. Wren was now bound to the Latin cross plan; at the same time the Great Model had shown him the kind of church he wanted, a centralized domed space, a successor to St Peter's and to François Mansart's project for the Bourbon Chapel at Saint Denis. A portico was also needed to replace Inigo Jones's as a means of keeping secular business outside the church, and Wren considered something taller than a dome desirable as a landmark. Already before the Fire he had written that "many Unbelievers would bewail the Loss of old Paul's Steeple, and

[28] 1903 ed., p. 137.

despond if they did not see a hopeful Successor rise in its stead''. The Warrant Design meets all these requirements except Wren's own. It lacks inspiration, and it is hard to see, after the Great Model, how even at his most rationalistic he can have accepted it as more than a paper solution. The history of St Paul's now becomes the history of the transformation of the Warrant Design, while retaining and fulfilling all the stated needs, into the building we know. The licence is not in the Warrant, but according to *Parentalia* "the King was pleas'd to allow him the Liberty in the Prosecution of his Work, to make some Variations, rather ornamental, than essential, as from Time to Time he should see proper". Wren disregarded the implication of the Warrant's "built and finished by parts"; undoubtedly (and probably rightly) afraid that if he finished the choir first the rest would be postponed indefinitely, he started work on the nave by 1684 while the choir was not opened until 1697. He also saw proper to change much more than a modern architect would be allowed to do, but quite apart from pleading that the result justified the liberties taken we should remember that seventeenth-century standards of accuracy were not the same as ours. When in the Middle Ages a building was commissioned to be "like" another the resemblance was accepted as a very general one. The compiler of *Vitruvius Britannicus* and the architects of Castle Howard were apparently content to publish drawings of that house in which the main elevations disagree in details both with the fabric and with each other. The kind of detailed accuracy we now expect, and sometimes misapply to the past, seems to be the product of the machine age, photography and art history.

Wren had the confidence of the King, and had decided, his son tells us, "to make no more Models, or publickly expose his Drawings". Within a few months of the Warrant the choir had been begun to a similar plan but with different dimensions in both main and side aisles.[29] And though nothing was irrevocable for Wren until it was in masonry, and though the final design of the dome and towers was not settled until the body of the church was ready waiting for them, he must have made at the commencement of work (so as to allow for them in the thickness of the foundations) crucial decisions about both the shape and size of the crossing and the appearance of the outer walls. Whether he settled their decoration or not, he must immediately have decided to introduce the screen-walls which make a two-storey exterior out of a basilican interior (Fig. 11a). The steps leading to this decision cannot be retraced, but it is the key to the character of the building. In the Warrant Design he accepted the Gothic length of the Latin cross plan; in the final design he did everything possible to disguise it and emphasized the domed crossing, and the result is a masterpiece of Baroque illusionism.

Part of the effect comes from alterations at the west end. Instead of the five-bay nave of the Warrant, the fabric has three bays balancing the three of the choir, and then an extra large western bay, which is both longer and slightly wider across the nave than the rest (Fig. 11b). From the west it appears as a necessary vestibule, not as part of the nave; from the crossing (Pl. 33) its walls cannot be seen and its length cannot be appreciated. On the outside the effective nave is also reduced to three bays, balancing the choir, by the projection at the west end of the Morning and Evening Chapels (Pl. 28). Wren also shortened each transept by a bay. A study of the siting of the old and new cathedrals suggests that all these plan changes were also made at the outset.

The elevation itself is more complex. By using coupled pilasters instead of the buttress strips of the Warrant, Wren not only implied his intention of breaking up the length but

---

[29] For the sketches that followed the Warrant Design see J. SUMMERSON, "The Penultimate Design for St Paul's Cathedral", *The Burlington Magazine*, CIII, 1961, pp. 83–9. My conclusions about the early date of the screen walls and changes in plan are independent of Summerson's dating to 1675, of which I remain unconvinced, of the first elevation to show them (*Wren Soc.* I, pl. XIX). In view of this drawing's indebtedness to St Peter's it is worth noting that Hooke was collecting prints of the latter in 1677.

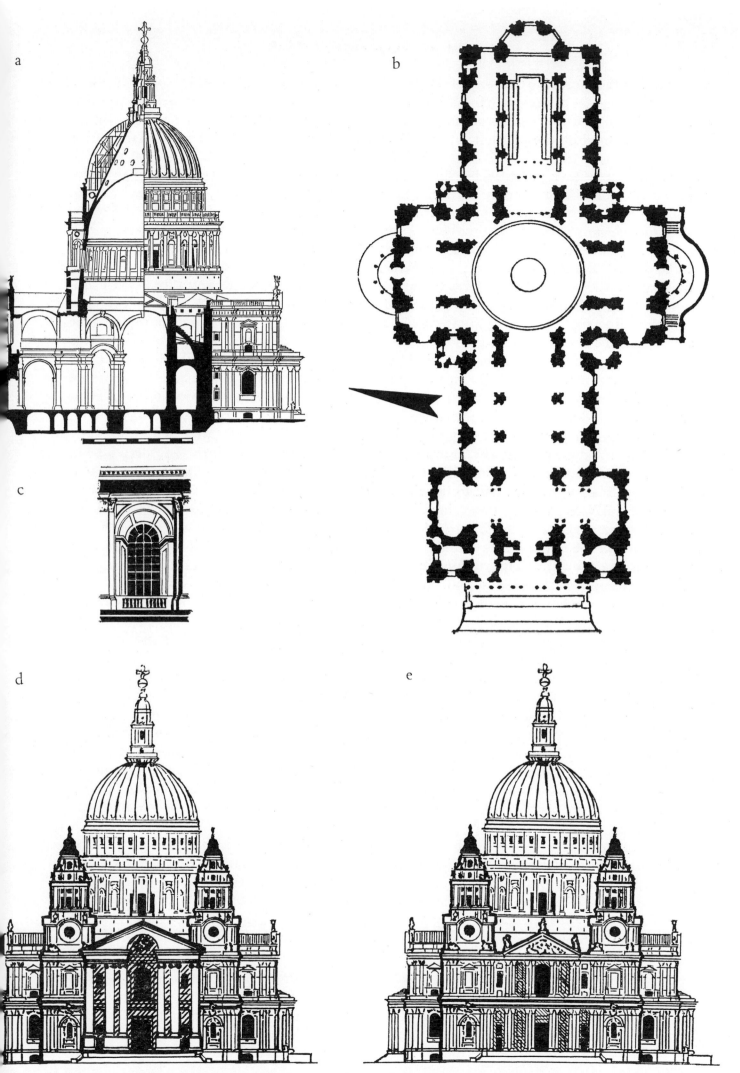

Fig. 11. St Paul's Cathedral. (a) Sections through transept and dome. (b) Plan. (d–e) West elevation with giant portico and as executed. (c) Rome. Palazzo Barberini. Perspective window.

also found the most effective way of shortening each bay, reducing the length of surface wall and enlarging the broken relief areas. But this alone was not enough to cancel out the long horizontals of the Warrant elevation, its two storeys separated in plane and in level by the aisle roof; coupling the pilasters and raising them into a second order are two parts of the same process.

The result is (or appears to be, since the upper walls are merely screens) a single great mass whose dominant lines are verticals (the pilasters). The shortened transepts appear not as cross-arms but as broad projections from the main block. This block is capable, unlike the Warrant elevation, of supporting *visually* the various domes its designer conceived for it, not least the one finally executed. The elevation of St Paul's has been compared with that of Inigo Jones's Banqueting House;[30] its texture and skeleton are similar indeed, and Wren took up the theme of the two-storey elevation a year or so later in Trinity Library at Cambridge. But St Paul's is much richer than Whitehall, and furthermore Wren took new and confident liberties with the language Jones had introduced, just as inside the building he suppressed the main architrave and frieze except over the pilasters. The screen walls have two other functions. They hide the flying buttresses Wren introduced while re-working the Warrant Design to take the thrust of the main vaults and which were too suggestive of Gothic for him to want them to be seen. They also add to the mass and number of cross supports around the main arches that carry the dome. It is typical of Wren that he should have thus combined structural with visual ingenuity; it is typical also that the aedicules he devised to fill the upper storey are both archaeological in inspiration (they derive from Serlio's reconstruction of the interior of the Pantheon) and Baroque in the way he treated his source. They appear at first to be windows; they are not, since the clerestory windows are some thirty feet behind them, invisible from below and separated by the width of the aisle. But below the complex form of niche within architrave within aedicule he has added, in the dado of the upper storey and almost unnoticed, real windows which light the tribunes that lie above the aisles. This running together of forms is a Baroque feature, of which there are other examples in the Cathedral. In the upper part of the transept ends outside, and the lunettes of the western nave bay inside, the relief decoration makes individual elements inseparable, though the detail itself, as in most of the building, is Renaissance Italian rather than Baroque (Pls 52, 48). The transept porticoes are indeed borrowed from Pietro da Cortona's portico to S. Maria della Pace in Rome, known to Wren through Falda's engraving, but the half-oval plan and uneven rhythm of the Roman example are significantly changed to semicircle and regular spacing in the English. The most obvious borrowing of a Baroque motif, the ground floor windows in the towers, was also transformed (Pl. 50). The famous perspective windows on the top floor of the Palazzo Barberini in Rome have illusionistic arches, to suggest greater depth (Fig. 11c). In St Paul's the motif becomes a decorative niche enclosing a window and the illusion is not of depth but of area: visually we accept the whole niche as the opening, but the structural aperture in the base of the tower is actually much smaller. (Wren's use of perspective arches in St Lawrence Jewry has been mentioned.)

Cleaning has begun to reveal the extent to which Wren's concern with surface texture and enrichment, ultimately French in inspiration and evident in drawings both for St Paul's and for the first Hampton Court scheme (p. 37), contributes to the effect of the Cathedral as a whole. The still-life naturalism which Dutch carvers had developed from the painters in the middle of the seventeenth century was transmitted through the Cathedral workshops to the elaboration of the wooden choir stalls (by Gibbons, 1696–8, Pl. 41) and the exuberance

---

[30] The similarity is increased by the Palladian balustrade with which Wren was obliged to finish the Cathedral instead of a solid parapet.

of the frieze panels of the main imposts (Pl. 31) and the Dean's Door under the south-west tower (Pl. 51).

If the whole exterior of St Paul's acts as a base for the dome, the interior too is subordinate to it. Interior and exterior are almost unrelated in scale and dimensions, and the same is true, in the device Wren finally chose, of the dome (Fig. 11a). Outside it is high enough to ride, even today, over the whole city; inside it is low enough not to appear shaft-like, and it is unfortunate that Thornhill's splendid false perspective painting of the inner dome exaggerates the very height that Wren had so cleverly reduced by the use of a double dome (Pl. 39).

The choir was originally closed at the west end by a screen with the organ on the middle of it; it is squatter (being raised on steps)[31] and narrower (because of the stalls) than the nave, and its separation from the latter was logical. Its decoration was also richer, even before the nineteenth century adorned it with unsuitable mosaics. The stonework of the apse and the wooden altar rail were painted to simulate marble, while the apse pilasters, which carry a full entablature (including originally a richly moulded frieze), were painted blue with gold veining. There was a painted golden "glory" over the upper window, and the choir had panels and cushions of crimson velvet and a great deal of gilding of details, while the woodwork was undoubtedly lighter than it is now (Pl. 40).

The organ screen also increased the feeling of enclosure in the central space under the dome. Its removal in 1860 and recent alterations to the apse have made a glaring vista through the whole length of the church, and imagination is needed to appreciate the original effect, with the help of engravings (Pl. 38). Wren was committed to a long plan, but at its heart is the centralized dome-church he had wanted. A comparison of dimensions makes this clearer; the central space is 107 feet across, that is only 17 feet (or about one-sixth) less than in the Great Model. Like the fourteenth-century octagon at Ely, which Wren must have known (his uncle was Bishop of Ely), this space takes the whole width of main and side aisles, and is surrounded by eight arches. At St Paul's the diagonal arches are narrower than the cardinal ones, owing to dimensional changes from the Warrant plan, themselves probably the result of the introduction of the screen walls. The uneven rhythm is only resolved by an illusion: the blind archivolts on the diagonals at the same level as the cardinal arches give the superstructure the appearance of resting on eight equally spaced points, and emphasize the integrity of the central space.

St Paul's, unlike Blenheim, is a comparatively unemotional building. Wren's architecture has a coldness that led Sir John Summerson many years ago to write of it under the title of *The Tyranny of Intellect*. But intellect did not have the last word. Ultimately the effect of St Paul's depends not on rules but on its appearance; that in itself is unclassical and halfway to Baroque. Its logic is first of all visual logic, which tells as little about the logic of its real structure as Verrio's painted elysiums do about the masonry of May's Windsor. In this visual logic a large place is held by ambiguity, a quality foreign both to the monuments of Renaissance Italy, from which our conception of the classic style depends, and to the monuments of English Neo-Palladianism. There is ambiguity at the core of St Paul's, between the equal and unequal rhythms under the dome, between nave-and-transepts and a centralized plan. There is a parallel here in St Stephen, Walbrook (Pl. 37) where in the middle of a rectangular grid plan of columns a dome rises on eight equal arches; this church can be "read" either along its main axes or around and outwards from the centre. There is ambiguity, too, in the form of the aedicules at St Paul's, and in the lack of relation between inside and outside.

The quality and feeling of the Cathedral lie in its total effect, not in the individual

---

[31] Originally the apse floor only was raised. After the removal of the organ screen the entire stalls were shifted some 40 feet westwards to their present position.

manifestations of Wren's eclecticism which led him to borrow from many sources. The dome and west towers were not finally designed until about 1704, but they fit both the earlier building, on which they stand, and each other (Pl. 34). The dome has a grand geometrical simplicity which reflects one side of Wren's genius; the periodic insertion of piers in the peristyle bays is the only unclassical enrichment. The towers show another aspect of their designer in their play of convex and concave forms and in the completeness of their open three-dimensional development. The relation between Wren, Hawksmoor and Vanbrugh is the crucial question in English architecture round 1700, and it involves not only St Paul's but Whitehall and Greenwich. There is no reason, however, to suggest the younger men's influence in the late stages of the Cathedral. The towers may be unique in Wren's work, but there is a drawing in his own hand for one of them, and their forms are hinted at in the steeples already discussed. Moreover, in their lacy openness they are complementary to the dome, and drawings show that some contrast of this sort had been in Wren's mind over many years. His concern for visual effect is further apparent in the illusionist treatment of the windows immediately under both the dome and the cupolas of the towers: they are all blind and filled with panels of Irish black marble.[32]

Wren is an uneven and often unaccountable artist as well as an eclectic one. It is true as a generalization that his later work, from the 1680's onwards, is increasingly Baroque in spirit. But while on the one hand explicit Italian Baroque forms like the tower windows of St Andrew, Holborn (Pl. 26) remain exceptions in a vocabulary basically French in origin, on the other hand there are already extremely bold Baroque implications in the Great Model of 1673–4, for all its classicism. In an undated discourse printed in *Parentalia* Wren expressed a general principle of his art, that straight lines are preferable to curves. Yet the powerful concave corner quadrants, perhaps derived from an engraved plan by Le Pautre, are basic elements in the Great Model exterior. The giant order is also essential to that design, though its scale is imperfectly considered in relation to building and to man, for instance in the colossal substructure. Perhaps because of this, Wren did not envisage giant pilasters for his final design. Only about 1690 did he plan a giant order for the west portico,[33] truly colossal and truly Baroque against the two-storey scaling of the other walls (Fig. 11d). According to *Parentalia* he could not get large enough stones at Portland for the entablature of such an order; since the portico was to project boldly the tower bases could not provide the abutment necessary for flat arches such as Wren used at Trinity College (Pl. 49). The west front was built with the same rhythm as the rest of the exterior but with columns in the portico; the construction, of smaller units, is still complex, and there is a gain in uniformity but a loss of dramatic effect for which Francis Bird's arresting pediment relief of the Conversion of St Paul (Pl. 53) cannot really compensate.

If St Paul's receives more space in this book than any other single building, it is not more than it deserves. Wren's achievement was not only a cathedral built in one life-span, unlike the medieval ones, but also a work as complex and full of diversity as they are. It is not wholly a Baroque building, but in the past it has been criticized as too cold, too theatrical, too Italian (in the Gothic Revival), too English (by eyes that have lingered on St Peter's, with which it has constantly and naturally been compared), and too French (by Shaftesbury). It has all the qualities on which these and other half-truths have been based. Unlike the City churches, and like English Baroque itself, it leads nowhere. But as an architectural creation it is the most important English building of the seventeenth century.

---

[32] *Wren Soc.*, xv, pp. 148, 152. Nevertheless the dome has deceived some draughtsmen into showing glazing bars.

[33] An elevation by Hawksmoor for this scheme (*Wren Soc.*, iii, pl. xv top) is inscribed, in part, *GVLIELM MARII R R*, which indicates a date after 1688.

WORKS INSPIRED BY THE ARCHITECTURE OF LOUIS XIV

England's awareness of her nearest neighbour has always been acute and has frequently encompassed both political mistrust or even hatred and "enlightened" respect for French taste. Charles II's admiration for Louis XIV's successful autonomy – which did not prevent his playing a skilful diplomatic game with his cousin and rival – was uncommon, and was by no means shared even by all his supporters; nevertheless the shadow of Louis fell on English state art from Charles's reign well into that of Queen Anne. Indeed Vanbrugh's remark about Colbert already quoted (p. 13) indicates the persistence in 1721 of an attitude receptive not so much to French taste in general as specifically to the achievements of the French king. Their effect can be seen in England quite apart from France's profound influence on English architects from Wren and Hooke to Talman and Vanbrugh, on English gardens of the period, and even on certain specifically "French" houses; the desire to imitate and outdo Louis lies behind the form or the very existence of some of the major monuments of the period.

Charles's attempts at this form of emulation were not confined to the new state rooms at Windsor. He tried early on to borrow Louis's garden designer, André Le Nôtre, who probably visited England in 1662 and seems to have designed a parterre for Greenwich (p. 125). Cibber's huge relief on the socle of the Monument (Pl. 17) shows Charles as a Roman hero rebuilding the city, in the pictorial language of Versailles. More important architecturally were Chelsea Hospital and Winchester Palace. The Royal Hospital at Chelsea, begun in 1682, was Charles's answer to the Invalides of Louis, and although the formal resemblance is minimal it must have been to this end that Monmouth had asked Louis's minister, Louvois, for plans of the Invalides in 1677 and received them the following year.[34]

If Chelsea, a relatively economical building, lacks the splendour of its prototype, Wren's concern to provide ample light and air for the wards gave his building an equivalent spaciousness without any real similarity in plan. The problems of scale raised by the large centre court, 230 feet square, were new in his work, and there is a curious separation between the simple "functional" stone-dressed brick architecture of the main masses, the hall and chapel, the ward blocks and lodgings, and the decorative elements introduced to give grandeur of scale and expression to a long and sprawling complex: the north and south porticoes and the frontispieces in the middle of the east and west ranges (Pls 13–14). It is not surprising that Wren had not employed a true giant order before, since he had had little occasion and no need for it; at Chelsea, however, it was almost the only solution, and the effect is Baroque not so much in scale as in the solely visual, not structural, logic of the solution. The porticoes frame the vestibule between hall and chapel; the vestibule is a less important part of the building but because it is on the main axis it is emphasized and the hall and chapel are not. Indeed the portico facing the court rides roughshod over the smaller order of the colonnade which provides a covered walk, while in the side frontispieces the insistence on massive scale at the expense of conventional fenestration patterns betrays a certain visual insensitivity which appears infrequently but in consequence all the more clearly in Wren's – and later in Hawksmoor's – work. The ideas planted at Chelsea, which may have sprung from Webb's Greenwich project (Fig. 1), were to bear further fruit with the planning of Greenwich Hospital under William III, and in his pamphlet on Greenwich (1728) Hawksmoor referred to the achievements of Louis XIV and Colbert in the arts and government of France, adding that "Lewis XIV had been truly a Royal Mecaenas had it stopt here".

In 1683 Charles began to build in the guise of a hunting retreat a new palace at Winchester, the old Saxon capital of England; it was nearer to the Channel than to London and

[34] WHINNEY and MILLAR, p. 217, n. 1.

to Parliament and thus easy of access for secret French missions. Wren's design had similarities with the contemporary Chelsea in the use of brick with stone dressings and in the intermittent use of giant columns, but it was the more interesting for being the most French-looking of Charles's commissions. Surviving preparatory drawings show that it was intended to raise over the central block a square mansard dome similar to Lemercier's on the Pavillon de l'Horloge and Le Vau's (now destroyed) on the south front of the Louvre; the engraving in Milner's *History of Winchester* (1798) shows a round dome rather suggesting Le Vau's Collège des Quatre Nations and purports to reproduce Wren's designs (Pl. 15). It is impossible to say whether the architect made this change, since when work was abandoned on the accession of James II in 1685 the dome had not been reached. The most direct link with France, however, was in the plan, which Wren no doubt thought appropriate: the long court facing the town and stepped gradually inwards towards the *cour d'honneur* at the inner end followed closely the layout of Versailles. There is some evidence, too, that Charles intended to build a new street on the axis of the palace leading to the cathedral. However, the interior arrangement did not correspond with Versailles; there the chamber on the main axis was the king's bedroom and the centre of the Bourbon world, whereas behind the portico at Winchester lay not the council chamber, as has been suggested, but the grand staircase leading to a roughly symmetrical left- and right-hand disposition of rooms.[35]

The effect of Versailles, soon to become the ideal of the German princes, was not lost on the Stadholder who became William III, King of England, and without Versailles and perhaps the Louvre, the Hampton Court of Wren would have been impossible. It is not unreasonable to see in the palaces of Louis XIV the ultimate spur for those who wanted to rebuild Whitehall Palace after the fire of 1698. William indeed cared little for Whitehall, but early in 1699 the Earl of Portland was procuring plans of Versailles, Trianon and Marly from J. H. Mansart, apparently in connection with "the design his Majesty is now forming". This was almost certainly the "Trianon" projected near Hampton Court by William Talman; once again the resemblance lay in the idea and not in the form in spite of the marked French character of Talman's work.

The architecture of William III requires separate treatment (below, pp. 35-45). The last and most defiant English architectural allusion to the Sun-king was Blenheim, for which the age of tourism has coined the title of "the English Versailles". Although a title can seldom have been more ill-judged, it was surely Vanbrugh's intention to match, in the monument to Louis's defeat, not only the scale and the rhetoric of Louis's palace but also its basic courtyard plan (Figs 37–8).

WILLIAM III AND THE ARTS

In his life of Matthew Prior, Dr Johnson relates from the former's *History of his own Time* an incident which occurred when the poet-ambassador was in France for the conclusion of the Treaty of Ryswick (1697). "As he was one day surveying the apartments at Versailles, being shown the victories of Lewis, painted by Le Brun, and asked whether the king of England's palace had any such decorations: 'The monuments of my master's actions', said he, 'are to be seen every where but in his own house'." To the extent that the king of England is not, like Louis in another phrase of Prior's, to be found "galloping in every ceiling", this

---

[35] The list of rooms in *Wren Soc.*, VII, pp. 17–19, is not identifiable in detail, but the position of the central staircase is confirmed by the foundation plan there, pl. II lower, and the description by Macky, *Journey*, II (1724 ed., pp. 19–20). Macky also mentions the new street. The palace was converted into a barracks and burned down in 1894; parts of the order were used in the modern barracks. Milner admits that the cupola in his plate is approximate and the statue an invention.

neat and rather smug reply is indeed true. But Prior's image of William was already, as ours still is, coloured by the Whig myth of the king created by Parliament out of a bloodless revolution.

William had been invited by Parliament to the throne of England, he depended on Parliament for money, public as well as personal, and he endeavoured to live *with* Parliament, not *without* it like his predecessors. Alien by upbringing and withdrawn by nature, sagacious politically, frequently abroad on campaigns, never popular, impatient of the ungrateful English he had come to save, William could and did use one weapon not available to his predecessors. This was the threat to return for ever to Holland, leaving England to internal party squabbles on the one hand, and on the other the danger from St Germains, where James II waited in exile as the guest of the French king. Indeed, the only moment of united support for William came in 1701 with James's death and the news of Louis's proclamation of the Old Pretender as King of England. But neither modern ideas of parliamentary monarchy nor Shaftesbury's talk of "the People", nor Walpole's dictum that "he contributed nothing to the Advancement of arts" should be allowed to obscure the fact that William was first and above all a prince and a grandson of Charles I. He was familiar with the splendours of the Huis ten Bosch and Honselaarsdijk, and with the machinery of court ceremonial and court art, the outward signs of government and state. He knew that the princely behaviour expected of a prince extended to patronage of the arts, and while such things as Purcell's compositions in honour of Queen Mary might indicate no more than his tolerance of the idea, there is evidence from his interest in building and in the royal pictures, and from the richness of Portland's embassy to Versailles in 1699, which dazzled even the French, of a more positive acceptance.

As royal foundations Hampton Court and Greenwich Hospital are remarkable by any standards. The very facts of his small popularity and the continual plots against him might suggest a symbol of authority and power such as Hampton Court, the nearest England came to a complete Baroque royal palace, to be a necessity. Hampton Court was for a brief spell the true English Versailles, for in his last two years William received embassies there in the newly completed section of the palace. And if he perhaps wished Hampton Court to tell us less about him than Versailles does about Louis or Würzburg about the Schönborns, it remains nevertheless unmistakably his monument. Not only did it become his principal home in England; although its decoration was discreet by the standards of Versailles it was full of references to his person, character and status.

The symbolism of Hercules appears in works of art connected with the House of Orange before William's maturity and seems to be connected with the new power and freedom of the United Provinces. The concept may have gained in attraction for him because of his own short stature and continual ill-health, and by the time of Hampton Court it amounts to personal identification. Thus he appears on the King's Staircase (Pl. 109) where Verrio painted, perhaps without understanding the programme, a complicated allegory of the triumph of Protestantism; in the ceiling too are the lions of Hercules and the zodiacal sign of Leo. The round window frames carved by William Emmett in the Fountain Court (Pl. 68) – some of the finest work of the period – take the form of Hercules's lion-skins with orange-wreaths (for the house of Orange) and the roundel fields in the south side of the court were painted by Laguerre with the Labours of Hercules in *grisaille*. In Cibber's pediment of the garden front (Pl. 54) Hercules tramples on Superstition (with a censer), Tyranny (with a crown and sword), and Fury (with serpent-hair) and is led by Fame to the Arts of Peace. In the three doorways directly below, carved with the English rose and Scottish thistle, while the middle hood has putti holding the crown, the side ones have the twin snakes that were strangled by the infant Hercules (Pl. 59). The south frontispiece bears the names of William and Mary and the keystones of the ground floor windows have the joint monogram W M R R, so marvellously undercut that birds have built their nests behind the letters. This is the language of Versailles and it is continued in the trophies over the entrances (Pl. 69); it appears most clearly in the full-size equestrian portrait painted in 1701 by Kneller for the Presence Chamber, where it still hangs, recognizably modelled on the Mignard of Louis XIV painted for an analogous position at Versailles.

The state of the royal palaces at the end of 1688 was not reassuring. At Whitehall, the picturesque assortment of buildings recently vacated by the flight of James, William immediately refused to live because of the damp of the Thames and because the smoke of London provoked his asthma. The same objections applied with less force to St James's, which in any case had not been much used since the Restoration. He received the younger Clarendon and his brother, Rochester, at Windsor on 16 December 1688, and later considered it worth commissioning from Kneller an illusionist portrait of himself enthroned to take the place in St George's Hall of the throne installed for Charles II, but the gaze of the latter from pantheon after pantheon cannot have pleased him and he preferred to live there infrequently. Winchester was a mere shell, and although in March 1694 Narcissus Luttrell reported that William was considering completing it, many of the materials had already been removed for use at Hampton Court. He had taken an immediate liking to the latter on his first visit (23 February 1689), and although the sovereigns found it old-fashioned, the decision to live there was almost immediate. The bed of state was brought there from Windsor,[36] and in April work was in progress on adapting for their use the Tudor palace, which Charles II had frequently inhabited but little altered apart from laying out gardens and building the canal through the Home Park; London was soon grumbling at the loss of the gay court of the two previous Stuarts for a king who only came to London on Council days.

THE ROYAL PALACES UNDER WILLIAM AND MARY AND QUEEN ANNE

The sovereigns must have decided almost as soon to make their own mark, to rebuild the palace, for new foundations were being dug in July. At the same time (June 1689) they bought Nottingham House as the nucleus of what is now Kensington Palace and was then well outside London. According to *Parentalia* Wren's buildings at Hampton Court were "a part only" of his design, and drawings in the Soane Museum show a plan (Fig. 12a) which would have swept away the whole Tudor palace, leaving only Henry VIII's Great Hall at the end of a new long court, the climax of an approach from the north through Bushy Park. The axis of this approach continued through a semicircular colonnade fronting the Hall and probably underneath it into another court and thence through a long garden down to the Thames. As the river was still a practical means of transport the western approach was to be regularized, by way of another long court leading to the main enclosed court and ultimately to Charles II's canal, which thus formed the second axis of the whole plan. Wren had seen Bernini's design for the Louvre in 1665 – and probably that of François Mansart also; his continued interest in French architecture twenty-five years later is known from other sources, and there is evidence of his royal patron's interest from the latter's correspondence and that of his friend and ambassador, William Bentinck, Duke of Portland. It is reasonable to suppose that, as with the earlier recorded case of the Invalides, representations were available to architect and king of the later stages of the Louvre and Versailles. In the long entrance courts and the general grandeur of scale the first Hampton Court plan looks via Winchester to Versailles, while the closed court recalls that of the Louvre.[37]

[36] H.M.C. Portland III, p. 431.
[37] A second design known from drawings (*Wren Soc.*, IV, pls XIII–XIV) is also strongly indebted to the Louvre, in particular to Perrault's north front.

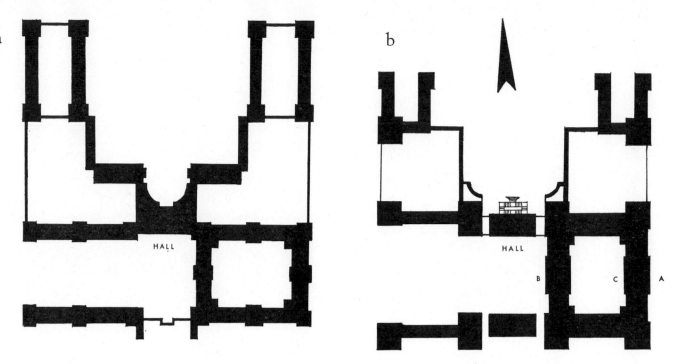

Fig. 12.   Hampton Court. Wren's grand scheme in two versions.

For this plan no elevations survive, but the main fronts of a related plan can be reconstructed from sketches in Wren's own hand (Figs 12b, 13). The Great Hall is here entered from the north by a grand staircase and is made to stand free from other buildings. In the court elevations both plan and silhouette are much more varied than at Chelsea or Winchester, and in effect Wren is composing with large block-like pavilions linked by lower smaller ones, and incorporating the Hall in his scheme, thus anticipating the composition of his 1698 proposals for Whitehall and his treatment there of the Banqueting House. The profusion of surface enrichment is French; the panels between the windows recall the Cour de Marbre at Versailles and there is probably a direct reference, in the stair towers in the angles of the court, to Bernini's third project for the Louvre. But in the handling of large masses in elevation and in depth, in the freedom of variation in bay-rhythms, and in the dramatic use of a giant order in the centre blocks, these elevations are Baroque in the terms not merely of Webb at Greenwich but of Maderno in Rome. Their assurance is surprising enough as an advance from the infelicities of Chelsea (Pl. 16); it is the more remarkable in view of the haste common to William's building works: the whole development from first to final design for Hampton Court can be placed between March and midsummer 1689.

It was probably speed rather than economy which led William to reject these schemes in favour of a partial rebuilding consisting of two new ranges, conforming to the usual division of "King's side" and "Queen's side" and facing respectively the Privy Garden on the south and the Park on the east; in the inner angle between them are the four sides of a new court of moderate size (117 feet by 110 feet, Fig. 14). Wren seems to have appreciated the difference between complete and partial rebuilding as one of kind, not of degree – the difference in fact between a fully three-dimensional composition and, in the later designs including the final one, two screening façades and the Fountain Court not directly related to them (Pls 57,62,66). All the final elevations share a uniform and unbroken parapet level and retain the division into a low ground storey, a *piano nobile* with an upper mezzanine, and an attic above a continuous cornice and fascia. The elevations are again conceived in large units, but they have been censured both for the richness of their close-set Portland stone dressings on a ground of scarlet-orange brickwork and for their lack of relief in height and depth. The

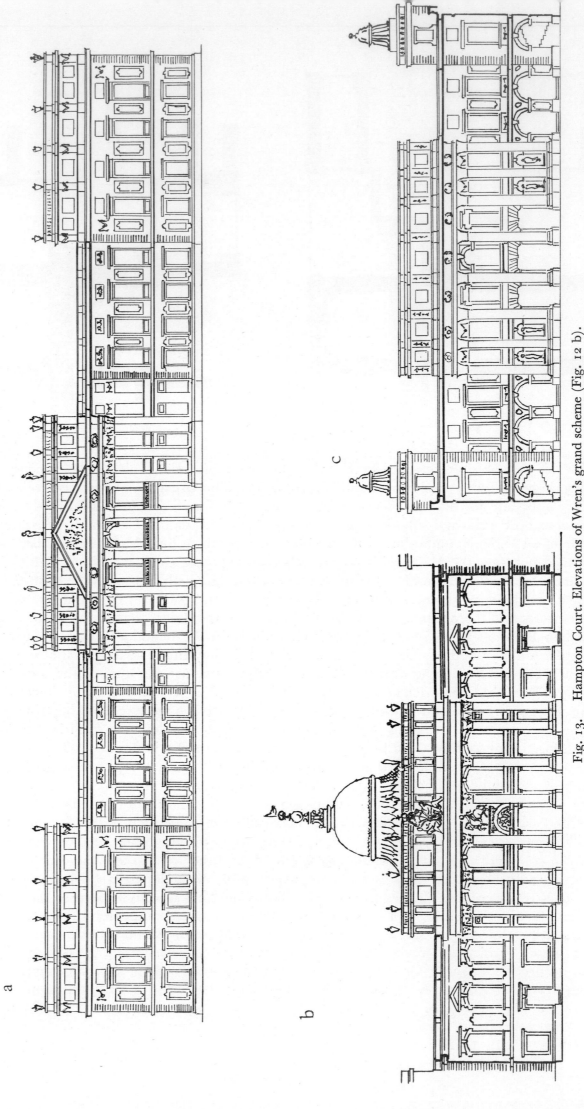

Fig. 13. Hampton Court. Elevations of Wren's grand scheme (Fig. 12 b).
(a) East front to Park. (b) West entrance front. (c) East side of Privy Court.

truth, which lies between these conflicting criticisms, is that they are, like the outer walls of St Paul's, screens, designed in this case to provide quickly and at least cost consistent with grandeur the illusion of a complete and regular palace – even the effect of the long flat garden front of the new Versailles of J. H. Mansart. In the interest of the illusion the mezzanine is treated as expendable; most of the round windows are real and light the mezzanine rooms, but in the larger state rooms of the main storey the ceilings are raised into the mezzanine for extra height. In the centre bays of the two outer fronts this device is screened by the entablature and frieze; the roundels on the north side of Fountain Court (the outer wall of the King's Gallery) are painted in *grisaille*. The four roundels nearest the centre of the south front were also decorated by Laguerre with emblems of the seasons but have been repainted matching a number of other false windows, placed to conceal internal irregularities, which have always had fictive glazing bars (Pl. 64).

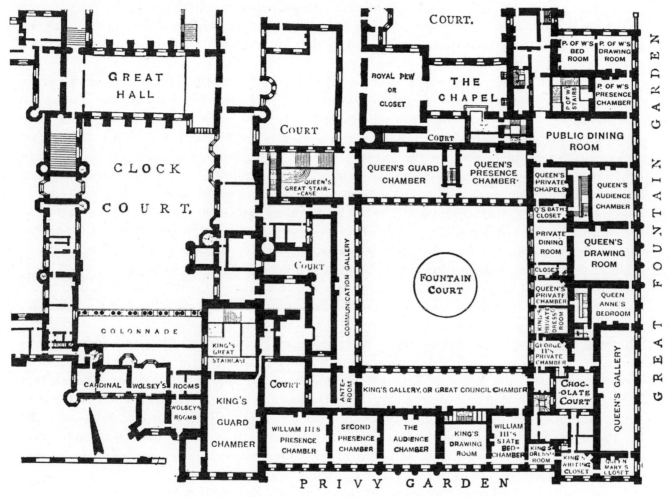

Fig. 14.   Hampton Court. First floor plan of Wren's building.

Wren's ingenuity appears further in the plan and elevation of the Fountain Court. In order to minimize demolitions he planned it on an axis two bays south of the centre of the Park front; he solved the consequent problem of symmetry by a shift of axis common in seventeenth-century Paris houses. He placed apses on either side of the court axis, one apse being blind and the other (Pl. 65) leading through a pillared hall to the central doorway of the Park front. In the elevation he repeated the device he had used at Trinity College, Cambridge (Pl. 30) of raising the archivolts of the loggia above the level of the floor above, but instead of a flat ceiling span he used low segmental arches and a low brick vault.

According to *Parentalia* the low level was the express wish of the king, and Wren was accustomed to elevations of two orders, as at St Paul's and Trinity Library, or of a giant order standing on the ground, as at Winchester and Chelsea, and not to the Palladian formula of a half-storey basement (Pl. 221). The state suites of Versailles and Windsor set a precedent in opening from a staircase and therefore being situated upstairs, and this precedent is followed at Hampton Court and at Kensington. The King's Gallery there (Pl. 83) as well as Hampton Court approach closely the Palladian formula, for in both the ground storey is lower than normal. Why the king preferred this arrangement we do not know at first hand, but the possibility that, because of his asthma, he wanted the minimum number of stairs from the ground to the state-rooms, is stated as a fact by a near-contemporary source (Macky's *Journey*, 1722). The problem of levels also contributed to the least satisfactory aspect of the palace, the stone-faced seven-bay centre of the Park front (Pl. 57). This "reads" as a single unit from ground to balustrade, and along the rest of the front the ground and first floor windows are linked by stone panels. Three low doorways inevitably make dark tunnel-like holes precisely where we should expect a solid base for the frontispiece at the focal point of the whole park.[38] The lengthening of the middle windows down to the continuous hood moulding just above them, which appears only in the last drawings, adds to the apparent instability.

Only a total re-designing could have saved this front from the appearance of a centre dropped under its own weight, and there was probably not time for such revision. The speed of work was probably the cause of a fall of part of the new south range in December 1689 (as it was of a similar accident at Kensington a month earlier) and was such that the east range was ready for roofing in the autumn of 1691, after two years' work, and the south range probably a year later. By this time a considerable amount of exterior carving had been done, including Emmett's lion-skin windows, the frieze and probably the hoods of the Park front doorways and the trophy relief by Grinling Gibbons, and the coats of arms on the south front by Cibber (Pl. 63). The latter's pediment relief on the east front (Pl. 54) was carved in 1694. Statues and urns for the gardens had also been provided; some of these, including the great urns by Pierce and Cibber, are now at Windsor (Pl. 73).

At the death of Queen Mary from smallpox on 28 December 1694, the structure of the palace was fairly complete, including the whole Fountain Court and the King's Staircase with its entrance colonnade in the Tudor Clock Court (Pl. 67). Work came to a standstill. The king was occupied with campaigns and diplomacy, and the finishing and decoration of the palace seem not to have been continued until 1697–8. But in June 1699 Luttrell reported 400 men at work; the Peace of Ryswick (September 1697) had given William recognition from Louis XIV and at least temporary security, and the fire at Whitehall Palace (January 1698) made the completion of Hampton Court the more desirable. According to an estimate by Wren of April 1699, the decoration of many rooms was "long since designed" and several of the fireplace designs by Gibbons in the Soane Museum have symbols appropriate to the joint sovereignty and must have been made before 1695.

Verrio, who had retired to work at Burghley after the Revolution, and was finally persuaded to return to royal service in 1699, painted the King's Staircase and the Banqueting House in the Privy Garden and the ceilings of the State and Little Bedchambers; all this was between 1700 and the summer of 1702. But the panelled and carved rooms and the few painted ceilings break no new ground, and the one building which did so, the Water Gallery, was demolished by the king's orders in 1700. This was a Tudor building at the river end of the Privy Garden to which Queen Mary had taken a fancy and which was entirely redecorated for her, with a marble room, a "japan" (lacquered) room, a looking-glass room, a "porcelain" room lined with blue and white tiles designed by Daniel Marot and, according to

---

[38] A similarly uncomfortable arrangement of three low entrances between the pedestals of an order occurs in the west front of the Greek Cross Design for St Paul's of 1672–3 (*Wren Soc.*, I, pl. XVII).

Defoe in 1724 (*A Tour through England and Wales*), a dairy. It was in the Water Gallery that Mary hung the "Hampton Court Beauties" of Kneller and kept her collection of Delft china some of which was also designed for her by Marot. The latter, a Huguenot, had been in William's service since the Revocation of the Edict of Nantes in 1685, styled himself "architecte de Guillaume III Roy d'Angleterre", and was responsible for the layout of the parterre in the east garden (Pl. 553). He was in England in 1695–6 and again in 1698, and though the work for the Queen is before this the assumption of earlier visits cannot be proved.[39] His personal influence (as distinct from the influence of his engravings) is not evident elsewhere in the palace, but he may have designed a good deal of the work in the Water Gallery, which stands, historically, between Le Vau's short-lived Trianon de Porcelaine at Versailles and the garden houses of Rococo Germany. William is usually said to have ordered its destruction because it reminded him of his dead wife, but as the order was made from Holland five years after her death it seems likely that he had never cared for the building and responded to suggestions that it blocked the view from the south front.

Marot's activity raises a more general question of William's choice of artists. A royal appointment was no doubt more eagerly sought, more likely to be assumed without warrant, and less often granted as an exclusive monopoly than it is today. William Talman is often described as favoured by King William, but beyond the existence of the "Trianon" designs and plans for a house of fifteen bays "Made by Direction of K. William" there is little evidence of partiality, although he was appointed Portland's deputy in the superintendence of the Royal Gardens. Talman may have owed to the influence of the Earl of Devonshire, for whom he was working at Chatsworth (p. 61) and at some time made plans for a London house, his appointment in 1689 to the Comptrollership of Works which had been vacant since May's death five years before. He certainly lost the post by an analogous process when, after William's death, Vanbrugh gained it through the influence of Lord Carlisle. Wren must have resented Talman's appointment; he possibly considered a Comptroller unnecessary and found in Talman a determined rival. The trouble started with the new man's efforts to make a scandal out of the building accident at Hampton Court (December 1689, p. 40) and culminated ten years later with an attempt to wrest from Wren the Comptrollership at Windsor Castle. In the Hampton Court affair the king upheld the authority of his surveyor, Wren; while Talman's salary and travelling charges appear with Wren's in the Hampton Court accounts, and while certain similarities may be noted, such as the four-columned vestibule under the middle of the east front and a similar arrangement in Talman drawings and in the Chatsworth grotto (Fig. 27a), there is no real evidence that Talman designed any part of the palace.

The "Trianon" drawings in the R.I.B.A. include a complete bound set of designs; its purpose as a country retreat from the court is shown by the garden front motto: VITO SUPERBA CIVIUM LIMINA (I shun the proud thresholds of the citizens). A plan shows the intended site to be across the Thames from Hampton Court in the neighbourhood of the modern Surbiton station; the south-east avenue of Hampton Court Park is continued over the river, the intended crossing presumably being by ferry as no bridge is shown. The

[39] A. LANE, "Daniel Marot, designer of Delft vases and of gardens at Hampton Court", *Connoisseur*, CXXIII, 1949, pp. 19–24. The same writer's later article in *Rijksmuseum Bulletin*, Amsterdam, VII, 1959, pp. 12–21, incorporates the same material and publishes a drawing of the Hampton Court parterre bearing Marot's name and the date 1689, but the orthography of the date is not above suspicion and the character of the drawing suggests a later date. In 1694 Marot was captured by the French on his way to England. The garden plan after Claude Desgots in the Nationalmuseum, Stockholm (CTH 7631) published by R. Strandberg, *Münchner Jahrbuch der Bildenden Kunst*, 3. FOLGE, XV, 1964, p. 180, as Hampton Court, shows in plan the buildings of Windsor Castle, and probably relates to the projected Windsor garden of 1698 (see p. 125 and note 125). The "1689" drawing is reproduced in *The Burlington Magazine*, XCII, 1950, p. 229, Fig. 19.

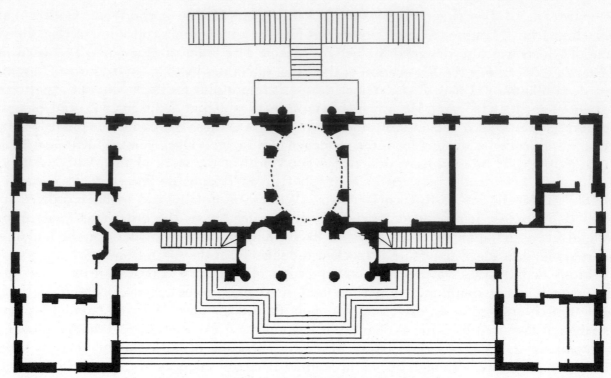

Fig. 15. William Talman's plan for a Trianon.

house, of one floor with a basement, is more French than anything built in England. The entrance front (Pl. 146) is closely related to Louis or François Le Vau's château of S. Sépulchre which was engraved in the *Grand Marot*; the garden front has a Flemish-looking double-pedimented frontispiece but the lateral bays have Doric pilasters and channelled arcading similar to Montagu's front at Boughton (p. 58). The garden terrace (Pl. 145) is grassed and flanked by arcades apparently, from their shape and the stipple of the drawings, cut out of evergreen and fronted by statues, urns and benches. In front are a semi-circular pond and a grotto with steps up to the terrace like those on the west front of Chatsworth. The interior decoration shown in the section is, perhaps at William's wish, close to the style of Marot whom Talman would by this time have met in England. The oval vestibule (Fig. 15) is French, but Talman's immediate source may have been May's entrance to Cassiobury (p. 18). The Trianon scheme, which came to nothing – presumably because of the king's illness and death – has great charm; if Talman's patrons saw similar drawings of other schemes they were no doubt eager to employ him in the face of any reports of his tiresome behaviour.

Hampton Court remains half a Tudor palace and lacks a grand entrance on the scale Wren planned. He seems to have presented his scheme for a northern court again in 1699 when the Bushy Park avenue was put in hand, but the scheme probably died with the king. The piers of the Lion Gates facing Bushy Park have Queen Anne's monogram, but they lead to a shrubbery. Anne's chief interest in the place was in hunting from a chaise, and the park avenues were improved to facilitate this amusement. Verrio's last work there, the over-pink decoration of the Queen's Drawing Room in the middle of the east range, was done in 1702–4, with scenes on the walls painted as feigned tapestries. The fitting of the rooms on the north side of Fountain Court continued into the Palladian period. The last work of the old school was the three fireplaces in what is now the Prince of Wales's suite at the north end of the east front (Pls 280–82).

William took a greater interest in Windsor towards the end of his life, revising the decorative programme by means of the Kneller portrait already mentioned and various alterations by Verrio after 1699; plans were also on foot in July 1698 for a new garden there, and the Office of Works at least considered a scheme for rebuilding the south front, in a similar style to May's refacing of the rest of the Upper Ward, and for extending it westwards as far as the Round Tower, making it symmetrical about a new entrance with an outside staircase leading down to a garden on the axis of the Long Walk which had been laid out by Charles II. Drawings for this survive by Hawksmoor (dated 1698) and probably by William Dickinson, and the scheme may have resulted from the destruction of Whitehall (Pl. 81).

The king bought the Jacobean Nottingham House in June 1689 from Daniel Finch, 2nd Earl of Nottingham, and immediately began to have it remodelled and enlarged as a suburban house within convenient distance, on foot if necessary, of Westminster. He renamed it Kensington House; the modern name of Kensington Palace was not used in his time, and the scale of building and decoration was much humbler than Hampton Court. Work on the addition of corner pavilions to the old house proceeded so fast that, although in November there was a fall of work already roofed, the sovereigns were able to move in before Christmas. Work continued until 1696 on piecemeal additional ranges and courts with disastrous effects on symmetry, and the rebuilding of the Jacobean core by Benson and Kent after 1718 and subsequent alterations have left a complex of buildings of great charm but of little relevance to this book. The early nineteenth century saw the loss of the Guard Chamber at the bottom of the main staircase (1692–3) which had walls of wainscot "colour grained", one or more chimney pieces of Portland stone painted with marble veining, and "a large Caesar's head & Busto bronzed" by the caster, Richard Osgood. The one building which combines heroic intentions with economy of statement, the outside of the south-east range containing the King's Gallery, remains unaltered (Pl. 83). It is of dark red brick with orange rubbed brick round the windows and a heavy wooden bracketed cornice; it was probably planned about 1690 but was built in 1695–6 and is very probably an early work of Hawksmoor who was Clerk of Works at Kensington from 1689 to 1715.[40] For Queen Anne Hawksmoor designed the Orangery north-east of the palace, which was built in 1704–5 and also survives (Pls 84–5). The most remarkable features of its interior are the rotundas at each end, which are clearly from the same mind as the gallery at Easton Neston; the exterior displays, in its curved attics and the variations of reiterated arches, niches and lunettes that fill its three-bay frontispieces and ends, the ingenuity in relief and surface pattern of one of the masters of English Baroque.

WREN'S WHITEHALL DESIGNS, 1698

On the afternoon of 4 January 1698 fire broke out at Whitehall; it burned all night, and by great efforts on the part of Wren and others the Banqueting House was saved; the assorted buildings that made up the palace, including the fabric of James II's Popish chapel, were ruined. On 20 January, Luttrell reported that Wren had surveyed and measured the site in preparation for rebuilding and that "his majestie designes to make it a noble palace, which by computation may be finisht in 4 years". But William had written to Heinsius three days after the fire that "the loss is less to me than it would be to another person, for I cannot live there. Yet it is serious." And by 3 March he had directed the building (never in fact carried out) of a council room and five lodgings; "the rest", wrote Luttrell, "will be omitted until the parliament provide for the same". The same writer's report in October 1702, that Queen Anne intended to set aside £100,000 a year for six years to rebuild Whitehall, was merely another flourish of the biggest architectural might-have-been of the Baroque

---

[40] For questions of attribution at Kensington see DOWNES, *Hawksmoor*, pp. 65–6, 81–2.

period. The disinclination of Parliament to allocate money for Whitehall may well betray a fear that a palace of such grandeur, on a site eternally associated with the earlier Stuarts (and centred in Wren's designs on the Banqueting House from which Charles I walked to the scaffold) would be halfway back to absolute monarchy; some ground for this fear may be adduced from the fact of Jacobite attempts to blame William for the fire. According to Macaulay, for whom the issue was political, it was the Tories who kept up the clamour for rebuilding, but the issue was also artistic. Shaftesbury, in the *Letter concerning design*, saw it as the great opportunity for the imminent National Style: "Hardly, indeed, as the Publick now stands, shou'd we bear to see a *Whitehall* treated like a *Hampton-Court*." Yet *Vitruvius Britannicus* contains no more than a resurrection in Volume II of a design supposedly by Inigo Jones for Charles I; Kent's larger publication of Jones's drawings (1727) was likewise an historical exercise. But before that eight or more independent designs are known to have been made for a new royal palace, either on or near the Whitehall site.

Pride of place inevitably goes to the two sets of drawings, numbered First and Second by the Wren Society (Figs 16a, b) which have come down to us in detail and which seem to be almost entirely the conception and largely the handiwork of Wren, assisted in drawing by Hawksmoor and probably also by William Talman. The collaboration and indeed the influence of Hawksmoor and Vanbrugh have often been seen in the design of these schemes, but this view, which would deny a great artist the faculty of surpassing his previous achievements, is not confirmed by closer examination of them. They must have been made in 1698, soon after the fire and before enthusiasm had cooled, and Vanbrugh was not yet connected with the Office of Works: the case against Hawksmoor's having been more than draughtsman is that the vocabulary of detail is Wren's as we know it from earlier works, not Hawksmoor's (Pl. 75). The ornament on the river façade of the "First" design, which confirms an early date in the use of William's initials and the relief of his landing from Torbay, has been put in by another hand – probably Grinling Gibbons, but architectural details such as the dormers in the round towers are Wren's (Pl. 76). In another block the elements of the Trinity Library façades are rearranged (Pl. 79). When the drawings in the Bute Collection were rediscovered and sold in 1951, All Souls College acquired an alternative of the river elevation, probably in William Talman's hand, showing different ornament (Pl. 77) and including two buildings known previously only in plan: the Thermae-like elevation of the proposed new Parliament House and the long corridor leading to it (Pl. 78). The French elements of these suggest Du Cerceau, Le Pautre and perhaps Le Vau, that is to say, the less classical side of French tradition.

There is also a sketch of the "First" design almost certainly in Wren's hand, showing the palace in perspective from St James's Park (Pl. 74), and bringing home the force of Wren's invention. This scheme, centred round Inigo's Banqueting House, and oriented to include such fixed points as Westminster Abbey and the Long Water in the park, is marked by such dramatic strokes as the giant portico fronting the House and the giant-columned stair-towers flanking it; by composition in massive blocks with strong projecting features, by flexible bay rhythms, by contrast in adjacent elevations. It picks up and develops the ideas set out nearly a decade earlier in Wren's big design, centred round the Great Hall, for Hampton Court. The plan includes gardens and canals.

The "Second" Wren design (Fig. 16b, Pls 80, 82) is smaller and is descended from a scheme of John Webb for a palace with the Banqueting House duplicated as a chapel. The giant order with a bold bracketed cornice, like that used less frequently in the larger scheme, directly recalls Bernini's Louvre design, and there are other links with France: the very elaborate central staircase is related to a Louvre plan by Perrault and the portico in front of it has the rhythm of Le Vau's Collège des Quatre Nations, afterwards to be used by Vanbrugh at Blenheim and Stowe. A common French source probably also explains the similarity

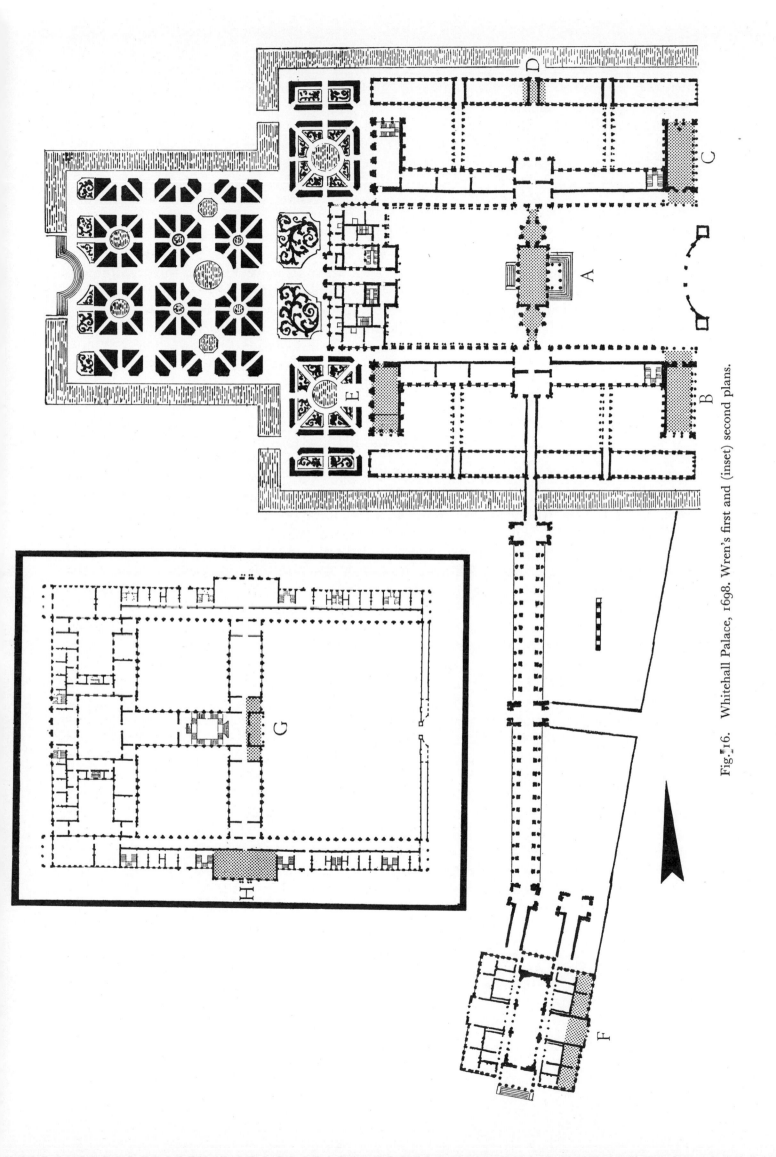

Fig. 16. Whitehall Palace, 1698. Wren's first and (inset) second plans.

between the centres of the side fronts and the Library of the Queen's College, Oxford, of 1692–5, which is probably by Aldrich (Pl. 531). Whereas the first scheme carries on the monumentality of the Hampton Court project, the second develops its tendency towards separating a series of large blocks by smaller linking buildings, in this case gate-towers.

Whitehall would have been Wren's greatest achievement in secular architecture. The elevations and plans give us some idea of it, and this we can supplement by looking at Greenwich Hospital, silhouetted in the misty greys of Thames-side winter or brilliant and strongly modelled in May sunshine. Flashes of genius like the apparent simplicity of Trinity Library or the Great Model for St Paul's should not blind us to the fact that Wren remained a learner and would have done so even if he had not been, as an artist, self-taught. Chelsea may be less successful than Trinity Library, but it attempts more. In 1698 the expansion to a larger scale of the free vocabulary he had built up throughout his career, and the handling of large masses which he had first attempted at Chelsea fifteen years earlier, were in the palm of his hand. Whitehall would have lacked the excitement of Blenheim, the imagery of Windsor and Versailles, the confectionery and the interior spatial organization of Würzburg, the plasticity in wall and detail of the Italians. Yet it would have been a great Baroque palace, and these are the comparisons it invites.

PALACES IN THE AIR

Other schemes are fragmentary. Sketches for a palace for Queen Anne by John Talman survive in the Royal Library at Windsor and the Victoria and Albert Museum;[41] the plan is vast but the wildly eclectic ornament seems to be the main interest of the elevation. William Emmett, the nephew of the carver of the same name and the owner of the drawings used by Campbell to present Inigo Jones's Whitehall designs in *Vitruvius Britannicus*, made drawings of his own, one of which is in the British Museum (Fig. 17). Features such as the perspective windows of the attic betray Emmett's knowledge of Wren, but the main inspiration of this overloaded design seems to be Italian engraving. Sketches for a palace by Hawksmoor are remarkably Palladian in vocabulary, and probably therefore datable about 1715–20, but neither the plan nor any complete elevations can be reconstructed.

Further designs for a new palace survive only in descriptions. One was made for William III by Jean Bodt or Bott (1670–1745), a Huguenot who went to Holland in 1685, was employed by William as a military engineer from 1690 to 1699, was in England in 1698, made designs for Greenwich Hospital, subsequently went to Berlin as architect to Frederick I of Brandenburg, and will be considered later as the architect of the south front of Wentworth Castle (p. 72). Bodt's Whitehall project is lost but from comparison with other surviving designs including that for Greenwich it must have been grandiose.[42] The Italian, Domenico Martinelli (1650–1718), who worked principally in Lucca and in Austria, is said to have designed a palace for William to be built at Brussels;[43] this is indeed possible, but the drawings, now lost, may have been connected with Whitehall. The Florentine dilettante, Paolo Falconieri, gave a design to the Duke of Shrewsbury in 1704.[44] A design was also made by another Florentine, Alessandro Galilei (1691–1737), whom The Hon. John Molesworth, English envoy to the Grand Duke of Tuscany, brought to England in 1714. Molesworth seems to

[41] A. P. OPPÉ, *English drawings at Windsor Castle*, London, 1950, cat. 609 (as William Talman); Victoria and Albert Museum, E.87–1940, E.306–1940.

[42] Information in COLVIN, *Dictionary* (under Bott) is supplemented by N. PEVSNER, "John Bodt in England". *Architectural Review*, CXXX, 1961, pp. 29–34.

[43] H. TIETZE, *Domenico Martinelli und seine Tätigkeit in Österreich*, Vienna, 1927, p. 7.

[44] H.M.C. Buccleuch II, p. 776.

have enjoyed the idea of keeping and showing off a tame architect; introductions included one to Sir Thomas Hewett, the nonentity who later succeeded the incompetent Benson (p. 7) as Surveyor-General. Galilei made drawings for the Fifty New Churches scheme and, encouraged by Hewett, for a royal palace. This was to have been shown to George I, but Hewett became non-committal and polite and finally regretful; possibly he hoped, but failed, to advance himself or to embarrass the Wren school through Galilei. The Florentine went home in 1719, taking an English bride and leaving in England one work which has only recently been recognized as his (p. 82). He seems to have taken his drawings with him, for he showed them to a Scottish traveller in 1733.[45] Some church designs survive in Florence, but for the palace there is only a hasty sketch and a written *Reflection upon the Scituation of the Royal Palace* of which Italian and English versions are in the Florentine State Archives. He reacted as strongly as William III to the atmosphere of the Thames and suggested for his enormous palace a site in the middle of St James's Park, aligned between St James's Square on the north and Westminster Abbey on the south and approximately between St Paul's on the east and Chelsea Hospital on the west. Alternatively he proposed the east side of Hyde Park with views to Hampstead and Chelsea and a broad road to Westminster.

Fig. 17. William Emmett. Design for
Whitehall. Detail.

Fig. 18. Layout of the Whitehall project
described by Defoe.

Ideas of grandeur were not restricted to the Italians, for a written proposal of 1712 among the Harley Papers is even larger; the writer envisages a palace in the middle of Hyde Park, facing south in distinction from Galilei's east, with an avenue southwards to a bridge over the Thames, another avenue south-east to Westminster, and one on the north to Hampstead Heath.[46] Yet another scheme, for a palace and government building 1,200 feet square, is described in detail by Defoe in his *Tour through England and Wales* (1724). He claims to have seen a model of it, to know its author and when it was proposed, but as there is no other record of the scheme the reliability of a writer of great powers of circumstantial invention must remain in doubt. Defoe's account of the plan is detailed (Fig. 18), and such decorative features are mentioned as domes of gilt copper with stone lanterns over the three

[45] I. TOESCA, "Alessandro Galilei in Inghilterra", *English Miscellany*, III, 1952, pp. 189–220; E. K. WATERHOUSE, "Rome in 1733", *Italian Studies*, XVII, 1962, pp. 48–9.
[46] H.M.C. Portland, x, pp. 148–51. The suggestion there that the hand is John James's is probably correct, and the scale of the scheme does not necessarily conflict with James's stylistic feelings.

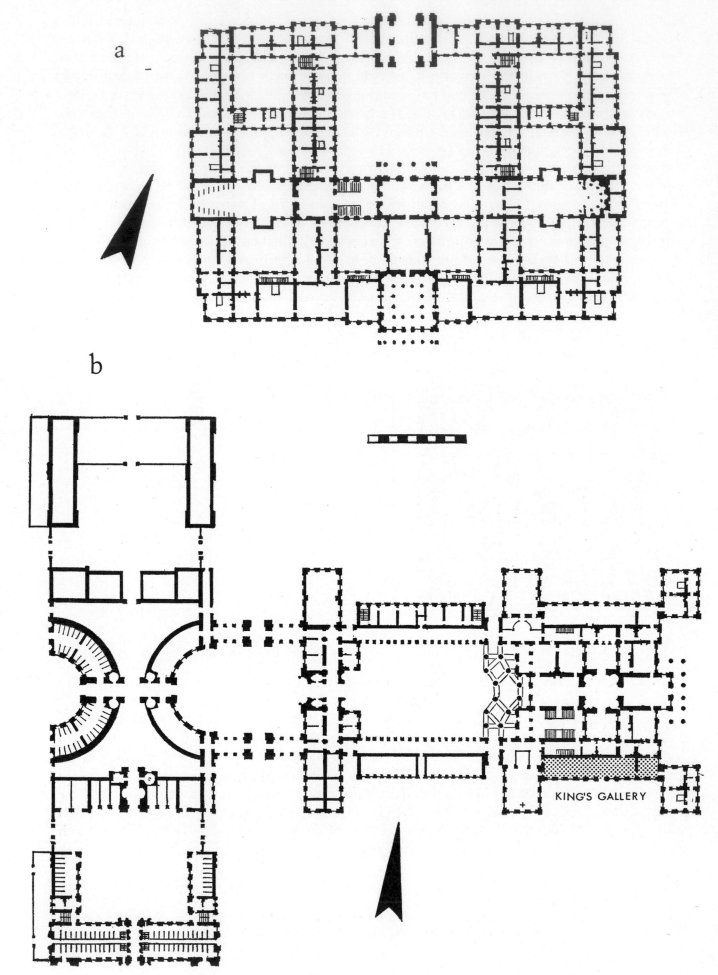

KING'S GALLERY

Fig. 19. Anonymous projects for (a) St James's Palace, (b) Kensington Palace.

chapels, "pavilions and pediments in their proper places" on the fronts, of the Corinthian order, marble columns 18 feet high flanking the altar of the big chapel, supporting life-size statues of St Peter and St Paul, "all as the king shall direct", an oval painted ceiling in the chapel, painted staircases and painted ceilings in the state apartments, marble door cases, gateways, and chimneys, stone or marble stairs, equestrian statues of William III and George I in the Great Court. But of the elevations, and thus of the real appearance of the design, not a trace is given.

The giant schemes of Galilei and the anonymous Harley writer took in or swept away St James's Palace and Kensington House. Plans were made in 1712 for rebuilding St James's and probably at the same date or soon after, for Kensington; several features suggest that their author was Vanbrugh, who had become Comptroller in 1702, though the draughtsman is unknown and some of the drawings are titled in French. The St James's plan (Fig. 19a) includes a colossal gateway to Pall Mall on the site of the present main north gate, recalling in plan the east gate at Blenheim, porticoes of Vanbrugh's favourite type with piers at the ends, a columned hall which implies a clerestory, a chapel similar in plan to that proposed for Castle Howard (Fig. 36) and a theatre balancing it. The Kensington plan (Fig. 19b) would have kept only the King's Gallery from the existing buildings. In position and shape the central rotunda and the room east of it apparently foreshadow the rooms built by Benson in 1718–19, but the whole build-up of the main block relates to Vanbrugh's designs for Eastbury of 1715–17. New courts were planned to the west, and spiral staircases on the plan suggest that the semicircular stable blocks, back to back, were to carry an impressive tower. Unfortunately no elevations have been found, and perhaps none was made; those suggested in the Wren Society, Vol. XIX, belong entirely to the twentieth-century revival of interest in English Baroque.

GREENWICH HOSPITAL

Nowhere in the history of English Baroque is the difference between great achievement and even greater intentions so clear as in the Royal Hospital for Seamen (now the Royal Naval College) at Greenwich; nowhere else was the English spirit of compromise so productive and at the same time so evidently inimical to architecture on the grand scale. Whereas a Vatican or a Versailles swept all before it, the designers of Greenwich accepted the challenges, but were at the mercy, of a strip of land on which they could not build and of two buildings which they could not demolish, and schemes to rival the scope of St Peter's Piazza and Versailles went by the board for lack of money.

The creation of Greenwich occupied the greater part of William III's reign, and the execution was drawn out well into the eighteenth century, eventually being terminated rather than completed. The official commencement of the project was the grant of Greenwich Palace by the sovereigns on 25 October 1694, but the initial impetus probably came from the victory of La Hogue (1692) and Luttrell's entries show that it was being discussed at that time and that Wren was involved from the beginning of 1693.[47] The Royal Warrant of 29 April 1696 authorized, as a modest beginning of work, the refitting of Webb's block built for Charles II (Pl. 86) and the addition of a base block behind it. The incorporation of Webb's building and, by implication, of the block Webb designed *en pendant* (Fig. 1) was the basis of the whole layout, which was also conditioned by the existence of the Queen's House of Inigo Jones. Queen Mary wished to keep the view open from the House to the river,

[47] LUTTRELL, II, pp. 472, 608; III, pp. 21, 23, 81, 83 (4 June, 3 November 1692, 26–28 January, 18–22 April 1693).

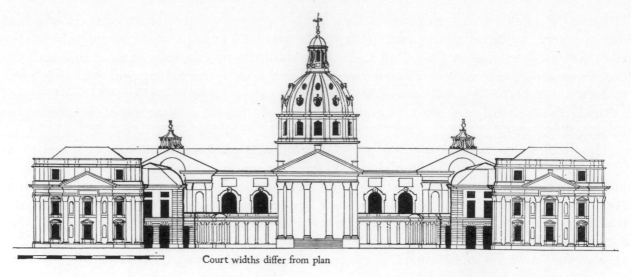

Court widths differ from plan

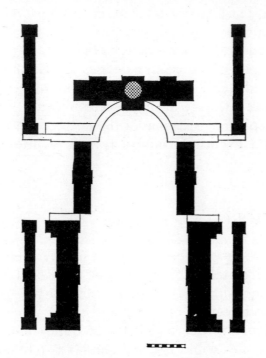

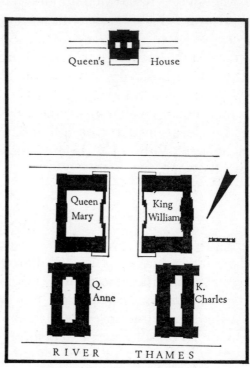

Fig. 20.   Greenwich Hospital. Early scheme.
Plan and north elevation.

Fig. 21.   Greenwich Hospital.
Plan as executed.

and although the Hospital gained the use of the House in 1708 or 1710 it remained Crown property and so did the strip of land between it and the river. The main axis of the whole Hospital was thus at once determined and made impossible to build on, and this ruled out Wren's first design (Fig. 20), a grander version of Chelsea with cruciform hall and chapel and a central domed vestibule. Its centrepiece and quadrant colonnades have more than a hint of Le Vau's Collège des Quatre Nations and in plan it repeats the Winchester sequence of narrowing courts. By June 1698, when Evelyn saw foundations for the hall, Wren had tried various schemes and arrived at a plan with the hall and chapel in their present positions and two ward blocks parallel to and south of each, joined by colonnades flanking and parallel to the central avenue. By 1700, and possibly by the end of 1698, this scheme of parallel blocks had been amended to the present one of courts closed by the colonnades (Fig. 21). Gradually the Hospital took its present shape. The main structure of King William Court, containing the Great Hall, was finished in 1704, but Queen Mary Court opposite, which contains the chapel, was taken above foundations only in 1735–9, when Thomas Ripley was Surveyor to the Hospital. Ripley's chapel exterior followed that of the hall (the chapel was gutted in 1779 and rebuilt by James Stuart) and his south block is a plainer version of its pair. His centre block, however, glares with Palladian dullness through the colonnades at the exuberance of King William Court. The carcase of Queen Anne base block and court was also completed in 1700–4, but the arcaded ends of the court (originally open) were not begun until 1716, and the stone front of Queen Anne building, facing and copying Webb's original elevation, had to wait until 1725–8 (Pls 96, 89). Meanwhile, in 1711 the decision had been taken to double the northern end pavilions, using Webb's design four times along the waterfront.

Hawksmoor's *Remarks on the Founding of the Hospital* (1728) refer to the "great Passion for Building" of its real foundress, Queen Mary, and "her Majesty's fixt Intention for Magnificence"; hence the desire, evident from Wren's first design onwards, to outshine King Charles's foundation at Chelsea. In those parts of Greenwich designed by or under Wren, although a large amount of brick is used, the only positively plain buildings were the King Charles's Base Block of 1696 (remodelled 1811–14) and the corresponding Queen Anne Block. The latter (Pl. 100) is of three storeys, unlike the 1696 block, and has the distinction of being entirely faced in stone; in this material its simple round-headed windows give it the severity and the monumentality of Bruant's Invalides, and perhaps an intentional reminiscence as well of Bruant's arcaded court. At first sight there might seem to be a connection between this part of Greenwich and the Palladianism of Ripley's work, but there is none. The Queen Anne façade is, to use the term of the period, a back front; like the court elevations it is important, but of secondary importance. We are behind the scenes of Baroque display, and the nearest parallel to the court is significantly in the internal courts of the main block of Blenheim or the kitchen side of Kimbolton (Pls. 256–7). The court arcades are Hawksmoor's only documented work at Greenwich, but H. S. Goodhart-Rendel's attribution to him of the whole block, made forty years ago, is likely to stand permanently.

The question of the authorship of the "Wren" buildings at Greenwich is raised more urgently by the elevations of King William Block. There is no problem in the colonnades, the hall and chapel, the exteriors or their twin cupolas (Pl. 90); these have always been accepted as Wren's, and in richness and plasticity the lanterns and domes match the slightly later towers of St Paul's. The west elevation (Pl. 87) and the corresponding court front (Pl. 88) carry on the block-composition and the scale of Wren's Whitehall project, conceived a few months earlier. The carved festoons of shellfish and Robert Jones's marine lion and unicorn in the west gable of the Great Hall (Pls 93, 95) follow the naturalistic carving of Hampton Court, and an early design for that building has the same prodigiously high channelled pedestals that support the aedicule in the centre of King William Court. But for the rest there is no precedent in Wren's work. The pilasters flanking the aedicule support entablatures but are too high to carry the depressed arch in the centre. Two different (though linked) patterns are set up, by the windows and by the order. Five different window-shapes are used, not counting those within the arch. The west elevation has a different but equally remarkable pattern, the middle block having all rectangles and the ends all curves. In either case the effect is dramatic and, if one can forget the standards of academic classicism, exciting and, as a heroic abstraction made from given architectural elements, extremely able. It is also necessary to allow for the effect of dirt on the balance between brick and stonework. Analogies with the front of Christ Church, Spitalfields and the north end of Easton Neston point to Hawksmoor as the author; Vanbrugh can be ruled out, since the western block was well advanced before he became Comptroller in 1702 and he did not attend a Greenwich meeting until 14 October 1703. The question remains unanswered – and it is one not only of attribution but of the history of English Baroque – how Wren, who was still the acknowledged architect of Greenwich in 1705–6, felt about designs which, on the evidence, were the work of his assistant. We do not know why he gave Hawksmoor an almost free hand, but it does not follow that Wren, because he conceived nothing of this sort, discountenanced it. One of his son's intentions in *Parentalia* was to show that Sir Christopher did not lack Taste, and his advocates have been trying to do so ever since. The Chelsea frontispieces (Pls 13, 16) are relevant here, although at Chelsea peculiarity is confined within them, and not woven, as at Greenwich, into the whole length of the elevations; moreover, it is far harder to believe that Hawksmoor had a free hand at Chelsea, when he was a junior clerk of 22, than at Greenwich fifteen years later when he was building up an independent practice. The City Churches are full of solecisms which Wren must have allowed, and the elevations of Hampton Court are not easy to pass by Augustan standards. The activities of the younger Edward Strong, who worked on King William Block with his father, are also relevant here. Strong designed and built in 1702–3 the gateway of St Bartholomew's Hospital, making the aedicule and the wreathed columns of the east front of King William the basis of a more conventional façade (Pl. 495). Strong was also the mason, and quite probably the designer, of Addiscombe House, Surrey, built at the same date for William Draper, Treasurer to the Commissioners of Greenwich Hospital (Pl. 163).[48] Addiscombe is significant not only for the Greenwich connection and the transmogrification of the King William façades but also for what Draper's father-in-law, John Evelyn, connoisseur, savant, writer on architecture and translator of Fréart's *Parallèle*, says about it (17 July 1703): "the Outsides to the Covering being so excellent Brickwork, Based with Portland stone with the Pillasters, Windows & Contrivement within, that I pronounce it, in all the points of good & solid Architecture, to be one of the very best Gent: Houses in all Surry, when finished".

Greenwich is still a building without a middle. Hawksmoor made a design for raising the Queen's House a storey higher to help fill the gap between the colonnades. At some time between 1702 and 1711 he also drew various schemes for a great southern court with a chapel displacing the House; in one case he intended to move it up the hill. One scheme (Fig. 22) is for an oval court which, with the domed chapel and its portico, relates directly to St Peter's Piazza. The spatial experience of Greenwich is vivid and exhilarating enough today; it would have been terrific if, after passing through the straits of the colonnades one could be released into this great closed court. But Greenwich was built partly by donations and mostly by taxes and levies; in 1711, if not before, Hawksmoor no doubt felt that the completion of St Paul's would release a revenue from the coal tax large enough for the largest scheme. The comparisons his schemes invite with Rome and Versailles support in architecture the perennial reply of the autocrat, that committees never achieve anything.

It is all the more interesting, therefore, that when Thornhill undertook in 1707 to paint the interior of the Great Hall he was apparently left to draw up his own programmes. The fact that architecturally the hall is entirely plain but modelled on May's St George's Hall at Windsor, suggests that Wren had initially intended it to be painted, but on the proscenium arch of the Upper Hall the *grisaille* relief decoration cuts across and contradicts the actual masonry relief. The capitals, cyphers, royal arms and some of the mouldings are carved; all the rest, including the division of the ceiling, is painted in this, the finest surviving painted ensemble in England (Pl. 103). The painter's theme in the central oval, ringed with the creatures of the Zodiac, and the four elements, is the Triumph of Peace and Liberty: King William presents the cap of Liberty to Europe and tramples on Arbitrary Power; William and Mary are accompanied by Peace, Piety and the Cardinal Virtues. Above,

---

[48] The house has been attributed to Hawksmoor because he measured joiner's work there in 1703 (COLVIN, *Dictionary*, p. 747).

Fig. 22.   Greenwich Hospital. Reconstructions of schemes for enlargement, with plans showing viewpoints. Uncertain features are left blank.

Apollo, the sun-god but no longer *le roi soleil*, drives the Vices down to the far end of the fictive oval, where they are subdued by Minerva and Hercules; Time discovers Truth, and Architecture displays a drawing of one of the Greenwich domes. The ends of the ceiling show British warships with Victory and the City of London, Fame, representatives real and symbolic of the nautical and military sciences, and the four great rivers of Britain, Thames, Tyne, Humber and Severn.[49]

The Lower Hall was finished in 1717; Thornhill then painted the Upper Hall, completing it in 1725. The programme there is more directly historical and for that reason less successful: William's landing at Torbay and George I's at Greenwich, and the return of the Golden Age under George. In the ceiling the World acknowledges Queen Anne and her consort as rulers of the seas. Yet even among the Hanoverian portraits in the Upper Hall there is a shift of emphasis from the Windsor of Charles II, or even from Hampton Court. William and Mary, the founders of the Hospital, were dead before the painter began work. There is no apotheosis; even the scenes of action in the Upper Hall are but the arrival of the two men invited in turn by the Nation to rule it. The language of Baroque decorative painting could hardly be strained further towards democracy. New and lighter decorative fashions were being established. And finally, the Painted Hall is not in a royal palace.

[49] The same rivers supported Cibber's Charles II fountain formerly in Soho Square.

III

The great age of house-building

THE VOGUE FOR ILLUSIONIST PAINTING

At the very beginning of our period Streater's Sheldonian ceiling (Pl. 105) bears witness to the importance for Baroque architecture of illusionist painting, which creates a fictive structure within a building. In a letter of 1702 the famous plasterer, Edward Goudge, attributes the falling demand for decorative moulded ceilings to two factors, "want of money occasioned by the war" and "the use of ceiling painting".[50] As so much decorative painting has been destroyed and so little adequately photographed, it is only since the publication of Mr Croft-Murray's first volume on the subject that the true amount of such work carried out can easily be estimated. Verrio's work at Windsor has been discussed (pp. 18-22). Between his arrival in 1672 and about 1720 at least fifty painted staircases were executed in new or existing private London houses and country mansions; ceilings and walls appeared to show, through an illusionist architectural skeleton, buildings, landscape and sky as a background for allegorical and historical figures. A smaller number of entrance halls and saloons also had walls painted as well as ceilings, for instance Verrio's stories of Hercules in the saloon of the first Montagu House (1682-3); in many other cases staircases and rooms had only painted ceilings. Deception on this scale is a convention, for while *trompe-l'œil* painting easily persuades us that individual flat surfaces are in relief or broken by solid objects, or that flat ceilings are vaulted, whole walls remain walls; nevertheless where the colour remains fresh perspective will almost trick the eye into accepting an extension of the real interior space. It is perhaps for this reason that the staircase, itself a spatial volume which is experienced in three dimensions by all who traverse it, was the favourite situation for spatial illusionism, in spite of the fact that different levels as well as directions of view greatly complicate the rendering of perspective. But first something must be said of the few large descendants of Verrio's state rooms at Windsor.

During his years at Burghley (1687-98) under the patronage of the 5th Earl of Exeter, Devonshire's brother-in-law, Verrio painted the suite known as the George Rooms on the first floor of the south front, working eastwards from the state dressing-room (*c.*1688, Pl. 108) towards the Saloon or Heaven Room (1692-5) and the ceiling of the Hell Room (1696-7, later a staircase). The coves of smaller rooms contain brilliant *trompe-l'œil* busts, putti, medallions, scrolls, pediments and wreaths and around the Feast of the Gods in the dining-room ceiling lie piles of golden plate, purple drapes and heaps of comestibles (Pls 111-12). The Heaven Room (Pl. 110) is painted from floor to ceiling, high in key and gay in feeling. In and out of a firm and very successful colonnade framework stand or fly Mars, Venus, Neptune, Bacchus, Vulcan and their attendants; flower-garlands hang between the capitals, and armour hangs from the columns above Vulcan's forge (beside which squats the artist, wigless) while a rainbow leads up to the assembly of gods and signs of the Zodiac in the ceiling. It would not be surprising to learn that Verrio was happier with pure mythologies

---

[50] H.M.C. Cowper, III, p. 3.

than with the heavy political programmes of Windsor or the King's Staircase at Hampton Court.

Louis Laguerre, Louis XIV's godson, who came to England as Verrio's assistant about 1684 and first worked independently at Thoresby, had benefited from his French training and was in general a better if not a more spirited painter than the Italian. The chapel at Chatsworth (1689–93, Pls 106–7) recalls the scheme of Verrio's Windsor chapel, with scenes of Christ healing the sick set in a colonnade opposite the windows and Christ in Glory in the ceiling. The conventional easel picture set into the altar-piece is Verrio's. Laguerre was sensitive to his surroundings, and at the end of his career he was to match the exterior richness of Blenheim in his decoration of the saloon (Pl. 118). At Chatsworth he painted feigned statues flanking Cibber's two figures on the altar-piece, while at the opposite end of the chapel the break is hardly discernible between Watson's musical putti and the painted cove above them (Pl. 104). He was fond of effective cast shadows in the coves, and in the decoration of the Hall (with histories of Julius Caesar) feigned and true relief are closely integrated. Laguerre had no difficulty in organizing large compositions (Pls 107, 113), though Mr Croft-Murray's researches suggest that his own figure style was more sentimental and less forceful than that of an anonymous assistant who appears only at Chatsworth.

Decoration in other houses was less extensive, with the exception of the young Louis Chéron's series of rather academic and totally unarchitectural ceilings at Boughton, c.1695, and possibly of the lost work at Cannons (p. 87).

The detailed discussion of either the iconography or the stylistic points of illusionist painting is outside the scope of this book; it is sufficient to stress its importance as a Baroque decorative medium and to illustrate a selection of examples. Thornhill is seen at his best at Greenwich (Pl. 103), at Blenheim (Pl. 122) and in the Sabine Room at Chatsworth (1706). This was originally an anteroom, and takes its name from the *Rape of the Sabines* which fills the north wall and continues upwards to the celestial marriage of Hersilea and Romulus in the ceiling. On the south wall (Pl. 121) a hemicycle of columns appears to extend behind the chimney-breast on which stands a feigned statue of Concord; this successful illusion is developed from the artist's earlier one in the hall at Stoke Edith (1704–5, destroyed by fire, 1927). Gerard Lanscroon, an insensitive but individual figure painter, who began as an assistant of Verrio at Windsor, deserves mention not only for his striking red marble columns at Powis Castle (for William III's nephew, Lord Rochford, 1705) and at Burley-on-the-Hill (before 1708, Pl. 124) where besides bronze figures there are lapis lazuli busts, but also for his ability to make the most of a small space as at Drayton (1712, Pl. 123).

All the skill in the world could not disguise the basic unsuitability of most decoration of this kind for the English house. It made, even for passage rooms like entrance halls and staircases, heavy demands on the suspension of disbelief. The gaiety of the Heaven Room at Burghley was a rare exception from a seriousness which seems to have been ingrained from the style's origin in Roman, Bourbon and Stuart propaganda cycles. Finally, for much of the year the English atmosphere is not bright enough for it. When the Venetian, Giovanni Antonio Pellegrini, brought to England by the Earl of Manchester, arrived in 1708 one of his first works was the little staircase at Kimbolton (Pl. 125) in the same manner; a little later, at Castle Howard, the painted area was reduced (Pls 126, 292). In the Saloon there was no cove and the edges of the ceiling were unmistakably flat. In the Hall painting is restricted to certain areas, the cupola, the pendentives, recessed panels. Fusion of painting, sculpture and architecture has given way to co-ordination. At Easton Neston (Pl. 212) Thornhill's *grisaille* is restricted to panels in the staircase walls; above, all is plaster. Thornhill's chapel at Wimpole (Pl. 296, 1721–4) represents the end of the style; *trompe-l'œil* ornament predominates, and even the decidedly Venetian *Adoration of the Magi* over the altar is more an altar-piece than a window into a further world. The gallery at Mereworth of the same date, decorated by the Venetian, Sleter (Pl. 297), puts the clock back, in good Palladian fashion, to Jones, Webb and the Venetian tradition.

THE TRANSFORMATION OF THE GREAT HOUSE

Sir Roger Pratt's Clarendon House, Piccadilly (Pl. 127) was built in 1664–7 for Edward Hyde, 1st Earl of Clarendon, Charles II's Lord Chancellor and the grandfather, through Anne Hyde, Duchess of York, of Queen Mary and Queen Anne. With an elevation fifteen bays long it was considerably larger than either Coleshill, its prototype, or Belton, which was modelled on it, or than its neighbours, Berkeley House and Denham (later Burlington) House, and it may fairly be considered a successor to the great houses built by the courtiers of Elizabeth and James I. Even during construction it drew comment from an envious public on account of its size and splendour, and praise from the better informed, Pepys, Evelyn and the architect's circle, for its regular design and fine workmanship. Clarendon was not popular, and no sooner was the house built than, impeached but not committed, he fled to France where he died in 1674. His heirs sold the house to Lord Albemarle, whose debts forced him after eight years to re-sell to an estate company who demolished it in 1683 in order to develop the Old Bond Street area. From Evelyn's diary and Pratt's notebooks we learn that the house was largely panelled in wainscot and enriched with wood carving and probably plasterwork. The plan is unknown, but there was probably a large entrance hall three bays wide on the centre axis with a saloon of the same width behind it facing the garden. This arrangement, which derives from Palladio by way of France, was afterwards adopted at Belton and by Hooke at Montagu House and Ragley, and became the core of both the Vanbrughian and the neo-Palladian mansion. As Pratt had approached it at Coleshill and was currently (1663–6) executing it at Horseheath (Fig. 23) it is reasonable to suppose that he introduced it to the Capital at Clarendon House. Costly cynosure though it was, this house, conceived in the early days of the Royal Society and at the height of its campaign against Fancy, appears to have been very sober, both inside and outside; in comparison the Baroque great houses of the end of the century stand out all the more clearly.

Whatever the Royal Society or its spokesman and first historian, Thomas Sprat, may have felt, one of its leading members, Robert Hooke, made the first moves away from the type. Hooke's French silhouette at Bedlam (1675–6) has already been mentioned (p. 5); Montagu House, Bloomsbury, begun earlier and finished later (1674–9), was markedly French in style. Ralph Montagu, English ambassador to France, succeeded as 3rd Baron Montagu in 1684 and was created Earl in 1689 and Duke in 1705. His francophile taste was well known, and he was also responsible for bringing Verrio to England from France in 1672. His house, which Evelyn persistently called a palace and also one "than which for painting and furniture there was nothing more glorious in England" was four bays shorter than Clarendon's and had an upstairs "great room" entirely painted by Verrio. The only picture of it, in Ogilby & Morgan's 1682 map of London (Fig. 24), shows that it was a tall house and had a pediment like that intended at Ragley. The house caught fire in January 1686; Evelyn's "burnt to the ground" may be an exaggeration, but if Ogilby and Morgan are to be believed (as, on account of their accuracy in other buildings, they must be) the reconstruction (1686–8) was larger by four bays even though it retained the general shape (Pl. 133) and perhaps part of the walls of the old. Evelyn also described the first house as "built after the French pavilion-way" which fits both the original and the reconstruction's separate mansard roofs over the projecting end pavilions and the raised central one. The building was bought in 1749 for the British Museum and was demolished to make room for the present museum. The redecoration of Montagu's interior was entirely French, being

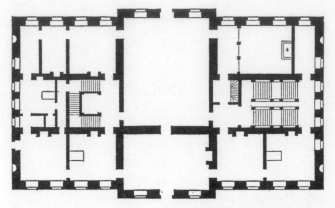

Fig. 23.   Horseheath (destroyed). Plan of main block.   Fig. 24.   Montagu House I (1675–86). South front.

Fig. 25.   Ragley. View from the east as projected, c.1698.

carried out by a team of painters brought over by Montagu under Charles de la Fosse, Jacques Rousseau, the landscape painter, Jean-Baptiste Monnoyer, the flower painter, and James Parmentier. According to Campbell,[51] who gives the wrong date, 1678, the architect was Puget, but this cannot on style be Pierre Puget, the architect and sculptor. Vertue's reference to "an architect brought over also on purpose" may not be more than a gloss on Campbell's note which he elsewhere copies; moreover the amount of work for another architect in the reconstruction is not at all certain. The original rather French court with gatehouse and colonnade behind the street front also survived the fire.

Montagu House seems to have had certain specific repercussions at Boughton, Ragley and Petworth. Montagu employed French painters again at Boughton, to which in the years before 1694 he added a fifteen-bay northern block which looks French in the careful contrasts of texture and the mansard roof which is nearer in effect to the monumentality of an attic storey than to the unequivocal slopes of Belton (Pl. 134). In 1679 Hooke designed Ragley, Warwicks, for Edward Conway, newly created Earl of Conway, with projecting pavilions and with the hall-saloon arrangement. Ragley was unfinished at Conway's death in 1683; little seems to have been done to it until 1750, and while the shell of the house is

51 *Vitruvius Britannicus*, I. See *Walpole Soc.*, xxv, 1937, pp. 93–6. Hooke's diary is missing for the years of reconstruction, though admittedly the extant section from November 1688 to 1693 contains no references to the house. The R.I.B.A. has some interior designs by "Mr Boujet" (*Architectural History*, v, 1962, p. 54); he could conceivably have undertaken the interiors of Montagu House.

Hooke's, most of what is visible now is due to Gibbs or to alterations made by James Wyatt. Kip's view of *c.*1697–9, however, shows the house with a form of mansard roof and with a feature which a plan by Gibbs (B.M.MS.Add.31,323) and an estate map in the Warwickshire County Record Office corroborate, a pediment resting on two widely spaced half-columns (Fig. 25); this seems to be the first English use of a Dutch motif which recurs at Thoresby, at Hanbury (by William Rudhall of Henley-in-Arden, dated 1701 and depending on Ragley, Pl. 131) and elsewhere.

In 1682 the heiress of Petworth, Elizabeth Percy, barely 16 years old and twice widowed, married her third husband, Charles Seymour, 6th Duke of Somerset. When she came of age in 1688, or possibly a little before, the Proud Duke (as he is known to history from his most memorable trait) prepared to rebuild the long and irregular Percy mansion. The east side faces the old court and offices, and seventeenth-century Petworth thus has only one major front, facing west (Pl. 135). Somerset's architect is unknown; John Scarborough was paid for eight days' measuring in 1690 but as his recorded employment in the Office of Works was chiefly as a measuring surveyor it is not very likely that he made the designs. A more significant though no more illuminating connection is with Montagu House. Elizabeth Percy's stepfather was Ralph Montagu and it was at the first Montagu House that she married Somerset. The irregular bracketing in the west frieze at Petworth is found in the second Montagu House (Pl. 133) and they share a French look which was originally more marked: accounts for 1689–90 refer to the "circular roof" and betray, with a background detail of Laguerre's staircase painting, the existence of a slate-covered central dome probably similar in shape to that on the rebuilt Montagu House. At the beginning of 1714 the southern half of Petworth was gutted and the dome was not replaced. The west front, intended as an entrance front but now faced by the park, is 322 feet long; such long low proportions are English rather than French. Nevertheless the classical restraint, the contrast between honey-coloured local stone and the Portland used for the centrepiece, window frames and carvings, the precise detailing and cutting, the proportions of the two main storeys and of the balustraded sections over the attic, all suggest a knowledge of France though not necessarily a French hand. Petworth also represents a more recent style than Montagu House; its attic storey makes much less of the roof and is nearer in feeling to Thoresby and Chatsworth. Like Versailles, the one long building which the Proud Duke might have deliberately wished to imitate, Petworth impresses by its size and its imagery (Pls 136–8) rather than by the more subtle architectural qualities of Chatsworth (Pl. 140). The same is true of the interior, decoration of which continued until 1696, and which is marked less by architectural invention than by richness. Most of the Carved Room, originally the dining-room, is by Gibbons, but the trophy between the central windows (Pl. 139) is more probably by the local carver, John Selden, who also worked the Marble Hall. Laguerre's staircase dates from after the fire.

Petworth is an exceptional house, and more decisive changes in design were already being made by William Talman at Thoresby and Chatsworth. Talman was born in 1650, the younger son of a Wiltshire gentleman who died when William was 13; this circumstance may have some bearing on the haughty manner which he adopted and which led to much strife with clients who thought less highly of him than he did. Such evidence as there is suggests that it was through the patronage of Edward Hyde's son, Henry, 2nd Earl of Clarendon, that he obtained in 1678 a virtual sinecure in the Customs.[52] Talman is not thought to have travelled, but he was receptive like Hugh May to both Dutch and French ideas. That he knew May is probable anyway – May was a friend of both the 1st and 2nd Earls of Clarendon – and is suggested by his use of an oval vestibule like the Cassiobury one (p. 18) in his Trianon plan (p. 42) and in other projects; Cassiobury's sculptured pediment,

[52] WHINNEY, *Talman.*

too, possibly inspired those at Thoresby and Chatsworth. Moreover, although May was not
the first to employ Verrio in a private house, the combination of illusionist painting and
lifelike carving of which Cassiobury is the first example apart from the royal work at
Windsor, was adopted by Talman. There is more interest than significance in the fact that
three Comptrollers in succession, May, Talman and Vanbrugh, were important designers
of country houses outside the Royal Works.

It has been established beyond reasonable doubt that Talman's first house, Thoresby,
Notts, was begun for William Pierrepont, 4th Earl of Kingston about 1683, the year after
his succession.[53] According to Vertue it was "most part burnt down when first building and
near finisht" and the fire was caused by the painters; Hawksmoor adds that the attic was
added at the refitting after the fire, but all the other walls remained as the fire had left them.[54]
Thoresby was of brick with stone dressings and frontispiece. Cibber and Laguerre were
working there in 1686–7, probably the date of the "refitting"; Vertue later saw Laguerre's
murals in the chapel, but the pediment in which Cibber carved "two figures flat" according
to a memorandum at Chatsworth, may have been earlier work damaged in the fire and not
replaced, as no representations of the house show it. Thoresby was burnt again in 1745, and
a Victorian mansion now stands on the site. Most of Thoresby remains a mystery, and we
have too few dates to be able to say more than that some of its important features precede
the better documented Chatsworth.

THE REBUILDING OF CHATSWORTH

Chatsworth owes much of its character and most of its peculiarities to William Cavendish,
4th Earl and 1st Duke of Devonshire, who succeeded to the earldom in 1684. He seems to
have inherited the building craze of his ancestor, Bess of Hardwick; his father had already
carried out such improvements to Elizabethan Chatsworth as the enlargement of the great
staircase and the introduction – an early example – of sash windows on all the fronts.
Nevertheless at the 4th Earl's accession the structure was reported to be "decaying and
weake". The new Earl was one of the seven statesmen who invited William of Orange to
England and his elevation to the Dukedom in 1694 was a result of his part in the Revolution.
Although a temporary retirement from the Court in evasion of a large fine in 1685 may have
forced on him the leisure to remodel Chatsworth, heredity and ambition were the major
forces in turning a large house into a palace. Between 1687 and 1707, the year of his death,
he rebuilt in turn all four ranges which had, around a square courtyard, formed the great
Elizabethan house. He employed three architects in succession and some of the finest craftsmen in the country; he constantly changed his mind and what had started as a rebuilding
only of the south range (Pl. 140) grew piece by piece into a complete reconstruction.

Chatsworth set the scale both for Baroque palaces and for the Palladian ones which
followed them, and thus marks the beginning of the decline in Royal patronage of architecture. The chapel and the upper-floor state rooms in the south range, decorated by Laguerre
and by Cibber, the local Samuel Watson and other carvers (p. 56), are unique except for
the contemporary Verrio rooms at Burghley. They emulate and perpetuate the lost splendour
of Stuart Windsor, of James II's Popish chapel, and of the original Montagu House which
was let to Devonshire and occupied by his family at the time of its destruction.

[53] *Ibid.* Campbell's date of 1671 is again wrong, as also is his 1681 for Chatsworth. Talman may have been in
charge of the alterations to Burghley which were begun about 1680.
[54] VERTUE, VI, pp. 24, 73; Hawksmoor's letter in *Walpole Soc.*,'XIX, p. 126. See also J. HARRIS's articles in *Architectural History*, IV, 1961 and VI, 1963.

Chatsworth is twenty-five miles from Thoresby and Devonshire was a distant relation of Lord Kingston; the latter may have recommended Talman, who had not yet made a name for himself. In a few years Devonshire was to regret his choice of architect, finding him expensive and intractable. His appointment as Comptroller, possibly with Devonshire's help, and the trouble he caused in the Office of Works, have been mentioned (p. 41). With his official position and a growing country-house practice Talman assumed the grand manner and would arrive at Chatsworth in a private coach and with his own servants. He acted as sole contractor, an unusual procedure for the time, which meant that the artificers were engaged and paid by, and were responsible to, him and not his client. They were London men at London rates, and all second thoughts were extra items outside the contract. In Devonshire's mind the expense and disputes with the workmen were his architect's fault, and after the completion of the east side in 1696 he made no further contract with him.

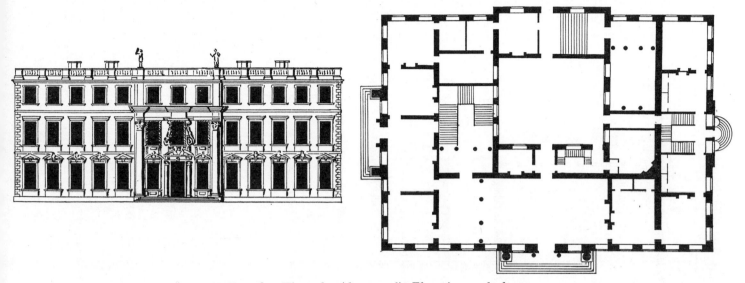

Fig. 26. Thoresby (destroyed). Elevation and plan.

Talman's south elevation (1687–8) was revolutionary. The logical development from Clarendon and Montagu House occurred at Thoresby, with the raising of an attic wall and parapet to hide the roof and provide a continuous façade with attic windows in place of a series of dormers, the pitch of the roof being reduced (Fig. 26). At Chatsworth (Pl. 140) there is no attic storey; two full floors rise above a substantial basement, and the top quarter of the elevation consists of a very heavy entablature and parapet, carried visually by fluted giant Ionic pilasters in the end bays and by the window and keystone system in the astylar centre. The massiveness of this capping, which is increased by the balustrade (apparently added in 1693) and large urns (added in 1700), immediately suggests Italy; the obvious source is in fact Bernini's third design for the Louvre, which was available in Jean Marot's engraving. The effect is grander, in purely architectural terms, than any previous building in England, and anticipates by over a decade Wren's Whitehall project and Vanbrugh's Castle Howard. The dramatic power of this rather plain façade is increased by the closer rhythm of the windows in the centre and by the unusual arrangement, only possible in an elevation other than the entrance front, of an even number of bays, twelve in all, with no centre bay. Consequently the eye takes the slightly recessed six-bay middle as a single unit and, by implication, accepts the three-bay ends also as units. Unfortunately the 6th Duke allowed Wyattville to replace the original quadrant staircases (Fig. 27a) by straight ones which obscure the centre instead of leading the eye into it. Wyattville also destroyed the more exciting quadrants within the Great Hall leading to the main staircase.

Talman's east front, (1693–6) which also has an even number of bays, suffered considerably at Wyattville's hands. Here there were attic windows in the middle section, again astylar, between the buttress-like stair towers designed by Talman to replace Elizabethan ones; Wyattville removed the attic windows and reclad the towers; the fine trophies which originally adorned their lower halves are now on the back of Flora's Temple (Pl. 153). The court side of the east range, containing the hall and great staircase, was rebuilt earlier (1688–92); this is the only side of the court not totally altered by Wyattville (Pl. 156). It retains Talman's top storey, but windows replace his ground-floor niches with statues of Mars, Prudence and Fortitude, by the Huguenot Nadauld, the channelled stonework of the piers was altered, and Watson's trophies (which originally ranged all round the court) were raised half a storey and shortened by the same amount by the removal of the huge stone knots from which they appeared to hang. Watson also carved the frame of the Diana relief (itself bought in London in 1692 for £16) in the grotto (Pl. 152). The grotto itself began life with the purely structural function of supporting the new staircase; when further rebuilding reduced the load upon it, one of Devonshire's happy strokes was to alter the grotto in order, in Celia Fiennes's phrase, "to supply all ye house with water".

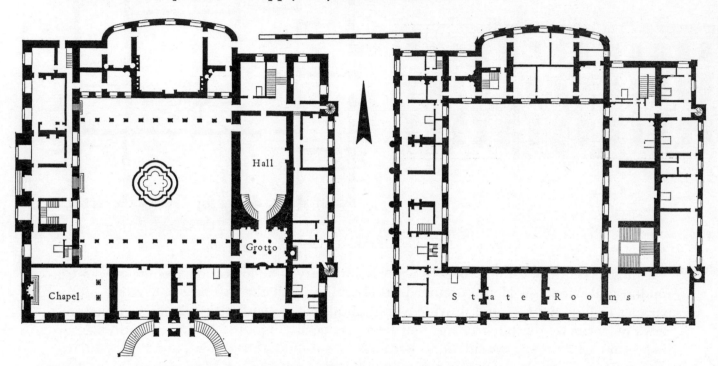

Fig. 27.   Chatsworth. Plans of ground and second floors.

Chatsworth is a building with four fronts, not with two main fronts and two ends; this was due to the shape of the old Chatsworth which it gradually replaced, rather than to deliberate imitation of Thoresby, which Talman had already built round a court. Just as other features of the house set a new standard for grandeur, this one gave new life and currency to an Elizabethan principle of plan. With the designing of the east front Talman amplified another idea which he had introduced at Thoresby: adjacent fronts are dissimilar in fenestration and in the rhythm and placing of projections. When Talman left in 1696 he had designed the terrace below the new west front, but not the front itself. The terrace was part of a scheme to modernize the existing west front and the Duke intended no more rebuilding. By 1700 he had changed not only most of his workmen (Watson remaining) but also his mind. John Fitch, the mason, arrived in June 1700 and in the next two years rebuilt the west front (Pl. 141) according to a drawing which survives with others at Chatsworth and whose author is unknown but may have been Thomas Archer. Archer was, as Devonshire apparently liked his architects to be, not yet established, and the fact that the Duke

Fig. 28.   Chatsworth. Reconstruction of north front.

Fig. 29.   Uppark. View from the east, *c.*1700.

left him £200 shows him as more congenial than Talman. He certainly designed the Cascade House (1702) as well as the north front (1705–7). The west front is indebted both to the south front and to the château of Marly, which seems, rather than the recently roofed Burley-on-the-Hill (p. 64), to be the source of the pilastered front with a pediment rising above the balustrade line. Devonshire no doubt gave directions, but it is too accomplished either for him or for a man like Fitch who is otherwise unknown as a designer – or, for that matter, for Thornhill who, in 1706–7 at the age of 30, painted rooms within and whom an obscure inscription in *Vitruvius Britannicus* suggests as the author. The west front is the richest in texture and decoration. Its armorial pediment relief, cypher keystones and enriched middle bay relate to Hampton Court; the stag heads on the lateral keystones and serpents in the frieze (both from the Cavendish crest) are repeated from those on the south front. All this detail, including the central frieze of putti and sea-horses, was worked by Nadauld, who also carved the dolphins on the Cascade House (Pl. 151).

The piecemeal growth of the palace left the west range longer towards the north than the east range, and the bowed centre of Archer's north front fairly effectively disguises this irregularity. Here again Wyattville reduced the fenestration to a discreet neo-classical rectangularity instead of the round-headed windows and oval carved attic lights of the centre bays (Fig. 28, reconstruction).

GREAT HOUSES BEGUN AFTER THE REVOLUTION

Rigid sociological theories of culture are apt to be upset by the fact that cultural events happen first. Thus Devonshire, whose interests were too wide and too worldly to confine him to politics, began Chatsworth well before the Glorious Revolution. Somerset, whose great passion was his own family although he became a promoter of the Revolution, began Petworth without relation to political events. The fact remains, however, that during the period of the achievement of constitutional monarchy private building on a royal scale of size and decoration became a common instead of an isolated phenomenon.

Daniel Finch, 2nd Earl of Nottingham, was one of the first to build on the new scale. His Toryism, acknowledged if mild, did not prevent his following Whig fashions in building (by the time of Rysbrack's Roman bust of him he had become a Whig), or his serving William and Mary as Secretary of State, 1689–93, and selling them his Kensington house

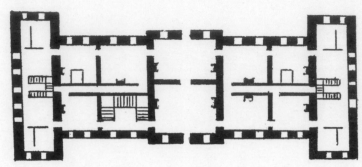

Fig. 30.   Burley-on-the-Hill. Sketch plan.

(p. 43). In 1694 Nottingham bought the estate of Burley-on-the-Hill, Rutland, from the trustees of the 2nd Duke of Buckingham, and after extensive preparations began to build in 1696, the walls being finished in 1698; some details of his expenditure have already been given (p. 12).[55]

As a friend of Sir John Lowther and nephew of Lord Conway, both patrons of Hooke, he might have sought the latter as his architect. The only known names of any relevance are Sir Henry Sheeres, Surveyor of Ordnance, Thomas Poulteney, a joiner who worked on the City Churches and who made a model of Burley, and the superintending masons, Henry Dormer and his successor from 16 April 1697, John Lumley. Certain features of the house, however, suggest that Hooke did help with the design. Burley is regular in plan and unusual in elevation (Fig. 30, Pl. 148). The end projections on the main fronts make a much wider H-plan than the Clarendon-Belton type and, like the corner pavilions of a French house, they contain each a suite of three rooms making one *appartement*; this arrangement had appeared at Ragley. The elevation of Burley is also related to the first Montagu House, which had a "great room" upstairs although how extensive it was we do not know. The most impressive room at Burley is that on the first floor behind the pilasters, nearly 60 feet by 40 feet and originally 33 feet high, taking in the attic storey and running right across the house from front to back. In recent times (its decoration was destroyed in the fire of 1908) it has been called the Ballroom, but in an early plan in the Clarke collection at Worcester College, Oxford, it is called the Great Room. Moreover, an elevation which is almost certainly for the garden front of the first Montagu House and is certainly by Hooke has an upper loggia opening from the great room, and also a first floor order above an astylar ground floor which itself is clearly above the basement.[56] This same disposition of the order is found at Burley and also occurred in the pavilions of Hooke's Bedlam (Pl. 130). Both fronts of Burley follow the entrance front of the first Montagu House in having a pediment, but Burley differs in having a roof hidden behind the parapet and balustrade, and the pediments thus appear on the skyline. As Salvator Musco was paid for carving on the north one in 1698 the idea precedes the west front of Chatsworth, and the most probable source, if one is sought, is in this case the Perrault fronts of the Louvre.

Burley-on-the-Hill has one further feature unusual for its time, the corridors running to the subsidiary staircases at the ends of the house; like those of Coleshill forty-five years before they are hidden in the core of the house, passage-ways for convenience rather than visual effect. No other seventeenth-century houses are known to have corridors; the outside court passages of Chatsworth were begun in 1691, but it was left to Vanbrugh (p. 76) to exploit the corridor.

[55] See reference in note 13 above, p. 12.
[56] British Museum MS. Sloane 5238, No. 56 (*Walpole Soc.*, xxv, pl. xxxviii).

Nottingham took great care with the surroundings of his house. On the north side he enclosed an enormous forecourt, with office wings joined to the main pile by quadrant colonnades on the pattern of May's Berkeley House (p. 6) or of Hackwood, Hants, in the 1680's. He terraced the falling ground on the south, which gives an extensive view even from ground level. Most of his gardens and the forecourt lodges were swept away by Humphrey Repton and the 1908 fire destroyed much of the interior; nevertheless Burley-on-the-Hill remains an impressive house and one whose importance is not always realized.

William Talman built a number of houses in a much more restrained manner than Chatsworth; Uppark (c.1690, Fig. 29) is of this type, which was set by the houses of the early Restoration period, with tall hipped roof, dormers and the minimal use of the orders. Only a tendency towards greater depth in the plan – towards a square house – marks Uppark as a building of the end of the century. Kiveton or Keiton, near Sheffield, 1694–1704, appears to have been in an intermediate class (Pl. 147). It was based on Hugh May's Eltham with a central pediment over four pilasters and a roof with dormers. It was, however, a long house with forecourt wings and therefore more imposing in appearance.

Talman's additions to Dyrham, Glos, are much grander. William Blathwayt, who served both James II and William III and became the latter's Secretary for War and Acting Secretary of State abroad, inherited Dyrham from his father-in-law in 1688. Between 1692 and 1694 the west range and the great hall behind it were rebuilt to the rather insipid but pleasant design of Samuel Hauduroy, one of a number of Huguenot artists of that surname.[57] Talman's connection with the house begins in 1698 with the stables south of Hauduroy's front; Talman's letter to Blathwayt of September 1699 (*Wren Soc.*, IV, p. 59) shows the east range to have been designed, but it was not begun until the following spring. This front, taller and grander than the west (Pl. 149), originally faced the garden. Its projecting ends and flat top repeat the theme of Talman's original Chatsworth front (Pl. 140), but Dyrham is less imposing and depends for its distinction on the restrained relief detail and, to a considerable extent, on the great stone eagle (Blathwayt's crest) carved by John Harvey and hauled up in 1703 (Pl. 161). Talman's letter suggests that Blathwayt approached him through the Office of Works as one senior Civil Servant to another; the east front of Dyrham represents the Whig palace at a lower level than ducal Chatsworth, and both the interiors in the earlier portion and those in Talman's range, undertaken when Blathwayt's power was declining, are restrained affairs of wainscot with light plaster ceilings. It is tempting to suggest that Talman made use of the drawings sent over by J. H. Mansart in 1699 (p. 34). The centre window on the first floor (Pl. 160) is flanked by two halves of an Ionic pilaster, recalling the grotesquely broad Ionic piers on the gallery front of the Grand Trianon at Versailles, but Talman had already used the motif in the panelling of the Chatsworth chapel (Pl. 157). The Orangery at the south end of Dyrham, however (balanced on the north by a loggia running into the hillside), is close in the windows and the order to the Orangery at Versailles; the heavy attic, while characteristic of Talman, adds to the similarity (Pl. 150).

Talman's buildings on the whole are not conventionally attractive. It is dangerous to read personal character into buildings, but just as Blenheim has the *bravura* of Vanbrugh's correspondence Chatsworth has a quality rather near arrogance which accords with what we know of Talman's behaviour. He did produce, at the time of his dismissal from the Royal Works, one building of very great, though concealed, charm. On 24 August 1702 his usual mason, Benjamin Jackson, contracted to build according to Talman's design the court front of the hall at Drayton, Northants (Pl. 173), and certain other works including

[57] M. GIROUARD, "Dyrham House", *Country Life*, CXXXI, 1962, pp. 335–9, 396–9; these articles are based on the Blathwayt papers.

the two little hexagonal cupolas above the main block.[58] Drayton retains to this day the core of a medieval house, extensively added to in the later sixteenth century, and, by the 2nd Earl of Peterborough, in Charles II's reign. The Earl's work included the gatehouse (Pl. 176) which was described as new in 1676 and the buildings either side of it which were begun in that year; both were thus contemporary with May's medievalizing exteriors at Windsor (Pl. 5). On the Earl's death in 1697 Drayton passed to his daughter, Lady Mary Mordaunt, Duchess of Norfolk, who had for some years been estranged from her husband and was the mistress of Sir John Germain, a Dutchman and probably an illegitimate brother of William III, who made him a baronet in 1698. In 1701 Norfolk died and his widow was able to marry her lover; as the garden gate is dated by a cypher of MDCCI and another gate is dated 1699, work was in progress before 1702. Talman may have been introduced to Germain by the king; he was perhaps also responsible for the main south forecourt gates (Pl. 172) bearing the arms of Germain and Mordaunt and the Mordaunt eagle supporters, and for the colonnades at both ends of the inner court (Pl. 173). These are not in Jackson's contract and their heraldry shows that they were built after Lady Mary's death and Germain's second marriage in 1706; their heavy parapets must be Talman's.

Much of Drayton's stone-carving is heraldic, as if Lady Mary had inherited some of her father's passion for arms. Besides the features mentioned so far, the ducal coronet of Norfolk appears on one forecourt pier with the Mordaunt crest, a Saracen's head (Pl. 181), and while one of the outer piers has the customary trophy, on the other flowers hang from the linked arms of Germain and Mordaunt (Pls 179–80). The hall front is full of heads and masks, even to the urns over the pediment (Pls 177–8, 182), and the doorcase has the rather parrot-like eagle adopted by Germain worked into its Corinthian capitals. Drayton is enchanting and its spell grows with familiarity; its whole effect is picturesque and dramatic. The cupolas (Pl. 175) integrate the old and new work and, as can be seen by covering them up in the photograph, give life and rhythm to the forecourt view by the simplest means. The surprise as one enters the inner court is both spatial and pictorial; the hall front, a façade like a stage set concealing the structure behind, is immediately in front and stretches far to either side of the shallow court, and its symmetrical assortment of details suggests, more powerfully than any collection of antiques, a continuity with the past which Germain may have been at pains to emphasize precisely because he could not claim it.

The houses of Hawksmoor and Vanbrugh will be considered separately (p. 73). By 1700 the new block-like house was becoming increasingly common, and had appeared in simpler brick- and stone-form (Pl. 186) at Newby, Yorks, West Riding (not to be confused with the Palladian Newby a few miles away in the North Riding, now known as Baldersby).[59] A more adventurous work is Cound, Salop (Pl. 162), dated 1704 and apparently built by one Prince of Shrewsbury, of whom nothing else is known. This is a three-storey house, again of brick with stone dressings, with a fine giant pilaster order supporting a continuous cornice.[60] That the designer quickly knew the King William Block at Greenwich (Pl. 88) is apparent from a general similarity in the recession of the ends, the stone strings and parapet and the isolation of the pilasters.

[58] N. V. STOPFORD SACKVILLE, *Drayton House*, privately printed, 1939; *Archaeological Journal*, CX, 1953, pp. 188–9, where Jackson's contract is printed. Mr. John Cornforth has recently suggested (*Country Life*, CXXXVII, 1965, p. 1287) that Captain Winde, who was called to Drayton in 1697–8, may have given a design for the south forecourt gateway, which has affinities with one of the Hampstead Marshall gates. Cf. Pls 172, 183.

[59] If Weston Park, Staffs, begun in 1671, had originally its present form it antedates all the houses discussed in having a three-storey elevation and flat balustraded top.

[60] *English Homes*, IV.i, pp. 417–24. From the illustration on p. 420 I suspect that the elevation depicted there is not, as stated, the architect's original but a much more recent drawing. A John Prince acted as surveyor on the Harley estate in St Marylebone in 1719–23 (Colvin).

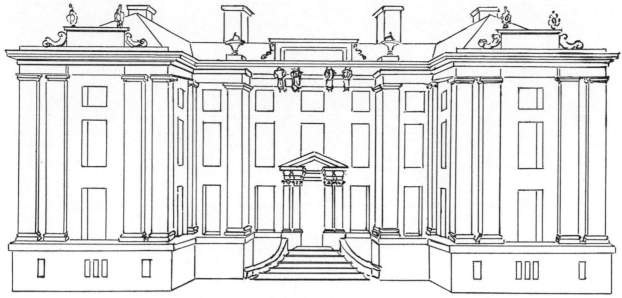

Fig. 31. William Dickinson? Design for a large house.

The use of a fairly high-pitched roof and the incorporation of the attic into the area below the main cornice is also a feature of Herriard Park, Hants (Pl. 168), demolished 1965, again dated 1704 (rain-water heads). Herriard is singularly gaunt and must have been so before the brick walls were covered in plaster; it has a look of permanently raised brows for which the plinth over the centre of the entrance front does not compensate. Experiments were certainly made in the Office of Works, for a drawing at All Souls with a similar feeling but a more broken plan (Fig. 31) is one of several in the Wren Collection very probably by William Dickinson (c. 1671–1725). As the old attribution of Herriard to Talman cannot be upheld it is tempting to see in Dickinson the architect of Herriard – and perhaps also of Cound. Waldershare, near Dover (before 1712) is possibly by Talman, but a fire in 1931 and re-modelling leave its historical value in doubt.[60a]

Another strange house, Appuldurcombe, Isle of Wight, shows knowledge of London work (Pl. 188). It was built for Sir Robert Worsley, 4th Baronet, of Appuldurcombe, who took up the estate on his marriage in 1690 but according to Campbell did not rebuild the medieval house until 1710 (*Vitruvius Britannicus* III, 61). This beautiful building, of a greenish local stone with Portland stone dressings of high quality, was completed and much altered by later Worsleys, and little remained inside from the early eighteenth century before the house fell into ruin as a result of neglect and vandalism in the 1930's and 40's. It is now in the care of the Ministry of Public Building and Works, who have restored the gutted masonry (all that remains) and have now opened it to the public. In a list of patrons and other "Persons of Quality" who would give him a good character, sent to Harley in 1711, John James includes Viscount Weymouth, Worsley's father-in-law. This by itself would not justify an attribution to James, but there are other small indications. Campbell's plate precedes those of Longleat, Weymouth's seat. Moreover, there is a relation, admittedly more evident in elevation than in perspective,[61] between Appuldurcombe and the end-pavilions on the river front of Greenwich Hospital, a building which James knew well; the doubling of the pavilions was not put in hand until late in 1711 but the architects undoubtedly

[60a] Mr Colvin has plausibly suggested John James as the author of Herriard. For an obituary of this house see *Country Life*, CXXXVIII, 1965, pp. 18–22.

[61] *Cf. Wren Soc.*, VI, pl. XLIV. See also *Country Life*, LXXII, 1932, pp. 568–72; RICHARD WORSLEY, *The history of the Isle of Wight*, 1781; H.M.C. Portland, X, p. 121. Dr Lindsay Boynton has recently discovered documentary evidence of James's connection and established that, while the house was begun in 1701, most of the structure was built in 1707–10.

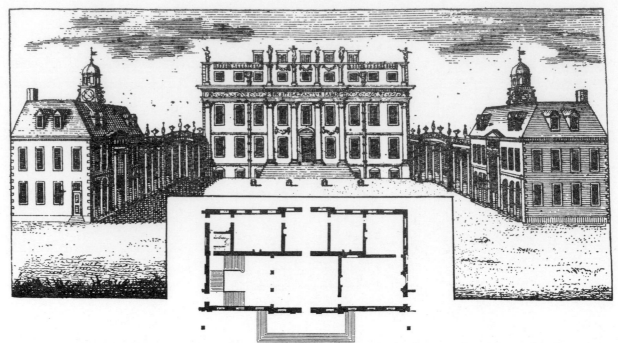

Fig. 32. Buckingham House, Westminster. View from the east and plan of main block.

considered the idea some time previously. Finally, the arched chimneys occur in James's own house, Warbrook, Hants (Pl. 369).

The part played in the diffusion of the new style by Captain William Winde or Wynne (d.1722) is doubtful but must be examined. He was born of an English Royalist family and brought up in Holland, returning to claim his patrimony at the Restoration. He took over the completion of Hampstead Marshall, Berks, for Lord Craven after the death of Sir Balthasar Gerbier in 1677 and the two may have collaborated a few years before on Ashdown (p. 5). During the 1680's he built up a fair practice in domestic architecture, but only after the Revolution did he retire from a long army career which embraced both cavalry service and fortification. He was an early Fellow of the Royal Society and something of a mathematician. Of Hampstead Marshall only the nine pairs of gate piers (Pls 183–5) survive and much of his work has been destroyed. Most of it was of the type of Belton (Pl. 129) of which he may have been the designer. On the authority of Vertue[62] he is credited with Cliveden, Bucks (burnt 1795, rebuilt by Barry 1850–1), while in *Vitruvius Britannicus* (I) and elsewhere Buckingham House, part of which survives in Buckingham Palace, is given to him. Both these houses are known to have been massive and flat-topped and more advanced in style than anything else by Winde.

Buckingham House (Fig. 32) was built for John Sheffield, 1st Duke of Buckingham and Normanby, in replacement of Arlington House which he had leased in 1698 and bought in 1702. There is good evidence that the traditional starting-date of 1705 is wrong and that the house was built 1703–5, the painter, Laguerre, being at work there in 1706.[63] Vanbrugh's letter of 15 June 1703 includes the Duke ("my Lord Normanby") among Talman's vexed clients; he is not known to have been building elsewhere, and Buckingham House was his principal residence. The screen of columns at one side of the entrance hall leading to the grand staircase, a major feature of both Buckingham House and Talman's Thoresby (Fig. 26), adds to the probability that Buckingham initially employed the architect of Thoresby to design the high attic and pilastered frontispiece of his London house. A drawing in the Sheffield family collection shows an astylar garden front, but the engraving at the end of the

---

[62] IV, p. 11.

[63] J. CORNFORTH, "The Sheffields at Buckingham House", *Country Life*, CXXXII, 1962, pp. 86–8. See also WHINNEY, *Talman*.

1729 edition of Buckingham's *Works* shows pilasters like those on the entrance front. The quadrant wings may have been the Duke's suggestion in imitation of Berkeley House at which he had previously lived.

Buckingham House helped to advertise the Thoresby type, which was imitated into the 1730's especially by Francis Smith in the Midlands (p. 95). Calke, Derbys (Pl. 383), dated 1703, may be his first house.[63a] Wotton (Pl. 187, designer unknown) was begun in 1704; the first floor windows were lowered and the attic reduced by Soane after a fire in 1820, but otherwise the exterior survives. The flanking pavilions suggest a direct imitation of Buckingham House, and Wotton remains the best guide to what the latter looked like.

The problem of Cliveden is more complicated. It was begun for George Villiers, 2nd Duke of Buckingham (an earlier creation), probably about 1670, but what evidence there is suggests that it was not finished for him. Hugh May, who had been his servant during the Commonwealth (p. 6), was no longer in his favour and cannot have been the architect.[64] Evelyn, who visited Cliveden in 1679, was impressed by the terrace overlooking the Thames Valley, but did not describe the house or give any sign that it was occupied. Brian Fairfax, the Duke's obituarist, also restricted himself to the extravagant cost of the terrace. The development of Cliveden was connected with Buckingham's liaison with the Countess of Shrewsbury; work was in progress in 1674 and 1677, but his mistress's remarriage in the latter year, while he was in the Tower, probably meant the abandonment of Cliveden. He was allowed out of the Tower for a day in June 1677 to go there because "a little mistake in my builders at Clifden may cost me £10,000 because I shall certainly pull it downe again if it be not to my owne mind".[65] A great deal of work was certainly done, and Buckingham was trying in 1675, already heavily in debt, to arrange for payment to the plasterer, joiner and carver; after his death in 1687 the estate passed through several hands, being bought in 1706 by the soldier Earl of Orkney. Orkney had received his title, his estate and his wife, Elizabeth Villiers (Buckingham's second cousin, William III's former mistress) from the king during the winter of 1695–6. Vertue, writing in the 1730's, understandably confused the two Buckinghams, the Villiers sisters, Elizabeth and Mary, and their husbands. He was wrong about the owners and he may well have been wrong about the architects. For according to *Vitruvius Britannicus* (II) (1717) it was "greatly improved and adorned" by Orkney and the wings and quadrant colonnades were added for him by Archer. Orkney seems to have been the first to care about Cliveden since the amorous Buckingham, and the house's final appearance was probably due to Archer (Pl. 170). Cliveden's pictorial relief panels under the windows are only paralleled in a drawing (Pl. 171) which is very close to Archer and may even be connected with Cliveden. If this interpretation of the evidence is correct, while the scenic potentialities of Cliveden go, as they did in Evelyn's mind, with Charles II's Windsor, the major part of the house belongs in sequence with Heythrop, well after Chatsworth.

Heythrop, Oxon (gutted 1831 and remodelled inside forty years later) was Archer's most important country house. It was designed for his patron, the Duke of Shrewsbury, one of the seven signatories who invited William III to England. Shrewsbury was in Rome from 1700 until the end of 1705. Woolfe and Gandon, on whose continuation of *Vitruvius Britannicus* we depend for the plan, give a date of *c.*1705; it was probably begun on Shrewsbury's

[63a] Calke is built round an irregular court and thus appears very large. It was roofed but unfinished in 1703 (rain water heads). About or after 1800 an Ionic portico was added, the Corinthian capitals were altered to match, the interior was refitted and the steps removed.

[64] See EVELYN, 23 July 1679; Cal. S.P.Dom., 1677–8, p. 205; WINIFRED LADY BURGHCLERE, *George Villiers, 2nd Duke of Buckingham*, London, 1903; *Country Life*, LXX, 1931, pp. 38–44; H.M.C. House of Lords (1678–88), p. 305; (1689–90), pp. 218–19. On May and Buckingham see PEPYS, 21 March 1669.

[65] BURGHCLERE, pp. 327–8.

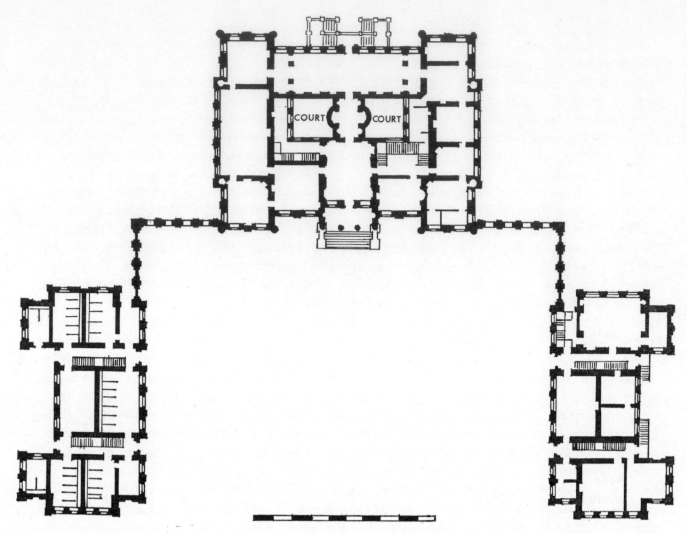

Fig. 33. Heythrop. Original plan.

return early in 1706, but was not roofed in 1709 and unfinished in 1716. It is possible, as has been suggested,[66] that the design given to Shrewsbury by Falconieri in Rome with his Whitehall plan (p. 46) might have served as a model for Archer. Details of Heythrop such as the eared windows (Pl. 198) and that on the north end are taken from Roman Baroque sources, but undoubtedly by way of Rossi's *Studio d'Architettura Civile* (1702). Archer's literal borrowing of the more fanciful and exuberant types of Roman detail is noteworthy because of its abundance and its homogeneity: all Heythrop's external detail looks mature Roman Baroque (Pls 196–202) and sources could no doubt be found for all of it. But in other respects Archer's eclecticism was broader and nearer home. The marked differences between adjacent elevations (Pls 191, 201) and the interesting detail of spiral staircases hidden in the salients of the ends (*cf.* Fig. 27) recall Talman's fronts at Chatsworth. The cupolas on the service blocks (Pl. 191) suggest, in intention though not in form, those of Vanbrugh's Castle Howard (Pl. 227). The vestibule in the middle of the house was later used by Vanbrugh for Eastbury (Fig. 41b), but its nearly oval plan again suggests Talman's experiments with this shape; it was probably to the nearby Blenheim that Archer looked for the two small internal courts which were necessary for light. Vanbrugh's references to Heythrop in letters indicate its contemporary importance; it was a palace in the Chatsworth sense, with large

66 WHIFFEN, *Archer*, p. 22.

state rooms. The staircase, however, was relatively small and apart from the vestibule there seems to have been little complexity or surprise in the shapes and sequence of rooms (Fig. 33).

Archer remained an amateur, deriving from sinecures under the Crown a considerable augmentation of his private means. His first-hand knowledge of Continental Baroque (p. 3) showed him the kind of detail he wanted, on his return, to quarry from engravings and the kind of three-dimensional development he wanted, as in the pavilions at Chatsworth and Wrest (Pls 154, 571), to achieve. But, just as not every bizarre doorway is his (Chicheley, p. 95, for instance), the conception of architecture underlying his ornament, his great broken pediments and his curving walls, is basically simple. The wings he added to Aynho, Northants, 1707–11, are plain but their central doorcases are Borrominesque (Pl. 197). Bramham Park, Yorks, was begun, traditionally about 1710 but probably earlier, for Robert Benson, later Lord Bingley. He is not known to be related to the Palladian Benson; his father was Lord Mayor and M.P. for York. Bingley's account with Hoare's Bank includes payments in 1699 and 1700 to "Mr. Archer" and twenty years later Archer designed a London house for him. Bramham is an extremely plain house (Pl. 189) but has a dramatic device of straight Doric colonnades connecting it to the wings, and was intended to have urns and statues on the skyline. There is some connection of idea between the sloping coachway and Archer's design "for a staire to ascend Windsor Terrace with coaches".[67] Bramham was gutted in 1828 and little of the interior survives except the walls of the pillared square stone hall and some of the woodwork.

Archer at his most fantastic is represented by Roehampton House, for Thomas Cary, 1710–12, which partly survives as the nucleus of Queen Mary's Hospital (Pls 167, 169). It is uncertain whether the giant pediment was ever built, but a similar one formerly rose above Monmouth House on the south side of Soho Square as Archer rebuilt it, probably shortly before 1718 (Fig. 34).[68] The most interesting surviving feature of Roehampton is the convex quadrant arcades flanking the main pile.

Besides Bramham, Archer had a connection with the north at Wentworth Castle (below) and may also have been responsible for Beningbrough, Yorks, completed in 1716 (date in parquetry on the staircase) for John Bourchier. The plan is simple and convenient, with rooms opening on both sides from a central corridor running the length of the house. Upstairs similar corridors run from the ends to balconies overlooking the cubic hall (Pl. 192). The window over the front door (Pls 190, 195) is very like the ground floor windows of Heythrop; it should be recorded, however, that Talman also used it in a design for Welbeck of c.1702 (Soane Museum). Other interesting Baroque details are the doorcases in the hall and at the foot of the stairs (Pl. 193) and the corridor arches with splayed jambs which have a suggestion of false perspective (Pl. 194).

In spite of the French or Dutch character of certain English buildings and the Italian or Austrian features in Archer's work, nearly all English Baroque is recognizably English. A building which does suggest that England shared in an International Late Baroque style is the east front of Wentworth Castle (or Stainborough), Yorks.[69] Thomas Wentworth, Lord Raby, bought the estate and seventeenth-century house in 1708 to increase his substance and thus further his claim to the extinct Earldom of Strafford; it had the advantage of being close to Wentworth Woodhouse (p. 92), the family estate which had passed over him to his nephew, Thomas Watson, who added the name Wentworth to his own. Raby was Ambassador in Berlin and commissioned the design for an additional front containing a

[67] H.M.C. Marquess of Bath, I, p. 231; G. W. BEARD, "Thomas Archer and Bramham Park", *Country Life* CXXIV, 1958, p. 1421.

[68] M. P. G. DRAPER, "The great house in Soho Square", *Country Life*, CXXXIV, 1963, pp. 592–3.

[69] A. BOOTH, "The architects of Wentworth Castle and Wentworth Woodhouse", *R.I.B.A. Journal*, ser. 3, XLI, 1933, pp. 61–72; J. HARRIS, "Bodt and Stainborough", *Architectural Review*, CXXX, 1961, pp. 34–5.

Fig. 34. Monmouth House, Soho (destroyed).

180-feet gallery from Jean Bodt, who had been in England in 1698 (p. 46) and was now Prussian Court architect. Bodt's first design is now in the Victoria and Albert Museum; in revision it became more monumental, more like the Louvre of Bernini, Le Vau and Perrault, more Baroque (Pl. 205).

In February 1710 Raby still wanted a front in "brick and stone as Hampton Court is" – the grandest example of the cheapest materials. The building was probably roofed in 1714 but the gallery on the first floor was decorated only in the 1720's, in a rather dull Palladian grandeur; Raby emerges as more concerned for show than for a work of art. By 1714 he was in correspondence with Archer about his building, probably having been introduced by Benson of Bramham, and Archer was presumably in charge of the work and responsible for such details as the eared windows on the first floor and the curious relief balusters under the ground floor windows (Pls 207–8).

Wentworth Castle stands at the top of a hill (which Bodt probably never saw) and rises imposingly through two-and-a-half storeys to a continuous balustrade. The carved fields above the door and above the very French arrangement of triple round-headed windows upstairs are characteristic of Bodt, but the actual detail of fruit, flowers, trumpets and trophies (Pls 206, 209) follows the tradition of Hampton Court. Monumental elevations of this kind can be found in Piedmont, in Rome and Naples, and in Central Europe. Raby's carver and his cosmopolitan architect proclaimed not "territorial Whiggery" (p. 12), but purely personal prestige. Wentworth Castle is superior as architecture to Cannons (p. 87) and speaks more directly, if with as little reason, the language of the great German palaces.

EASTON NESTON AND CASTLE HOWARD

Among all the great houses of the age of Wren two especially are conspicuous, not as a pair but as the first major works of Hawksmoor and Vanbrugh and as extraordinary attempts to modify the course of English house planning. Of Castle Howard most of the important dates are known; of Easton Neston little more can be said than that its commencement must have been the earlier by several years. Hawksmoor designed Easton Neston as a trained architect of considerable experience; Vanbrugh began Castle Howard without evidence – even apparently to his contemporaries – of any previous preparation for the task. Easton Neston is, as far as we are likely ever to know, Hawksmoor's work alone; Vanbrugh could not have realized his vision of Castle Howard without the abundant help, acknowledged and documented, of Hawksmoor.

Wren was evidently little interested in domestic architecture and seems, when approached by Sir William Fermor, a relation by marriage, to have delegated the commission for Easton Neston to Hawksmoor. The house bears the date 1702 on frieze and rain-water heads, and was probably begun about 1696–7. According to Bridges's *History of Northamptonshire*, compiled from his notes after his death in 1724, the wings (of which the north one survives) were built about 1682; thus although the new house was carefully sited the unknown designer of the wings limited any successor to a court about 125 feet wide. Fermor bought a large part of the Arundel Collection of antique marbles in 1691 and was created Baron Lempster the following year, soon after his third marriage to Sophia Osborne, daughter of the Duke of Leeds. According to Luttrell the match gained Fermor both the Barony and a gift of £10,000.[70] From the scale and appearance of the house and early descriptions Hawksmoor seems to have accepted a challenge to produce a building combining the modern dignity – admittedly not the size – of Chatsworth and the austere "antique" gravity of the old sculpture gallery at Arundel House. The hall has been completely altered and the sculpture, whose arrangement was unfinished at Lempster's death, is now in the Ashmolean Museum, but it is still possible to appreciate the unconventional merits of a house designed by a young architect anxious, perhaps, to show off his command of plan, elevation and interior space (Fig. 35).

The exterior is of great distinction; the precision and the rhythmic subtlety of the giant composite order on the main fronts (Pls 203–4) leave no doubt of the deliberateness of the north end (Pl. 210), in which the lower members of the entablature are dispensed with and, perhaps in imitation of Ammanati's Palazzo del Collegio Romano, mezzanine windows are inserted in the intermediate bays. The patterning of windows is as diverse and as far abstracted from our expectations of a classical façade as the east front of King William Court at Greenwich; in fact the epigrammatic neatness with which all the features are fitted together, shape answering like shape, without overcrowding, gives this front a refinement above the rhetoric of Greenwich and appropriate to the elegance of the main fronts. The fenestration is related to the interior planning of the north end, where Hawksmoor introduced mezzanine floors in order to produce more *appartements* in a small space; as these floors run behind some of the large windows, function is clearly subordinate to appearance in the elevations.

The rooms fill the house like parcels expertly packed into a case, and the importance of this skilful disposition was evidently such that it was not altered from the preliminary model which, although already flat-topped, differs in proportions and in having superimposed orders. Over half the building is used for a sequence of state rooms which are related most dramatically. The entrance originally opened unexpectedly into one end of the hall, the middle portion of which rose through two full storeys, both ends being of one storey

[70] LUTTRELL, II, 380.

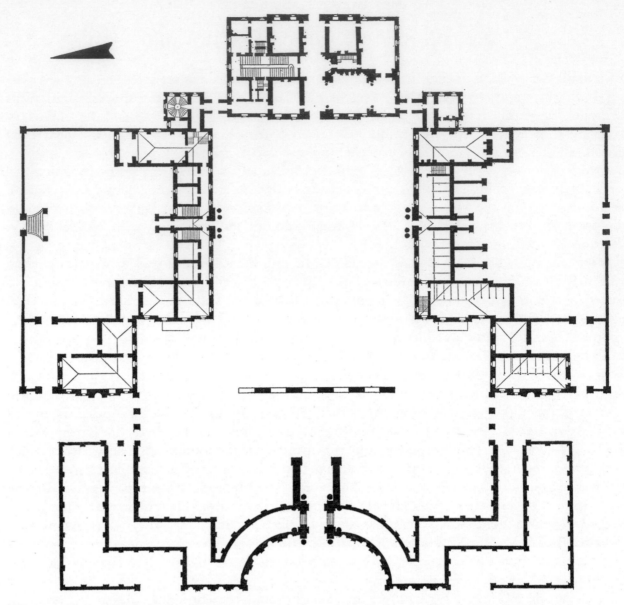

Fig. 35. Easton Neston. Plan of 1715 showing main block and projected forecourt and enlarged wings.

(Pl. 223). This dramatic stroke was succeeded by another. In the centre of the house, through the end of the hall, is a low dark vestibule, from which the grand staircase extends as far to the left as the hall did to the right, rising the whole height of the house and lit solely by the big window in the middle of the north front (Pl. 212). The change of direction at the halfway landing under the window leads to yet another change, for at the top of the stairs is a gallery running across the house at right angles to the stair-hall, giving access to the main upper rooms (Pl. 213).

Easton Neston was well served by craftsmen: by the unknown mason who worked on the façades and the shell-niche at the bottom of the staircase (Pl. 290), the unknown plasterer who decorated the staircase and gallery and the smith who made the stair-rails, and by Thornhill who painted the staircase walls in *grisaille*. In the artifice and the flexible but urgent rhythms of its elevations and in the surprises of the interior it is a Baroque house. In retrospect its debt to Chatsworth is clear, but its importance lies not in the development of country house design but in its individual character. When Lempster died in 1711 it was as complete as we know it (the drawing room is a generation later and the fine garden is modern) and the engravings in *Vitruvius Britannicus* (I) probably represent an attempt of Hawksmoor's to interest the 2nd Baron in enlarging the wings (which he later described as "good for nothing") and adding a cupola in the knowledge of what had by then been done at Castle Howard (Pl. 220).

The creation of Castle Howard was due to the efforts of four men. Charles Howard, 3rd Earl of Carlisle, was the owner of Henderskelfe Castle and Vanbrugh's friend, junior by five years, fellow-Whig and patron. As architect for his new house he chose Talman, first architect of the first Whig palace; plans by Talman exist for a rectangular house with giant pilasters and also for a forecourt with quadrants linking the main house to front wings.[71] The latter may even imply that a change from a westerly aspect to the present northerly one was suggested by Talman before he was superseded. He and his mason, Jackson, visited Henderskelfe more than once, but Carlisle found his charges for these trips and for drawings excessive and relations ended in a lawsuit in 1703 in which Talman gained only part of his fees. Meanwhile – and before the autumn of 1699 – Carlisle had received designs from Vanbrugh, drawn for the most part, if we may go by the earliest surviving studies,[72] by the fourth man, Hawksmoor. One of the strangest events of architectural history is the partnership between Vanbrugh and Hawksmoor which produced Castle Howard and Blenheim. In 1699 Vanbrugh, retired soldier and writer of successful comedies, with apparently no experience but with ideas and assurance enough to gain Carlisle's ear, needed a draughtsman, an administrator, and a detail designer. Hawksmoor, then developing his own practice, seems to have been willing to act as all three, and it is now beyond doubt that he did so from the start.

From a letter of Christmas 1699 we learn that Vanbrugh had been at Henderskelfe that summer "and Seen most of the great houses in the North as Ld Nottings: Duke of Leeds Chattesworth &c." It is interesting that two of the examples in his mind were Talman houses; Kiveton, roofed but not yet finished, for the Duke of Leeds, Lord Lempster's father-in-law, and Chatsworth, still incomplete. By the time the south front of Vanbrugh's main pile began to rise in 1702 it would be seen to be indebted to Chatsworth's west front, begun two years earlier. Lord Nottingham's was Burley-on-the-Hill (p. 64), also roofed but unfinished in 1699, and whose corridors probably inspired the inclusion if not the drama of those at Castle Howard (Figs. 30, 36, Pl. 226).

Devonshire had understood from Carlisle that Vanbrugh's first design was "a plain low building like an orange-house" and when the architect displayed his designs at Chatsworth, Devonshire was struck by the low wings and the "Ornaments of Pillasters and Urns". The first design we have (Pl. 214) shows a pilastered house such as Hawksmoor was building at Easton Neston and Talman had intended for Castle Howard, with the wings mentioned, but as yet neither urns nor other carved work. The most significant additions to the south elevation as the design evolved were the pediment with a carved tympanum and the carved frieze. The windows are round-headed unlike those of the west front of Chatsworth, and the order is Corinthian instead of Ionic, but the resemblances outweigh the differences, running even to the same winged sea-horses in the frieze under the pediment in both buildings (Pls 229–30).

The two respects in which Castle Howard immediately differs from preceding houses are the wings on the south front in addition to those flanking the entrance court on the north, and the dome which lights and crowns the hall and gives the whole exterior an unparalleled dramatic climax. The wings figure in the earliest drawings; the dome was an addition which both disguises the debt to Chatsworth and raises and transforms Castle Howard from imitation to invention. It seems clear that the designs Vanbrugh showed Devonshire in 1699 had no dome, as his Christmas letter does not mention it; the idea first appears in an

[71] In the R.I.B.A. Library; see WHINNEY, *Talman*, pp. 132–3 and pl. 37.
[72] Now in the Victoria and Albert Museum; mostly reproduced in WHISTLER, *Vanbrugh*, 1954.

intermediate elevation at Welbeck[73] and in a plan in which the supporting piers are clearly an addition. The idea of architectural design as a process of experiment is recognized in Wren (for example, in the development of St Paul's) and is not only evident in Hawksmoor's work but formulated in his phrase "experience and tryalls"; with Hawksmoor and, it appears with Vanbrugh, design might also be a matter of growth. The kitchen and stable courts, which do not appear on the early plans, exemplify the tendency of Vanbrugh houses to spread ever outwards and become, as Horace Walpole said of Castle Howard, "a palace, a town, a fortified city". It was planned on a scale previously the prerogative of royalty; the increase over Chatsworth, however, is not in the number of state or private rooms but in ground area, and the main block, on the now familiar hall-saloon pattern, contains few rooms. The north front has the variable rhythms but the plan has none of the ingenuity of Easton Neston, and initially only the open quadrant arcades ran between the main house and the north wings; the enclosed passages behind were only conceived later, perhaps as late as 1709–10.[74] The two east-west corridors are not primarily functional, since they open to few rooms, but their tunnel-like perspectives have a dramatic effect unattainable in the conventional enfilade of the south front which they by-pass. Unfortunately the west side of the house was unfinished at the 3rd Earl's death (1738) and was completed by Sir Thomas Robinson to his own design for the 5th Earl, thus destroying the intended symmetry. In 1940 a disastrous fire ravaged the hall and most of the south range, but while most of the decoration is lost for ever the interior of the hall and dome and the structure of the south front have recently been restored.

One of the characteristic features of the Clarendon-Belton house type is the wooden cupola containing the stairs to the roof top. The cupola at Castle Howard is much larger, it is of stone, and it forms an upward extension of the hall. Vanbrugh and Hawksmoor probably knew the Oranjezaal of the Huis ten Bosch in The Hague, which is cruciform and has a central lantern; they certainly knew May's Queen's Staircase at Windsor (p. 20) which was also lit from above by a small lantern, and although Phaeton and the Four Elements were popular subjects Carlisle and his architect may have deliberately taken them from the cupola and pendentives of Windsor as suitable for incorporation in the new Whig palace. The effect within and without is as though one of the Greenwich domes or the crossing of St Paul's in miniature had been inserted into the house; rather than on painted illusion it depends on real relief and illumination, on the Baroque use of light flooding down from the eight tall windows to the painted panels, carved piers and capitals and marble and stucco ornament below. By the time the decoration was undertaken (1707–12) Vanbrugh was established; his advancement at Talman's expense had culminated in his obtaining the older architect's post of Comptroller in 1702, soon after King William's death and at the end of Carlisle's period of office as First Lord of the Treasury, and as Blenheim began to rise from the mud in Woodstock Park Vanbrugh (with Hawksmoor in attendance) could point northwards to the richest entrance hall ever completed in England (Pls 126, 292).

Carlisle was unwilling to pay London rates, and unlike Devonshire before him managed to avoid them; the principal masons were William Smith and John Elsworth of York. The stone carving, which is more profuse than on any later Vanbrugh house, was undertaken partly by them but largely by Samuel Carpenter of York and two Huguenots, Daniel

---

[73] WHISTLER, *Vanbrugh*, 1954, Fig. 1, showing a much smaller dome and probably between (but loosely related to) the two plans in Figs 11 and 12 there; the latter shows the piers for the dome, and in the original they are clearly visible as additions. I no longer consider (*cf.* DOWNES, *Hawksmoor*, p. 274) that this plan and the Welbeck drawing are before June 1699. Work began on the north-east wing in 1700 and they may be as late as that, the introduction of a larger dome even months later.

[74] WHISTLER, *Vanbrugh*, 1954, p. 89. Fig. 36 is based on the second (1717) edition of *Vitruvius Britannicus*; the 1715 plate is erroneous.

Harvey (originally Hervé) and Nadauld (or Nedos) who brought his frieze designs from the west front of Chatsworth to the south front of Castle Howard. The figures, urns and metopes on the north front and the frieze and pediment on the south are bold and telling, even stagey in comparison with the softer realism and flowing relief of Hampton Court. Carpenter's composite capitals in the hall, however, are of fine quality (Pl. 243) and worthy of Isaac Mansfield's plaster work in the pendentives, that of Bagutti and Plura in the chimney-piece, and the paintings in the hall, the garden room, the two saloons and elsewhere by Pellegrini, who was at Castle Howard between 1709 and 1712. Gibbons received £35 for carving, traditionally for an overmantel in a room west of the saloon, destroyed in 1940.

With the main pile and one wing complete, work slackened. Carlisle and his architects turned their attention to the creation of the unique park-landscape of Castle Howard (p. 125). At the junction of the west drive to the house with the road from Coneysthorpe to York they built a 100-foot obelisk in 1714–15. The inscription was not added until 1731 but a letter of Vanbrugh records before its erection his patron's intention, with which he agreed, to raise his own memorial to the hero of Blenheim.

BLENHEIM

There is no reason to doubt Vanbrugh's retrospective account of the commissioning of Blenheim, that at the beginning of 1705 "Viewing a Modell which Vanbrugh then had in Wood of the Earl of Carlisles House, the Duke said that was ye sort of House he liked, onely with some alterations and additions as a Gallery etc." Thus were determined the architect, the size and the heroic associations of Marlborough's palace, which was to be the nation's gift in gratitude for the victory which was the turning-point of the war with Louis XIV. Marlborough accepted the glory as no more than what was due to him, yet – curiously for one so ambitious – impersonally, for the deed not the doer. In Kneller's sketch for a painting recording the reward and his written explanation of it the figures are, at the Duke's wish, allegorical, except that of the Queen, who presents a drawing of Blenhcim to "Military Merit".[75] From the beginning Blenheim was not merely a house but a national monument, and as such Vanbrugh saw it. He wrote to Sarah, Duchess of Marlborough, that "tho' ordered to be a Dwelling house for the Duke of Marlborough, and his posterity, [it] is at the Same time by all the World esteemed and looked on as a Publick Edifice, raised for a Monument of the Queen's Glory through his great Services", and he told Harley that he looked "upon it much more as an intended Monument of the Queens Glory than a private Habitation for the Duke".[76] The Duchess cared more for her husband than anything else in the world. Vanbrugh she disliked (the feeling was mutual) and Blenheim she suffered from the first with unconcealed distaste for the expense and extravagance of time, money and ideas. Yet after she had provoked the architect's resignation in 1716 she determined to make the place habitable (appointing a cabinetmaker named Moore as her "Oracle"), and in 1722 as a widow of 62 she took as a duty and a challenge the £50,000 left her by the Duke to finish the palace. She recalled Hawksmoor, who had been Vanbrugh's assistant from the outset, and for whom as an architect her toleration amounted almost to admiration. Blenheim had already cost £240,000; of the further £50,000 she spent only half, but the west (stable) court and the grand gateway and closing wall of the entrance court went unbuilt. Immense financial trouble had beset the building all along; this was firstly because of the shortage of money common to all Treasury building projects of the time, secondly because,

[75] GREEN, *Blenheim*, pp. 315, 298–9.
[76] WHISTLER, *Vanbrugh*, 1954, p. 237; VANBRUGH, *Letters*, p. 46.

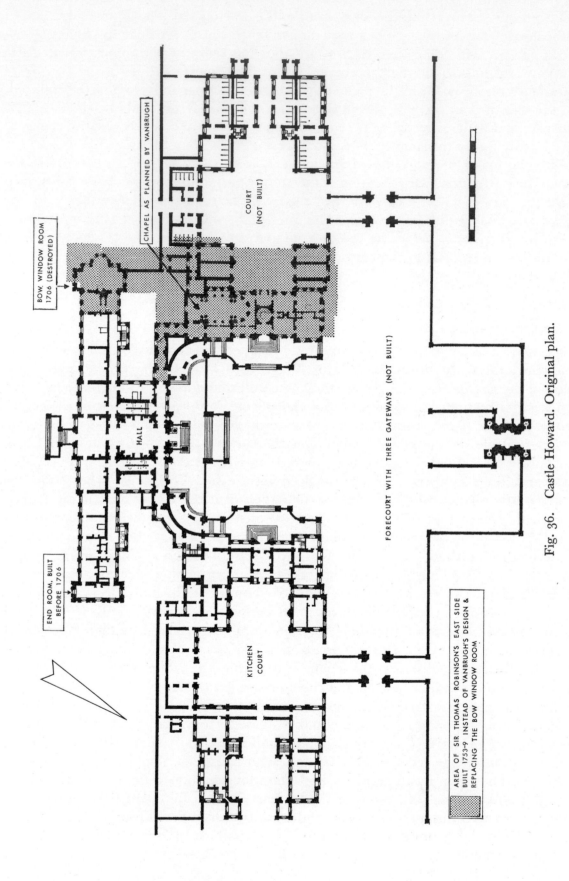

END ROOM. BUILT
BEFORE 1706

BOW. WINDOW ROOM
1706 (DESTROYED)

CHAPEL AS PLANNED BY VANBRUGH

HALL

COURT
(NOT BUILT)

KITCHEN
COURT

FORECOURT WITH THREE GATEWAYS (NOT BUILT)

AREA OF SIR THOMAS ROBINSON'S EAST SIDE
BUILT 1753-9 INSTEAD OF VANBRUGH'S DESIGN &
REPLACING THE BOW WINDOW ROOM

Fig. 36.   Castle Howard. Original plan.

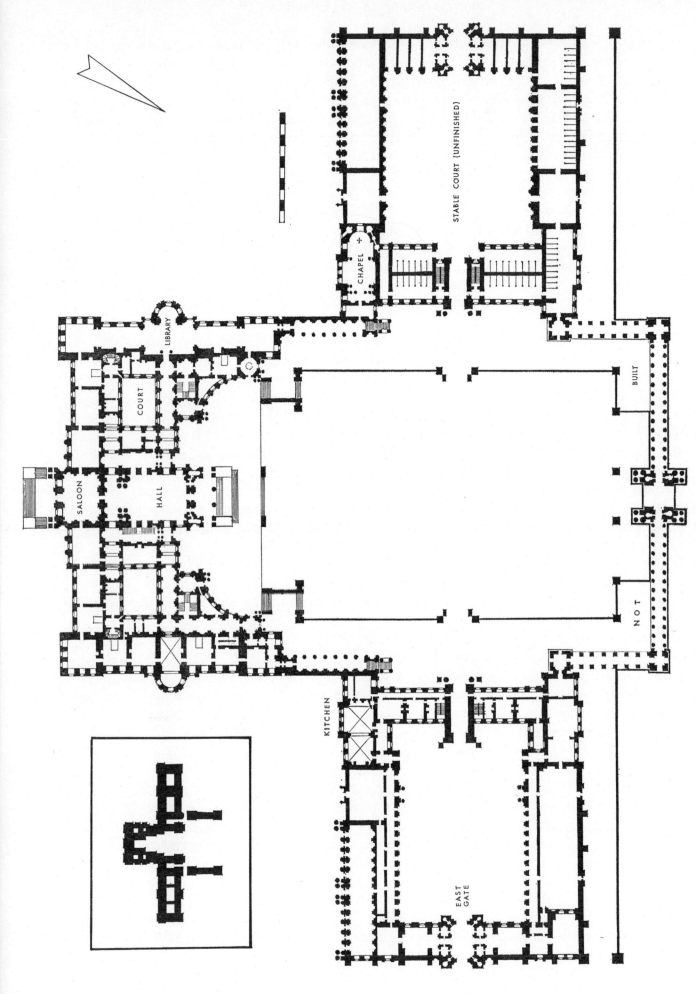

LIBRARY

COURT

SALOON

HALL

CHAPEL

STABLE COURT (UNFINISHED)

BUILT

NOT

KITCHEN

EAST
GATE

Fig. 37.   Blenheim Palace. Plan. Fig. 38 (inset). Outline plan of Versailles, *c.*1700.

although the gift of Woodstock Park was definite and that of the house project promised
though apparently undocumented, no price limit was ever fixed for the latter, and thirdly
because in 1710–11 Tory intrigue brought the disfavour and finally disgrace of the Marlboroughs, a stoppage of money and a train of litigation. For the Duchess (taking over a
phrase of Vanbrugh's from her husband), Blenheim became a "Monument of Ingratitude";
in finishing it in her own way, she made it, with an economy proportionate to her wealth,
a personal monument to Marlborough himself. That is the message of Hawksmoor's inscribed
Triumphal Arch at the Woodstock entrance (1723, Pl. 235), of the "historical pillar" which,
after many designs for obelisks and columns by Hawksmoor and others, became in 1727–31
the Doric column carrying the Duke's statue in lead, designed by Lord Herbert, amateur
architect, later 9th Earl of Pembroke (Pl. 241). These were the accepted symbols, as was the
great machine of sculpture, designed by Kent and executed by Rysbrack, which forms Marlborough's tomb and fills Blenheim chapel. Nor did Sarah take the quarrel with Queen Anne
to her grave; in 1738 she commissioned a statue of the Queen from Rysbrack and placed it
in the Long Library. But in the architectural meaning of Blenheim she had little interest or
understanding.

The first known design for Blenheim (Pl. 217), with a lower Doric order instead of Corinthian, with no attic over the hall and without the final multiplicity of towers and finials, has
unmistakably both the air of a palace and a dour solemnity beside which even Castle Howard
seems gay. The final design (Pls 218, 228) is richer and more varied in surface, outline and
detail, but it is essentially the same. The roof-top "eminencys" designed and so called by
Hawksmoor, but conceived by Vanbrugh, are no mere ornaments but sculptural structures
of a high order of imagination; besides obvious prototypes in the lanterns of Borromini
they indicate, as do the bow windows and projecting towers on the plan, inspiration from
the wild skylines and tower-fringed plans of great houses of a century or more before, such
as Burghley, Wollaton and Hardwick. Those houses were themselves romantic creations
which had associations with medieval castles, and the chain of association is completed with
Vanbrugh's attempt, two years after Blenheim was begun, at the "Castle Air" at Kimbolton (p. 17). It can hardly be accidental that Henderskelfe became Castle Howard and
that Blenheim was called Blenheim Castle by the Office of Works.

Blenheim is not only the richest building of its kind, the epitome of English Baroque and
worthy of ranking with Schönbrunn or Stupinigi. It is architectural rhetoric; on the north,
approached as it should have been by the Grand Bridge or Viaduct, with the "eminencys"
and the attic over the hall fully visible, it is all fanfare and cannons (Pl. 228). This is partly
due to the dramatic composition of masses, to the progressive narrowing of the court on the
Versailles pattern, to the sweep of the quadrants, enclosed and more fully developed than
at Castle Howard, and to the frequent changes of scale and texture between adjacent parts
of the whole, culminating in the giant pilasters of the main block which seems to overfill
and project forwards from the space left for it in the quadrants. But a great deal of the effect
comes from the objects above the cornice, from the progression from the kitchen and stable
court lanterns to the main corner towers and thence to the central attic, and from the
ornamental detail. Statues – though they are modern replacements of Gibbons's originals –
stand on the main block; the 9th Duke, who did much to restore Blenheim, moved trophies
from the east front to the north to flank the main steps in place of the larger ones intended but
never made; further trophies (Pl. 120) crown the ends of the colonnades leading to the side
courts. Caryatids stand over the west bow window (Pl. 119). The finials of the corner towers,
originally picked out in gold, consist of ducal coronets carried on reversed fleurs-de-lis
(representing the downfall of France) standing on cannon-balls on scrolls, while over the
gateways to the side courts the British lion savages the French cock (Pls 237, 247). The kitchen
court is battlemented, and the massive east gate beyond it rests, in appearance, on cannon-balls

(Pls 246, 252). The engraving of the garden front in *Vitruvius Britannicus* (Pl. 219) shows an equestrian Marlborough crushing his enemies, supported by ludicrously large figures of the lion and the cock; by a happy stroke of effrontery Marlborough obtained the 30-ton bust of Louis XIV from the city gate after the sack of Tournai in 1709, and placed his conquest, like a head on a stake, above the garden front (Pl. 216). The language of Versailles was used for the gate piers of Petworth (Pl. 234) and the garden pedestals of Chatsworth (Pl. 159); it could be diluted, through the pediment of Castle Howard (Pl. 230) to those of minor houses like Hale Manor and Woolton (Pls 341, 232) and even to the chancel gable at Chicheley (Pl. 233). Nowhere was it more appropriate, nowhere stronger, than at Blenheim.

Inside the house, little decoration was done before the break between Queen Anne and the Marlboroughs, apart from the hall (Pl. 245, almost certainly designed by Hawksmoor), one of the four identical doorcases in the saloon (Pl. 248, designed by Hawksmoor and cut, like the hall capitals, by Gibbons) and some fireplaces. Thornhill's hall ceiling (Pl. 122), showing Marlborough presenting a plan of the Battle of Blenheim to Britannia, came in 1716 with *grisaille* trophies on the upper walls; Laguerre (who was cheaper) painted the apotheosis on the saloon ceiling and the illusionist architecture around representatives of the four continents on the walls in 1719–20 (Pl. 118). In 1716 after Vanbrugh's departure most of the craftsmen and artists gradually left, and it was not until 1722 that the Duchess recalled Hawksmoor to design the hanging ceilings east of the saloon (Pl. 238) and the finest interior in the palace, the Long Library (Pls 249, 251). This room, which Vanbrugh had intended as a picture gallery and which takes up the whole west side of the house, was transformed by Hawksmoor into something much grander than its contours, determined by general symmetry, would suggest. It is a sequence of spaces of different height, width and treatment; it has the angular plasticity of Easton Neston, but it gains warmth from Isaac Mansfield's plaster work.

Vanbrugh's bridge (Pl. 242) was one of the casualties of Blenheim; it lacks its towers and arcades, and Capability Brown, for whom a bridge could not be complete in itself without water round it, raised the level of the stream by several feet to make the present lake. Brown also destroyed the great formal parterre on the south of the house, where now the lawn rolls up to the windows. From the Long Library windows, looking out westwards over Duchêne's formal garden created for the 9th Duke in 1925–30 (Pl. 240), one can form some idea of its appearance.

VANBRUGH'S LATER HOUSES

The Castle Howard-Blenheim style was the product of a partnership, and it is distinct from, though recognizably connected with, the independent work of Hawksmoor and Vanbrugh. Apart from Easton Neston and fragmentary or inadequately recorded work Hawksmoor's achievement lies outside domestic architecture, whereas Vanbrugh was predominantly a house designer, for all the interest he showed in other buildings and schemes. That they did not collaborate again on a great house is less remarkable than that two men of such individual genius did work together on two occasions. Vanbrugh took Hawksmoor with him to Kimbolton in July 1707 to discuss with the Countess of Manchester the rebuilding of the south front after a collapse. With Coleman, the local mason who had been first consulted, they "all Agreed Upon" a design "which Differs very much from what Coleman had drawn".[77] But while Hawksmoor is known to have made drawings for Kimbolton in the next three years his hand is not to be found in the building and it looks as if he acted purely as a

---

[77] Vanbrugh to the Earl of Manchester; *Letters*, p. 13.

draughtsman, just as did Henry Joynes and one "Arthur" in later years; the drawings for Vanbrugh's Eastbury are in three distinct hands none of which is Hawksmoor's.

Vanbrugh's intention to give Kimbolton (Pls 254–6) a "castle air" based on May's work at Windsor has been mentioned (p. 17); this is the key to his whole design, and in a later letter to Lord Manchester (September 1707) he referred to its "Manly Beauty . . . produced out of such rough Materialls", adding that "'tis certainly the Figure and Proportions that make the most pleasing Fabrick And not the delicacy of the Ornaments".[78] Kimbolton was a late medieval house, roughly symmetrical round a rectangular internal court; the court had been refaced shortly before Vanbrugh's time. By 1710 he had refaced all the exterior fronts, except the east portico, the last front to be done being the north or kitchen side with its depressed arcade (Pl. 256). On the west he retained the earlier gateway, and the slight concavity of the front is probably the result of using old foundations. The yellow ashlar, the grooved corners which imply the presence of a giant order and the bold projections, different on each front, justify the architect's confidence in the effect of his design.

It has been frequently remarked that the east portico is too large for the front in which it stands. A plan and elevation in the Huntingdon County Record Office (Manchester papers), certainly by an Italian hand, together with letters from Manchester to Galilei in June and July 1719 just before he returned to Italy, leave no reasonable doubt that this enormous afterthought was not Vanbrugh's but the only traceable work in England by the designer of the Lateran portico in Rome, with which it has obvious similarities.[79]

Vanbrugh designed Kings Weston for Edward Southwell in about 1710–11 and the masonry was completed by 1714, apparently using the foundations of an earlier U-shaped house on the edge of a plateau with a westward view over the Avon-Severn confluence towards the mountains of Wales. The staircase was being floored in 1719 but the house was not finished, and much of the interior as well as the steps to both the entrance (south) and the garden (east) fronts were carried out to his own designs between 1763 and 1772 by Robert Mylne, who also built, in a sympathetic style, the nearby stables.[80] Mylne or a later architect also altered the north and west fronts, and during the last fifty years the house has suffered not only from varied and not always suitable tenancy and insufficient funds for its upkeep, but also from vandalism. At present it is ideally occupied by the Bristol School of Architecture but its maintenance cannot be predicted with confidence and its restoration is not yet complete. It is Vanbrugh's least photogenic house but one of his most attractive; the warm pleasant texture of the reddish-yellow stone (from a quarry south-west of the house) gives it a softness and warmth of appearance which mitigates the sternness of its plain walls and unframed windows. Kimbolton was a special case of remodelling; at Kings Weston Vanbrugh started from the ground, and principles which can be found at Blenheim are now fully evident. Sir Joshua Reynolds was the first to recognize and to assert that Vanbrugh "composed like a painter"; Kings Weston is at once massively prismatic, in its simple general lines, and picturesque, in its lack of cut relief. The *sfumato* softness of its windows is best conveyed by comparison; they are neither punched deeply out of the wall, like Hawksmoor's at Limehouse (Pl. 400), nor circumscribed by precisely cut mouldings, like those of Easton Neston (Pl. 204) or a Palladian house. The colossal applied entrance portico has no plasticity, no projection from the wall; mouldings are reduced to the minimum of detail. Everywhere the effect is of drawing with a brush rather than a pen (Pls 261–2). And without Hawksmoor

[78] *Ibid.*, p. 15.
[79] The letters are quoted in *English Miscellany*, III, 1952, pp. 214–15. A phrase in a recent guide to Kimbolton and a note in the Huntingdon Record Office indicate that my conclusion about this drawing had previously been reached by Miss Toesca after the publication of her Galilei article.
[80] C. GOTCH, "Mylne at Kings Weston", *Country Life*, CXXIII, 1953, pp. 212–15.

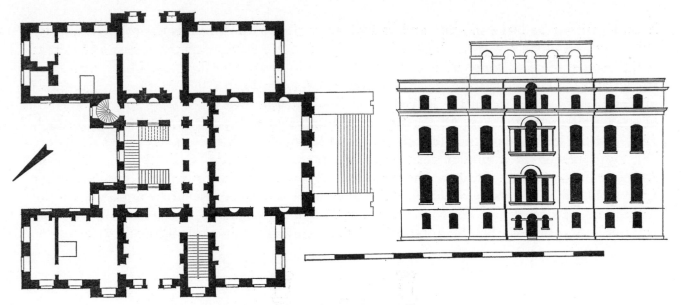

Fig. 39. Kings Weston. (a) Plan. (b) Original west elevation.

the Blenheim skyline becomes, formally primitive but no less dramatic, an arcade of chimneys.

Within the house, the staircase rising its full height is Vanbrugh's (Pl. 266); the feigned niches (Pl. 263) must date from his time, but the overhead roof lights are later and perhaps due to Mylne. The hall originally had a single door on the central axis leading into the staircase flanked by two fireplaces (Fig. 39). This arrangement was reversed by Mylne who rearranged the hall as a portrait gallery; although he made drawings for the ceiling in 1767 he may have retained some of the original mouldings.

The outbuildings at Kings Weston include a rusticated banqueting loggia at the end of a walk on the axis from the east front (now ruinous),[81] a brewhouse in Vanbrugh's "fortified" manner (Pl. 265) and a loggia on the western edge of the plateau (Pl. 267) which probably dates from 1718–19 and shows the exterior treatment of the house applied to the Venetian window motif. As Vanbrugh's later houses show, his reaction to Palladianism was idiomatic but definite. An album of drawings formerly at Kings Weston, containing drawings for the estate as well as for buildings elsewhere, will be further mentioned later (p. 89); one drawing shows that the building known as Penpole Gate, demolished in 1950, was built partly to the design of the rival Colin Campbell, to whom Southwell's patronage also extended.

In or before 1702 Vanbrugh had made designs for rebuilding Welbeck for his friend, John Holles, Duke of Newcastle. The Duke showed them to Talman, who in 1703 produced a revision of them, dressed up à la Drayton. It is to this that we owe Vanbrugh's account, written to Newcastle, of the Talman-Carlisle lawsuit and of the numerous clients who had met with "vexations" at Talman's hands.[82] The scheme came to nothing; eight years later the Duke died after a fall from his horse, and his nephew and heir, Thomas Pelham Holles, became both the architect's friend and his client. Some time before 1715, when he was 22, he bought Vanbrugh's little house at Esher (Fig. 40); created Earl of Clare the previous year he renamed the house Claremont, and before he was made Duke of Newcastle in October 1715 Vanbrugh had begun to enlarge it for him almost beyond recognition. He removed the battlements and added a pediment; the house was at the foot of a slope, apparently on a raised terrace, and he built this out, and instead of making a deep forecourt added long side wings raised on arcaded basements. Thus the small centre remained at the front, where

---

[81] *English Homes*, IV, ii, pl. 197. Vanbrugh drawings for the Penpole Gate are at Elton Hall.
[82] WHISTLER, *Vanbrugh*, 1954, pp. 35–8.

it could appear as large in scale and as high in outline as possible, being topped only by chimneys and clock towers and, on a higher foundation at the rear, the two-storey "great room" some 100 feet long, added asymmetrically in 1719–20 (Pl. 260). Fifty years later Brown and Holland swept the house and gardens away for Lord Clive, and nothing remains of Vanbrugh's work except the Belvedere on the hill to the west (Pl. 258) and the nucleus of a farm village to the east. Of the big house Vanbrugh seems to have built at Swinstead, Lincs, for the 1st Duke of Ancaster before 1720 little remains again except a plainer Belvedere (Pl. 259), placed in a similar relation to the house and facing Grimsthorpe, the other Ancaster house (p. 86). At about the same time (c.1719–24) Vanbrugh enlarged Stowe for Lord Cobham, adding service wings at the sides of the seventeenth-century house; again the extension was lateral and not round a court. The north portico of the house, of the same rhythm as Vanbrugh's Blenheim type, is all that remains of his work (Pl. 287).[83]

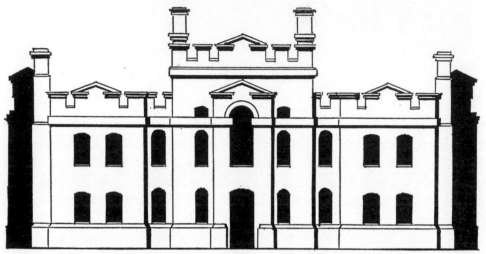

Fig. 40.   Claremont (destroyed). Vanbrugh's original house.

Vanbrugh's planning of new houses remained simple and symmetrical but impressive, and became more compact. His second design for Eastbury, Dorset, for George Dodington, 1716 (*Vitruvius Britannicus* (II)), has a long hall flanked by staircases, as at Blenheim, but lined with niches between half-columns, and there are no corridors (Fig. 41a). On the garden side he planned a tripartite room with a large bow window, rather like the Long Library at Blenheim. Dodington died in 1720, having built only the forecourt, wings and base courts. At about this time Vanbrugh made a third design, which was begun by, though possibly not before, 1724 and was uncompleted at his death in 1726. The house was lavishly finished on this last plan by 1738 by Roger Morris, having cost £140,000 or nearly half as much as Blenheim. Morris omitted Vanbrugh's crowning feature (Pl. 269), the central attic which was to light the twin staircases. In this plan (Fig. 41b) the light and expanse of the hall and long saloon were separated, as in Archer's Heythrop, by a long dark narrow vestibule in the middle of the house. Eastbury's fate was sadly dramatic. Bubb Dodington died in 1762 and thirteen years later the house, unfashionable and untenanted, was blown up, leaving part of the north wing and base court (Pls 270–1).

Vanbrugh's practice continued until his death in 1726. Seaton Delaval was commissioned in 1718 by Admiral George Delaval and completed for his nephew, Francis; work did not start until about 1720, the architect's representative on the site being William Etty of York and of Castle Howard.[84] Vanbrugh was there in 1721 and 1724 but did not see the house

---

[83] *Country Life*, CXXII, 1957, pp. 68–9; CXXV, 1959, pp. 352–3.
[84] *Leeds Arts Calendar*, No. 46–7, 1961, p. 8.

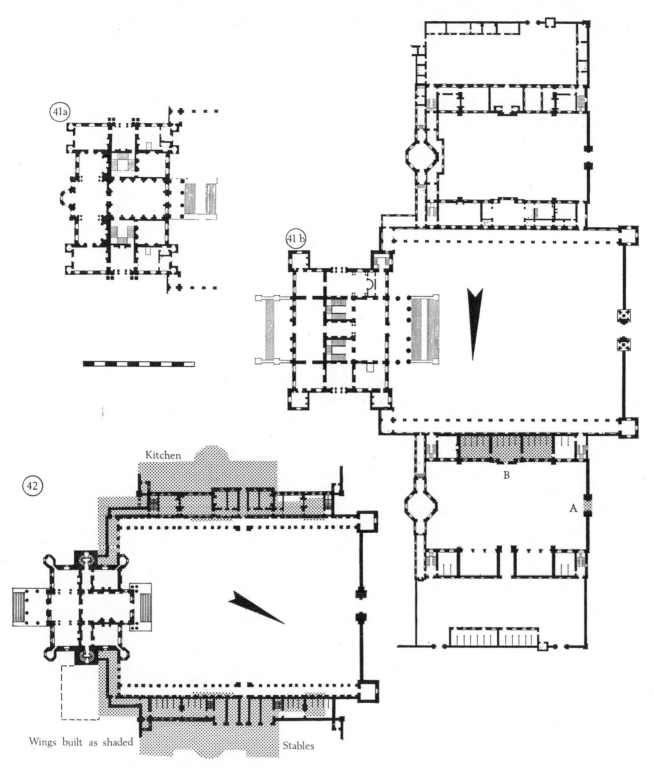

Fig. 41. Eastbury (destroyed). (a) Second plan, main block. (b) Third and final plan, with surviving portions shaded. Fig. 42. Seaton Delaval. Plan.

finished; the north-west tower has the dates 1721 and 1729 scratched on the balustrade. Most of the house was gutted by fire in 1822 and only with the recent completion of restoration of the structure has it come to life again instead of being a romantic ruin. Paintings and drawings in the house show that a long garden front was considered, and although *Vitruvius Britannicus* and most later sources conceal the fact, the external masonry confirms that a south wing of six bays was actually built on the east side. Nevertheless the Admiral could not afford the scale of Eastbury, and while the arcaded forecourt is as deep and narrow as

Eastbury's the main pile is small and high, taking over the tripartite garden saloon of the second Eastbury plan (Fig. 42).

In about 1715, that is the launching time of Palladianism, Vanbrugh's vocabulary became more Italianate. There is little of it in the Kings Weston elevations, but the first design for Eastbury (Pl. 268) uses Venetian windows. At Seaton Delaval and at Grimsthorpe, begun 1723, this tendency is more marked. At Seaton, however, the Venetian windows and pedimented windows are worked into a picturesque house worthy of its wild site between the Northumberland moors and the sea. The entrance front, facing north and dark against the sky, presents in both silhouette and plan the developed form of that debt to Elizabethan houses like Wollaton which was noted at Blenheim and Eastbury. Octagonal turrets stand out from the corners and larger square ones flank the sides; in the centre the hall again rises into a clerestory. As at Blenheim textures of stone coursing are varied and contrasted and the masses of the building alter in their relation as one's viewpoint changes. It is wrong to think of Seaton as devoid of ornament, for it is richer than Kings Weston if plainer than Blenheim (Pl. 293). But after Blenheim Vanbrugh never again used a giant order round a block. Having found that mere mass and void could speak, he used an order, preferably full columns, for gigantic punches of the highest drama. Thus the tripled ringed columns appear on the north front of Seaton, thus too the fluted Ionic portico is thrust out between the bare blocks of the garden front in an elegance heightened by its situation (Pls 272, 274–5).

Of the interior it is no longer possible to write adequately. The stable in the east wing, still used, is a reminder of what Vanbrugh's Castle Howard and Blenheim stables, never built, would have been like (Pl. 277). The west wing, including the great vaulted kitchen, is furnished (Pl. 289). The arcaded hall remains, calcined, with a finely corbelled gallery and a series of plaster statues of the Arts (Pl. 276), a design that goes back in essence to the earliest drawings for the hall and saloon at Blenheim.

Grimsthorpe, Lincs, Vanbrugh's last house, was commissioned by the 1st Duke of Ancaster shortly before his death in 1723 and carried on for his son, the 2nd Duke. Plans and elevations for a complete rebuilding of the old court-plan house are given in *Vitruvius Britannicus* (III), but only the north side, replacing a Restoration block of the Eltham type, was executed; by Vanbrugh's death in 1726 money or enthusiasm had been exhausted. The north side consists of an entrance hall flanked by towers and joined to them by staircases; the towers were to have been repeated on the south with a tetrastyle portico and pediment and the fenestration, rusticated ground floor windows and rectangular upper ones, was to have continued round all four sides. The arcading of the entrance front is repeated on both storeys all round the hall (Pls 273, 278); feigned bronze and gilt figures of English kings repeat the formal theme of Seaton Delaval, and the oval ceiling moulding is mirrored in the grey marble patterning of the floor. The economy is the same as in the Blenheim hall of nearly twenty years before; the creamy stone is worked only in floral panels high up in the end walls (Pl. 291), and in the chimney-piece (Pl. 279) which looks directly to Blenheim, being a larger version of that in the Duchess's Bedchamber. Vanbrugh's most dramatic stroke is the arcades at the ends of the hall. At Audley End in about 1708 he had inserted a screen between the hall and the staircase (Pl. 284) of which he also must have designed the pseudo-Jacobean strapwork ceiling. The scenic and spatial effect at Grimsthorpe is finer and richer, the arcade-screens being doubled in depth. Beyond them the stairs part, turn and rejoin, and we go through doorways of Michelangelesque inspiration to galleries joining the rest of the house (Pl. 285). Hawksmoor's sale catalogue contained drawings for the Duke of Ancaster's Chapel, so that it is possible that the chapel in the north-west tower (Pl. 283) is his; he too in later years made use – entirely unorthodox – of Palladian vocabulary, but there is no real reason to suppose that Vanbrugh did not design the gallery doors.

A catalogue of Vanbrugh's houses would include a number of others, but nothing finer or more representative than those discussed here. His genius was very different from Hawksmoor's. Hawksmoor cared about detail for its own sake, and could give its source; his mind was so grounded and trained in the classics that he could evoke without quoting. Vanbrugh was altogether simpler. History, glory, grandeur and above all castles and the theatre, these were his concepts and he did not define them much more closely. There is no reason to doubt Swift's jest that

> Van's Genius without Thought or Lecture
> Is hugely turnd to Architecture.

Only a prodigious man could do so and succeed, and that Vanbrugh succeeded there can be no questioning. That he did so without the continued help of Hawksmoor is finally proved by the known independence of his last work of all, the Temple at Castle Howard (Pl. 562).

CANNONS

In 1713 James Brydges, afterwards Earl of Carnarvon and 1st Duke of Chandos (p. 12), married for the second time, moved into the Jacobean house of Cannons near Edgware which he had bought from his first wife's uncle, resigned his lucrative post of Paymaster of the Forces abroad, and appointed William Talman as rebuilder of his house. Talman built the offices but proved too haughty; at the end of 1714 John James replaced him and as Brydges wanted fronts "as plain brick work as possible except the middle part of each, which I would willingly have compos'd of some noble design in architecture in stone" James had some opening for his belief in beauty in "ye Greatest plainness of the Structure" (p. 11). In May, 1715 Brydges had enquired about chimney-pieces carved in Italy by Baratta but rejected them as the carving made them too expensive. A year later James was replaced by James Gibbs, who was still in charge in September 1719 when the Duke, as he had become, had settled on the final articulation of the south and east fronts (Pls 298–9) and had decided to encase them in Portland stone. Engravings of these fronts almost identical – are signed by J. Price, 1720, but most of what they show must have been due to Gibbs and has similarities with his work at Ditchley (Pl. 300).

The chapel, of which the ceiling paintings by Bellucci and windows painted by Joshua Price after Sleter survive at Great Witley, Worcs (Pl. 397), must also have been designed by Gibbs as it was opened in August 1720, and it is probable that the moulded ceiling at Great Witley in papier mâché was made from squeezes taken from the Cannons stucco work of Bagutti.[85] Vanbrugh, whom Brydges consulted in 1715 but did not let "me be his Architect", dined at Cannons in 1720 and found the "Fronts . . . very fine . . . but the inside is of poor Invention". Work inside the house and in the extensive gardens continued until 1725. Chandos died in 1744 and within four years the whole building had been sold piecemeal and demolished. Macky (1722) and Defoe (1724) thought it "inferior to few Royal Palaces in Europe" and "the most magnificent in England" and it was popularly identified with Pope's "Timon's Villa". Chandos was rich, evidently (from the Stowe papers) tight with money but quite unpractical in personal and domestic expenditure. He had a household of eighty-three in 1718, including an orchestra which played in the parish church of Whitchurch (rebuilt for him by James, 1714–15 and decorated in *grisaille* and colour by Laguerre (Pls 116–17)) and in the Cannons chapel from 1720; in both buildings he listened from the

---

[85] F. J. B. WATSON, "A Venetian Settecento chapel in the English countryside", *Arte Veneta*, VIII, 1954, pp. 295–302. See also COLLINS BAKER, *Chandos* and I. DUNLOP, "Cannons, a conjectural reconstruction", *Country Life*, CVI, 1949, pp. 1950–4.

west gallery. The orchestra also played in the house for his meals. Pepusch and Handel both served him and the latter wrote for Whitchurch the Chandos Anthems. Apart from the chapel there were seventeen painted or partly painted ceilings by Laguerre, Sleter, Bellucci, Grisoni and Kent. The gardens, stocked with exotic birds of every kind, had a canal, a lake, parterres, fountains, gilded urns by the dozen and some in gold and vermilion and gilded lead statues including an equestrian George I similar to those surviving (ungilded) at Stowe and Birmingham (Pl. 303). Six lead figures surmounted the centre bays of each front of the house. In the mausoleum in the north-east corner of the church (Pl. 114) stands the Duke's monument. Gibbons was paid for it in 1717–18, but it was enlarged in depth with painted wood when the mausoleum was built in 1735–6. The mausoleum was decorated by the painter Gaetano Brunetti.

All this added up to a style and colour of living unparalleled in England and equal to the magnificence of the German Electors. The descriptions of contemporaries became, with the destruction of the original, a myth which has persisted even in spite of modern research. The elevations of Cannons are, though elegant, not remarkable for their date. The house was a rectangle 147 feet by 123 feet, or rather smaller than Chatsworth. Its main staircase was of marble. But Chandos's taste was uninformed and unsure. At this distance the enthusiasm of Macky and Defoe seems to have been generated by the complete ensemble; in its own way, and on a lower level than Chatsworth or Castle Howard, it was a fusion of all the arts. For this reason – but to some extent because it fits nowhere else – Cannons belongs to the history of English Baroque.

IV

The diffusion

THE BAROQUE COUNTRY HOUSE

Cannons symbolizes, if with a certain bathos, the end of the era that began with Chatsworth. While great men (Shaftesbury's phrase) and many lesser ones turned to Palladianism, the diffusion of the Chatsworth style which had begun about 1700 was carried on in the houses of the more conservative and rural nobility and of ambitious and newly or temporarily wealthy middle-class patrons. Their architects were usually local craftsmen with some knowledge or working experience of one of the great Baroque buildings (p. 14); their engagement as designers of houses is frequently only to be inferred from their recorded activity as the builders, and as they would copy unusual details while diluting the generality, the attribution of undocumented designs is even more difficult than in those cases which, for convenience or for special points of relevance or importance, have already been considered.

Some idea of the practice and the ability of these local men can be gained from the Kings Weston book of drawings (p. 83), a collection compiled during the early eighteenth century but pasted up in its present form a century later. While it includes plans, elevations and details of Kings Weston the majority of the drawings are for other houses and garden buildings, built or projected. Some are apparently the work of one of Vanbrugh's draughtsmen, but others are drawn and annotated in the compiler's hand, firm, round, and distinctive, but unidentified and unprofessional. Some of these are titled as copies, and the annotations are also found on some of the drawings with Vanbrugh connections. The copies include projects for out-buildings at Kings Weston by Price of Wandsworth and George Townesend of Bristol (the master mason at Kings Weston until his death in 1719 when the compiler perhaps succeeded him) and a copy of a drawing and agreement dated 1717 by Thomas Sumsion of Colerne for two of the roof urns for Kings Weston (Pl. 264). There are also plans connected with Spettisbury, Dorset, by one of the Bastards of Blandford and a Mr Wilson. The compiler's own designs include projects, dated 1717 and 1726 but not executed, for Charlton House near Wraxall in Somerset; one dated 1717 has chimney arches similar to those of Vanbrugh's first design for Eastbury (Pl. 268). The album thus indicates both a general and sometimes a detailed interest in Vanbrugh and an area of acquaintance and activity extending from north of Bristol through Somerset and Wiltshire to south of Blandford, a distance of over fifty miles; it is an instance, the more valuable because it is on a lower plane, of the same collector's interest in drawings shown by Wren, the Talmans, Hawksmoor and others, and it suggests that local or regional builder-designers exchanged ideas with each other. At the same time another elevation for Charlton, showing a plain alternative "That the Owner may choose which sutes his humour or Conveniency best" and giving plain door and windows which "may be enriched . . . as the Owner pleases" implies a lack of conviction about Baroque detail, quite different from Hawksmoor's nonchalant offers of alternative styles or even from Vanbrugh's emphasis on "Figure and Proportions".

The central south-west of England indeed had something like a Baroque "school", deriving from the Vanbrugh houses at Kings Weston and Eastbury and through George

Townesend from Oxford and Blenheim, as well as from a continuous stone-building tradition both in country towns and in fashionable Bath and mercantile Bristol. In 1715 Thomas Archer bought an estate at Hale, on the Dorset border of Hampshire, and rebuilt the house there for himself; unfortunately it was drastically remodelled before 1800. In the present state of knowledge the extent of Archer's direct influence on local architecture is uncertain and it may have been small. Thomas Bastard of Blandford (died 1720) and two of his sons, John (c.1688–1770) and William (c.1689–1766) were among the leading builders. Others were Francis Cartwright of Bryanston (1695–1758) and Nathaniel Ireson (1686–1769), who came from Warwickshire, built Stourhead 1720–2 under Colin Campbell, settled in Wincanton and may have been the compiler-draughtsman of the Kings Weston album.

According to Hutchins's *Dorset* Chettle House (Pl. 306) was built for George Chafin in 1710 and this date, if correct, would establish by its priority the origin of the school. On style, however, a more probable date seems about 1720–5, which is also the most likely date for Marlow Place, Bucks (Pl. 312). There are grounds for attributing to Archer both houses, which share a unique and curious debased type of Doric corner capital (Pls 313–14).[86] The similarity was originally greater, before the addition in 1912 of rounded ends to Chettle, matching the original bowed front. Both houses have also been altered internally, but the Doric hall of Marlow, one-and-a-half storeys high, survives intact (Pl. 365). Marlow also shares with a number of buildings in the south-west a composite capital with inturned volutes, ultimately Borrominesque (Pl. 310). Almost identical examples were applied in Blandford itself (Pl. 353), and at Crowcombe, Somerset, which Ireson contracted in 1734 to complete (Pls 305, 307, 311). Ireson took over stables and offices which were built ten years earlier to a lower ground level and which account for the asymmetry of the main fronts.

Ven, Milborne Port (Pl. 308) would be datable about 1730 on grounds of style; the traditional date of 1698 cannot be upheld, and the drawings by the otherwise unknown Richard Grange are surveys rather than designs. Ven's affinities in general elevation and such details as the window aprons support an attribution to Ireson. Ven carries on the Thoresby-Buckingham pattern; the elevations of Crowcombe are more complex, having both pilasters and quoined pilaster-strips, while the addition of bare pediments and Venetian windows is a characteristic eclectic mixture of Baroque and Palladian aspirations. The same Venetian window in a pediment occurred with the inturned capitals at Spettisbury, Dorset, c.1735 (demolished), which is also attributable to Ireson.

Vanbrugh's work also affected in a very literal fashion the builder of Bishopsworth Manor House, now in the southern suburbs of Bristol (Pl. 315). The contrast of whitish rough stone with yellow stone quoins and dressings, the tall windows and the mansard roof give the house a fortuitously French appearance, and the present plate-glass windows belie the early eighteenth-century date which is betrayed by the door and window details. The general scheme of the elevation, of five bays with the centre one projecting as one vertical unit, is not uncommon for the West Country, though more common in town houses (e.g. Weymouth House, Bath, Pl. 318, demolished), but over the roof is a chimney arcade obviously modelled on that of Kings Weston.

An elevation of great distinction and of more orthodox appearance is the south front added to Widcombe Manor, Bath, about 1727, for which no satisfactory attribution has been made (Pl. 317). The richness given by coupled fluted pilasters, channelled ashlar in the centre and masked keystones is foreign to the general character of Georgian Bath, and there is a

---

[86] G. WEBB, "Chettle House", *Country Life*, LXIV, 1928, pp. 466–72; H. M. COLVIN, "The architectural history of Marlow", *Records of Bucks.*, XV, 1947, pp. 8–9; A. OSWALD, *Country houses of Dorset*, 1959 ed. pp. 30–38, discusses the whole "Blandford School". The inturned volutes of Marlow also appear in Archer's design for Harcourt House (Pl. 368.)

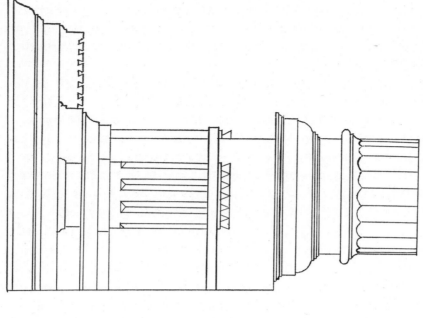

Fig. 44. Doric order, after Perrault.

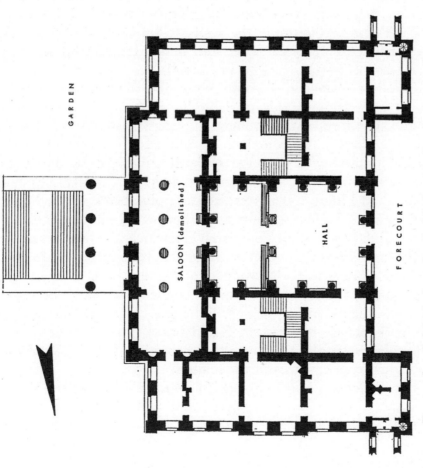

Fig. 43. Duncombe. Original plan of main block with (hatched) present disposition of hall and garden portico.

GARDEN

SALOON (demolished)

HALL

FORECOURT

Baroque complexity in the arrangement of doorcase and windows in the centre part and in the ambiguity by which it reads either as three bays or as one wide one. Freer but rather less successful invention is to be found at The Ivy, Chippenham, c.1728 (Pl. 320) where several of the elements of provincial Baroque are combined: quoining strips, fanciful gable-ends, round headed and square headed windows mixed, and a two-storey frontispiece with a window breaking into the pediment.

The influence of Vanbrugh was not confined to the south. Little is known of William Wakefield, a Yorkshire gentleman who died about 1730, in spite of the praise he received from contemporaries, who credited him with Duncombe and Gilling Castle. Sir Charles Duncombe, banker and Receiver-General of Excise, died in 1711 leaving to his niece's husband and his business colleague, Thomas Browne, the Helmsley estate he had bought from the trustees of the 2nd Duke of Buckingham. Browne took the surname of Duncombe, and if the date of 1713 in *Vitruvius Britannicus* (III) is correct he was not slow to begin a house in the manner, if not on the scale, of Castle Howard (Pls 321–3, 327, Fig. 36). After a fire in the 1890's the interior was remodelled, the hall reduced to a square, the garden front recessed and the portico moved inwards with it. The detail of the hall now looks decidedly Edwardian, but its general scheme appears to be original. The plan has affinities with Vanbrugh's second plan for Eastbury (Fig. 43) and may have been provided by him; nevertheless, while Duncombe's giant Doric pilasters and the four-faced urns over the entrance recall Castle Howard and the arched turrets over the spiral stairs of the north front have a Vanbrughian quality the total effect is unlike anything of Vanbrugh. Contemporaries recognized Wakefield's skill and knowledge; he also had the local man's eclectic awareness, and at Gilling (Pls 324, 329) he added an entrance court and hall, using "Gibbs" windows (with rusticated architraves) outside and a completely un-Palladian series of Venetian window motifs inside. Of Atherton, Lancs, begun 1723, only the flanking buildings in brick survive (Pl. 326); a portrait of Robert Vernon Atherton in the Paul Mellon Collection shows them to be about half the height of the stone-dressed house and makes it doubtful whether the pediment shown in *Vitruvius Britannicus* (Pl. 325) was executed.

It is conceivable that Wakefield was also responsible for the west range added to Wentworth Woodhouse and demonstrable on heraldic evidence to have been built between 1725 and 1728 and therefore for the younger Thomas Watson Wentworth. Wentworth was second cousin of the Lord Raby who had established Wentworth Castle (p. 71) and an element of rivalry in display is common to both buildings. In about 1734 Wentworth dwarfed his own west range with an eastern one designed (and closely modelled on Wanstead) by the Palladian Flitcroft. The west front, of pink brick and light stone, is a curious mixture. The window rustication suggests an earlier period altogether and sources in Serlio or Du Cerceau, and the partly blind Venetian window over the door resembles the structures in the hall at Gilling. The pilastered frontispiece is Baroque in scale and in its unusual details, the niche-doorway, the window pediments, the coat of arms breaking into the entablature and window frame, and the carved emblems in relief (Pls 331–6). One of the most peculiar details, the parrot on the door lintel, invites comparison with the garden front of Aldby, near York, which is dated 1726 and has a pheasant and foxes (Pl. 337). The rusticated hall fireplace of Aldby also suggests an acquaintance with Vanbrugh, and William Etty (p. 84) had some connection with the house.[87]

There are other distinctive houses for which no satisfactory attribution has been made. Barnsley Park, near Cirencester (Pls 359–62) was built for Henry Perrot, a relation by marriage of Chandos, and rain-water heads are dated 1720–1, but although this was the

---

[87] G. W. BEARD, "Architects and their craftsmen in Yorkshire", *Country Life*, CXXVI, 1959, pp. 254–6.

period at which John Price was Chandos's architect (p. 87) there is no evidence for identifying him with the Price of Wandsworth in the Kings Weston album, and no reason to believe him capable of elevations of the quality of Barnsley. The strong and angular modelling of the west front and the lack of exterior ornament, the heavy attic and the arcading and vaulting of the hall suggest knowledge of recent work at Oxford and Blenheim (Pls 253, Fig. 62). The hall screen materializes an early scheme for the Blenheim hall and the piers of the hall attic resemble the attics of the Long Library which are probably slightly later than Barnsley; from these links, the crowding of motifs on the walls and the high quality of the house one would suspect Hawksmoor's hand. Barnsley is also rich in plasterwork (Pl. 363) similar in style to that of the same date (1725) in the saloon at Ditchley, Oxon, executed by Artari, Vassali and Serena for Gibbs (Pl. 364). Finchcocks, Goudhurst, Kent, is a red brick house of 1725 (rain-water heads) with a very tall attic (Pl. 366); the round windows over the pediment and the convex quadrants leading to the wings recall Archer at Roehampton (Pl. 167) but are insufficient ground for attribution. The rear elevation is astylar with red and blue chequered brickwork. The existence of a local school is suggested by the presence of other pilastered brick houses in mid-Kent such as Bradbourne, Larkfield (1713–15) and Matfield (1728).

Thornhill made several excursions into architecture; the possibility (it is no more) of a connection with Chatsworth has been mentioned (p. 63), and in 1719 he tried, in opposition to Sir Thomas Hewett, to gain the Surveyor-General's post, gaining instead the enmity of the new régime in the Works by "demonstrating their ignorances in ye Art of Building" (Vertue). Of his responsibility for one building, Moor Park, Herts (Pl. 367), there is good evidence, since in his lawsuit against the owner, Benjamin Styles, in 1730 it was established that he "was employed as Surveyor and designer of that building". From a previous suit settled out of court in 1728 it appeared that Thornhill had also painted and supervised relief decoration in the house.[88] Styles, who had achieved a fortune out of the South Sea Company, bought Moor Park about 1720 as a brick house built fifty years earlier for the Duke of Monmouth; he encased the house in stone, preserving the original tall ground floor rooms, the cubic hall and the saloon behind it; rain-water heads are dated 1721. His anger against Thornhill seems to have been so strong that he had the house redecorated in the 1730's by Italian artists (Pls 294–5); of the earlier decoration there survive only the hall doorcases and the original Verrio ceiling of Monmouth's saloon, with borders by Thornhill (one is signed). The great portico may have been Styles's attempt to outdo Wanstead (Pl. 221); in formal terms it owes more to Hawksmoor's Clarendon Building or his unexecuted designs for All Souls (Pl. 518, Fig. 62) which Thornhill, who was consulted by Dr Clarke of All Souls in 1716, would have known. Moor Park stands on the ground and thus follows the Baroque rather than the Palladian formula, and the rhythms of the wall surface have basically a Baroque liveliness although in execution they are too repetitive. The house suffers from isolation; Thornhill retained the Monmouth wings, but these, although recased in 1763, were demolished in 1785. Moor Park is indeed surprisingly restrained for the work of the leading English Baroque painter, but the additions he made to Thornhill Park, Dorset, the ancient family manor which he bought back in 1720, are even more reticent (Pl. 370).

Reticence is not unexpected in the houses of John James, in view of his recorded opinions (p. 10). Wricklemarsh, near Blackheath, for Sir Gregory Page (1721, demolished 1789, *Vitruvius Britannicus*, IV, 58 ff.) was an essay in imitation of Inigo Jones but with the addition of a tetrastyle portico; this, which survives at Beckenham Place, Kent (Pl. 371), is smaller than those of Wanstead and Moor Park and originally ended in a flat parapet and not a pediment. Gibbs repeated the form in 1726–8 at Sudbrook, Surrey, for the 2nd Duke of

88 VERTUE, I, pp. 100–1, III, pp. 35–6, 46.

Argyll. Wricklemarsh at least was a *nouveau riche* house, but without a date the reason for the ostentatious portico at Avington, Hants, cannot be determined (Pl. 373). It is traditionally dated 1682 but must be some thirty years later: the brick wings on either side may be of the same date.[89] In 1724 James built for himself Warbrook House, Eversley, Hants, a very pretty brick house with stone dressings, which shows admirably (Pl. 369) how successful his "greatest plainness" could be and how far it was, in its implied giant order, tall chimneys and high attic built round the pediments, from Palladianism. Iver Grove, Bucks, for Lady Mohun, 1722–4 (Pl. 372), is probably also by James; the chimneys are similarly used though not identical, and while the elevations show a knowledge of Vanbrugh the closest similarity is with James's Twickenham church (Pl. 452). He may also have designed the original part of Hursley, Hants (after 1718), which has similar brick and stone pilastered frontispieces.[90]

Small country houses provided some of the strangest and some of the most charming examples of a Baroque language only partly understood. At Kettlethorpe Hall, Wakefield, dated 1727, an otherwise plain front has a gay and undulating series of pediments of various shapes (Pl. 328). The fluted order and carved frieze of Farfield Hall, Yorks, West Riding, 1728, are descended from the west front of Chatsworth (Pl. 330). Hale Manor, Lancs, built soon after 1700 for the Vicar, William Langford, has a military pediment and false oval windows by someone who had seen Hampton Court; the Doric end capitals and broken pediment are Baroque inventions (Pl. 341). Christopher Emmott's additions to the now ruinous Emmott Hall, Colne, Lancs, dated 1737 and marking his retirement from a prosperous career in London, consist of a six-bay ashlar façade with crude but vigorous pilasters and windows and a convex bowed porch (Pl. 342). At Brizlincote, above Burton-on-Trent, apparently of 1714 (Pevsner), Baroque conventions similar to these houses are topped on all four fronts by enormous segmental pediments on the scale of King William Block at Greenwich (Pl. 343).[91] The front of Woodnewton Hall, Northants (Pl. 345), is based on the formula of Hawksmoor and Archer of split and inter-penetrating pediments (Pl. 504). The Trumpeter's House at Richmond, Surrey, recalls the frontispieces of Chelsea, and perhaps has Office of Works connections (Pl. 339). Occasionally a farm or village house is dressed up with a façade. One of the most attractive brick houses of the period is one near Bredgar, Kent, dated 1719, of dark red and light red rubbed brick; the corbels above and aprons below the windows produce a lively wall and it is evident from the repetition of the modillions of the centre cornice at the ends that the latter were conceived as giant pilaster strips (Pl. 344). The front of Netherhampton, Wilts, is a Vanbrughian façade added to a plain house (Pl. 340).

The giant pilaster or pilaster-strip is the most frequently vernacularized Baroque device, and not every use can be explained as a descendant of Buckingham House or Thoresby. In some cases quotation replaced imitation: local builders who had copied doors, windows and other details from prints or books seem to have treated the engravings of the orders in Fréart or Perrault (Fig. 44) in the same way as sources of ornament, and pilasters singly at

[89] George Rodney Bridges the younger, half-brother of the Duke of Shrewsbury and cousin of Chandos, inherited Avington from his homonymous father in 1713; James, a Hampshire man, was Chandos's architect in 1714–16.

[90] Hursley was built for Sir William Heathcote some time after 1718 and much enlarged early in the present century. James may also have designed Kingston Maurward, Dorset, built in brick with a Corinthian frontispiece for George Pitt of Stratfieldsaye in 1717–20 but encased in stone in 1794. Pitt was one of James's references in 1711 (p. 67) and James was friendly with the Bastards (Oswald, *Dorset*, p. 37). The ashlar entrance front of Kingston Russell, Dorset, *c.*1730, has an applied portico and windows without architraves which recall Kings Weston; it has been attributed to Francis Cartwright (*ibid.*, p. 157).

[91] An even more bizarre pediment is at Bunny Hall, Notts, *c.*1725.

the ends or flanking the middle bay of a façade often have neither the force nor the organic relation to the elevation of a Vanbrugh building. This decorative isolation of the order is most apparent with Doric because of the sharp rectangular features of the Doric capital and the nearly invariable use of a triglyph in the piece of entablature above it which, although quite correct, has the effect of uniting the true capital and the entablature into a huge capital form disproportionate to the shaft below it. Chilton, Bucks, of about 1730, is one of the few Doric examples with a continuous entablature and no triglyphs. The type may have originated in the Office of Works with Herriard or its precursors (p. 67). The casually pilastered house is common in the Midlands, and there are numerous anonymous examples such as Scraptoft (Corinthian) and Ravenstone (Composite) in Leicestershire and Dallington (Doric) in Northants besides those known or thought to be by Smith of Warwick.

Francis Smith (1672–1738) was born in Tettenhall, Staffs, the son of a bricklayer of the same name; he settled in Warwick in 1697 and became known as "of Warwick" through his extensive practice as mason-architect. He has already been noticed in his capacity as contracting mason (p. 14). With the probable exception of Calke (1703, p. 69, Pl.383) the west range of Stoneleigh, Warwicks, begun in 1714, is his first major design (Pls.374, 378). Stoneleigh is impressive in scale and projection but lacks the variety and climax of the great houses. Other monumental houses attributable to Smith are the Doric Swynnerton (Pl. 387) and the Composite Trentham (demolished), both in Staffordshire, as well as a number of astylar houses such as Chillington, Staffs (1724, addition, Pl. 381), Wingerworth, Derbyshire (1729, demolished), Davenport, Salop (rain-water heads 1726), Kinlet (1727–9, Pl. 385) and probably Hardwick in the same county, which has a segmental centre pediment over pilasters and quoined ends. Smith may also have designed Elford, Staffs (demolished 1964, Pl. 382) which had the door common to Stoneleigh and the entrance front of Kinlet and the scrolls above it common to Stoneleigh and Sutton Scarsdale (Pl. 389). The latter was Smith's finest house; a lead plate found in the grounds recorded its commencement in 1724 and gave Smith as its "gentleman architect" at the head of a list of those who worked on the house, including Edward Poynton of Nottingham, "gentleman carver", Thomas Eboral of Warwick, "gentleman joiner", and "Albert Artari, gentleman, and Francis Vassali, gentleman, Italians, who did stuke work". Of the plentiful and rich stucco only fragments survive (Pl. 390), and even the exterior shell is now a ruin as total as that of seventeenth-century Bolsover which Sutton was built to face and to rival across the valley. Like most of these houses (but unlike Chicheley or the crowded elevation of Stoneleigh) it sits squarely on the ground with no visible basement. Its language is that of Talman and Vanbrugh but handled with sympathy and great competence. It is tempting to attribute to Smith the east front of Compton Verney, Warwicks, 1714, on topographical grounds; it reveals a knowledge of Vanbrugh and a competent eye (Pl. 338).

At Stoneleigh (Pl. 378) Smith used a Michelangelesque window form; the south door of Swynnerton derives from the north door of Castle Howard. Chicheley, Bucks, for Sir John Chester (Pls 375–80), which has recently been established as designed and built by Smith in 1720–5,[92] shows him reacting also, in the upswept curves of the entrance front and the curving doorcases, to influences usually associated with Archer. Within the house Smith had to give way to Kent and Flitcroft, but his joiner, Eboral, was employed, as was his carver, Poynton, on the exterior. Buntingsdale, Salop (rain-water heads 1721), for Bulkeley Mackworth (Pls 386, 388) has main fronts which are similar but not identical to each other and a broad bow in the middle of the south end; the Composite pilasters vary between fluted and plain. The interior, which seems always to have been simple, was altered in the

---

[92] J. M. TANNER, "The building of Chicheley Hall", *Records of Bucks*, XVII, 1961, pp. 41–8. Chester had already rebuilt in 1708–9 the chancel of the church (pl. 233).

course of the 1860 additions on the north and more recently completely resurfaced. At
Mawley, Salop (Pl. 384, rain-water heads 1730) for the Tory Catholic Sir Edward Blount,
generally attributed to Smith although Thomas White of Worcester has been suggested, the
exterior dressings and Doric pilasters of soft yellow sandstone have mostly needed renewal –
the house stands on a windy hilltop near Cleobury Mortimer – but the interior is exceptionally rich in well preserved decoration in wood and plaster. The hall and staircase and
several other rooms have stucco ceilings; the hall overmantel carries an elaborate trophy
above relief panels of garlanded scientific instruments (Pl. 395). Similar relief panels occur
at Davenport, where the hall walls are rusticated overall; the hall at Parbold, Lancs, of
about the same date, has rustication made of wooden blocks. At Mawley the wall opposite
the fireplace has a shell niche (Pl. 391). The capitals have inturned volutes beside which
those of the Blandford school are tame and into which are worked the heads of stags and
hounds and other animals (Pl. 393), and the capitals in one of the upstairs rooms enclose
kissing putti (Pl. 392). The staircase (Pl. 394) has stucco walls and the remains of a marquetry
floor; the stair-rail is in the form of a snake with its head at the bottom, the string under the
rich balustrades is carved with reliefs of musical instruments and emblems of other arts.
The doorcases on the upper landing probably derive, like those at Knowsley, Lancs (1733)
and the west range at Wentworth Woodhouse, from the upper saloon at Castle Howard
(Pl. 288). The Little Drawing Room at Mawley (Pl. 396) is, like the saloon at Davenport,
entirely finished except for the ceiling in marquetry; it is contemporary with the more famous
examples in South Germany but perhaps derives from the lost Water Gallery at Hampton
Court (p. 41) which was decorated when marquetry furniture was fashionable in England
and certainly contained the other exotic *décors* of the German palaces.

These houses have fewer surprises in plan than in elevation or decoration. Mawley, Calke
and Kinlet (Pl. 385) follow Sutton Scarsdale in that the centre of the garden front is recessed;
this reflects Baroque reaction to the plain rectangular house plan and is formally analogous
to the varied spacing of the order on the main fronts. At Mawley the staircase is behind the
hall (*cf*. Fig 39a); Kinlet and Buntingsdale have the common hall-saloon axial plan with the
stair opening from one side. Francis Smith and others like him were competent men capable
of following a pattern and of inventing in a slightly outmoded style. The houses included in
this section are not among the great masterpieces of English art, but they represent with
others not mentioned the varied range of the diffusion of domestic Baroque, in many cases
only partly understood or deliberately only partly imitated. As an art word, *gusto* was a
seventeenth-century English Italianization of *taste*. The variety and vigour of these buildings
are their claim to our present attention and to their survival from a period in which gusto
in our modern sense was a more common virtue than taste.

TOWN HOUSES AND INNS

The frequency with which country houses took fire was only exceeded by that in towns:
the Great Fire of London was more famous and larger but not otherwise more serious than
many provincial conflagrations. A series of London building acts, from 1667 into the reign
of Queen Anne, not only ended timber building in the capital but introduced certain
structural standards and indeed type-patterns for domestic architecture;[93] their effects were
gradually copied in the provinces, both in the ordinary course of rebuilding and new building
and, as in Northampton (1675), Warwick (1694), Blandford (1731), Tiverton (1731),
Wincanton (1747) and other towns, after disastrous fires. The town mansion free-standing

---

93 J. SUMMERSON, *Georgian London*, 1945, pp. 36 ff. See also T. F. REDDAWAY, *The rebuilding of London*, 1940.

in its own grounds was always the opulent exception, and Clarendon and Buckingham Houses, Monmouth House in Soho, or The Ivy at Chippenham have been discussed with country houses of the same date, from which they differed not in any essentials but only in their location. Similarly the engraved elevation designed by John Price in 1720 for the Duke of Chandos's house in Cavendish Square, never built, was an urban translation of Cannons (Pl. 301). Powis House in Great Ormond Street, finished 1714, was based on Buckingham House in plan and elevation but had a rusticated stone front (*Vitruvius Britannicus* (1), 41–2). In his design for Bingley House, Cavendish Square, 1722, Archer introduced Baroque forms and broken rhythms into an older formula based on the use of an upper storey order (Pl. 368). Where smaller free-standing houses of some pretention exist their setting is seldom strictly urban (e.g. the Cathedral Close at Salisbury, Pl. 347); a town house is almost by definition a street house, contained by street and garden fronts (the latter often plain) and party walls on either side. There were social as well as financial pressures towards sober exteriors, besides the requirements of by-laws and leasehold contracts. They produced the liberal uniformity of the London squares and Georgian Bristol and Bath, but they left little opportunity for Baroque individualism. Flamboyance was largely but not entirely restricted to the palaces, and Schomberg House, Pall Mall, reconstructed in 1698 for the 3rd Duke of Schomberg, the son of one of William III's generals, is exceptional both in scale and in the projections and cornice decoration of its façade, the only part which survives in a modern rehabilitation (Pl. 351).[94] Similarly Weymouth House (Pl. 318) and the more florid Rosewell House, both in Bath, are exceptional.

Nevertheless the craftsmen-designers of the lesser country houses also worked for the towns which were their centres, and their invention can be seen up and down the country. Hope House, Woodstock (Pl. 348) and Vanbrugh House, St Michael's Street, Oxford (Pl. 349) are exceptional in their closeness, stylistic and geographical, to Blenheim; Vanbrugh House probably belonged to Bartholomew Peisley II or III, the Oxford and Blenheim masons, in which case one or other remodelled it.[95] The presence of the Kempsters at Burford, Oxon, may account for the grand but not unique stone house (now only a façade) in the main street (Pl. 346). Simpler houses with or without pilasters occur in Lichfield (Pl. 352), Wincanton (1733, Pl. 358)[96] and many other towns, though their number continually decreases in the face of twentieth-century commerce.

Some houses or groups of houses display a degree of urban rather than simply personal pride; most of these are the products of rebuilding after fire. Of seventeenth-century Northampton hardly anything remains, but at Warwick the grand pilastered houses on the crossroads south of the church, built after 1694, survive (Pl. 350). Henry Bell of King's Lynn, who was consulted in the Northampton reconstruction, probably built the Duke's Head at King's Lynn (Pl. 357). This was begun in 1683 and was intended by Sir John Turner to accommodate visitors to his new Exchange (p. 5); it is exceptionally imposing for a hostelry, but its broken segmental pediment and other details belong less to Baroque than to the

---

[94] The roof originally had a balustrade and cupola on the Belton pattern. The present centre porch is later; the bases of the herms are signed COADE LAMBETH.

[95] The following is known: Bartholomew Peisley II (d.1715) owned property in St Michael's parish (GREEN, *Blenheim*, p. 239); his son Bartholomew III died in 1727 at his house in New Inn Hall Lane (COLVIN, *Dictionary*, p. 451); Henry Joynes, who married Bartholomew II's daughter (*ibid.*), frequently exchanged messages of affection and regard between Hawksmoor and the Peisley family, mentioning on one occasion "all friends in New Inn Hall Lane" (British Museum MS.Add.19607); New Inn Hall Lane or Street was formerly the street at right angles to the present one and was renamed St Michael's Street in 1899 (H. HURST, "Oxford Topography", *Oxford Historical Society*, XXXIX, 1899, p. 67).

[96] Nathaniel Ireson's house at the top of Wincanton was altered beyond recognition in the nineteenth century.

category defined by Sir John Summerson as "artisan mannerism".[97] The new buildings at
Blandford after the 1731 fire include three public and private houses in the market place
attributable to the Bastard firm: the former Greyhound Inn (Pl. 355), a big pilastered front
with charming detail, the former Red Lion Inn (Pl. 353) which has capitals with inturned
volutes, and a similar house almost next door (Pl. 356) with a pretty floral Composite, also
with inverted volutes. This type of façade with a pediment astride two pilasters recurs in
Blandford at Coupar House (Ionic) and in a house on the Salisbury road which is in fact
astylar (Pl. 354). John Bastard also built the house in Market Street, Poole, Dorset, 1746–9,
for Sir Peter Thompson, merchant and dilettante (Pl. 319).[98] At Bridgwater, Somerset, the
Duke of Chandos owned from 1721 to 1728 an estate on which he tried to develop residential
and industrial enterprises.[99] Some of the houses in Castle Street have interesting doorcases
(Pls. 302, 304), and Benjamin Holloway, Chandos's principal surveyor there, built for himself "The Lions" on the quay at the bottom of Castle Street (Pl. 316). Holloway was not a
very good builder, and Chandos considered him a knave but necessary to employ. Perhaps
in the pretension of "The Lions" we may find an echo of the whole story of Chandos and
Cannons.

THE FIFTY NEW CHURCHES

The Tory return to power in 1710 after twenty-two years in opposition provided the opportunity, and an accident of nature the final impetus, for the erection of a group of buildings
unparalleled in the history not only of English politics but of English architecture: the
so-called Fifty New Churches. St Paul's and the City churches had been paid for by a tax
on coal coming into London. In 1710 they were complete, and when old Greenwich Church
collapsed in a November gale the tax seemed to the vestry to be the obvious source to tap for
a reconstruction. Their petition brought to parliamentary notice the whole question of
established worship in the newer districts of London outside the City, both the well-to-do
West End and the poor industrial and mercantile districts to the east. There were indeed
chapels on the west, but East End religion was becoming alarmingly and rapidly non-
conformist. The Tory party was also the High Church party, and a scheme which combined
a work of piety with a powerful display of political prestige was embodied in Acts of Parliament of 1711 for prolonging the coal tax and appointing a Commission in order to build
"fifty new churches of Stone and other proper Materials, with Towers or Steeples to each . . .
in or near the Cities of London and Westminster, or the Suburbs thereof".

Greenwich was to be included in the fifty, and later supplementary Acts substituted the
rebuilding of St Mary Woolnoth, patched up by Wren after 1666, for one of the new
churches and provided for certain "Gothic" works, a tower for Wren's St Michael, Cornhill
and the west towers of Westminster Abbey (p. 121). In 1714 the Tories lost the government,
and the new Commission appointed by George I in 1715 to administer the Acts was predominantly Whig. It lacked both the missionary and the artistic zeal of the original one; the
expensive ideas of the architects had already used a great deal of money and started works
requiring a great deal more, the job became a routine one, and at the virtual winding-up
of the Commission in 1733 it had built a dozen churches, bought and dignified three chapels,
including St George, Queen Square (consecrated 1723, altered 1867 by S. S. Teulon
(Fig. 45)) and was financing, though it did not supervise, the rebuilding of St Giles-in-the-
Fields, St George, Southwark, and the parish churches of Woolwich and Gravesend.

[97] *Architecture in Britain.*
[98] OSWALD, *Dorset*, p. 36.
[99] COLLINS BAKER, *Chandos*, ch. x.

Fig. 45. St George, Queen Square. Interior before alteration.

Fig. 46. Deptford Rectory (destroyed).

The dozen, however, are remarkable. The original Commission included Sir Christopher Wren and Christopher, his son, Vanbrugh and Archer; as its Surveyors it appointed Hawksmoor and William Dickinson. Baroque and Office of Works representation was thus strong, and it is hardly surprising that nothing more was heard of the design Colin Campbell submitted in 1712. Dickinson took another post in 1713 and was succeeded by Gibbs, who had returned in 1709 from Baroque Rome and the studio of Carlo Fontana. The new Commission of 1715 included none of the architects, and Gibbs, a Scot, a Tory and a Catholic, was dismissed – the compatriot to whom he attributed this misfortune was undoubtedly Campbell – and was succeeded by John James. Of the twelve churches six were designed by Hawksmoor, one by James, two by them jointly, two by Archer and one by Gibbs. Dickinson made designs, of at least two of which models were made.

The churches and unexecuted designs were basically of two types, deriving from the two fundamentals of the Wren churches, the idea of the aisled and galleried auditorium and an inclination towards centralized planning (p. 24). Wren's own memorandum to the Commission recommended St James, Piccadilly as a prototype both practical and economical; it was followed by James at St George, Hanover Square (Pl. 431) and by the joint Surveyors at St John, Horselydown (mostly demolished 1948 after war damage) and St Luke, Old Street (Pl. 433), gutted 1960. A number of plans for unexecuted churches among the Commission's papers in Lambeth Palace Library are basically similar. The other nine churches are more complex and more exciting. Gibb's St Mary-le-Strand (Pls 408–9) is aisleless and of medium size, because of its island site, and is lit only from the upper storey, a practical measure which excludes much of the street noise. It is the nearest to contemporary Italy in its richly developed two-storey exterior and interior, in the emphatic though small chancel and in the detail over the apse windows (Pl. 423). Nevertheless, even in this early work Gibbs's eclecticism has begun to lose its Roman character in favour of English sources – specifically Wren whom he had evidently studied with some care: the shape of the apse inside and the whole east end outside derive from St Paul's, just as the semicircular west portico does from the cathedral's transept porticoes. The latter borrowing may be indirect, since the motif was considered common property in the Commission office; it was used by Archer and it appears in a plan by Hawksmoor and in one by Dickinson dated 1713 and Gibbs's church was not begun until the end of 1714, being structurally finished in 1717. Moreover, the foliage drops and cherub-heads of the exterior carving are markedly indebted to the vocabulary of St Paul's.

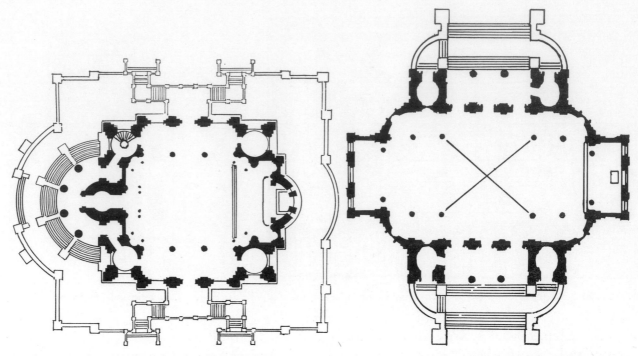

Fig. 47.   St Paul, Deptford. Plan.   Fig. 48.   St John, Smith Square. Original plan.

Of Archer's two churches St John, Smith Square (1713–28, Pls 412–13) is the more remarkable outside; the original interior was lost in a fire in 1742 and the replacement gutted in 1941. St Paul, Deptford (Pls 399, 402) is intact. Both are planned round two intersecting axes so that the side elevations are symmetrical with important entrances on the cross axis (Figs 47, 48). This modified form of centralized planning, which was also exploited by Hawksmoor, was adumbrated in certain near-square or Greek cross churches of Wren (p. 24) and represents an attempt to reconcile the requirements of High Church liturgy with Baroque spatial effects. The Commission specified that its churches should have proper chancels – a liturgical provision – and that wherever possible they should stand free on open sites – a provision both iconographical, in view of their propaganda value, and also of great importance for the architect. At St John, Smith Square, adjacent elevations are different and opposite ones identical; all are based on a giant Doric order like Hawksmoor's contemporary Greenwich Church, and Archer's characteristic detail includes large broken pediments and ornaments over the lower windows that join them to the upper ones and include (Pl. 413) cannon-balls worthy of Vanbrugh. Archer intended to repeat the disposition of the corner towers in four stone pinnacles on each tower (Fig. 51); these were under consideration up to 1718, but the towers were finished ten years later with lead finials which Archer did not authorize. From drawings and the accounts it is possible to reconstruct the interior.[100] A three-centred or "semi-elliptical" plaster barrel vault ran from west to east, and was crossed by a similar one joining the north and south transepts which contained major entrances. The corners, two bays by one, had flat ceilings. The twelve interior Corinthian columns were arranged so as to make a dramatic proscenium-like chancel arch on the east and a matching western one. The side galleries running behind the columns were reached by staircases in the base of the towers. The interior was quite clearly aligned from west to east, but the prominence of the north and south entrances made a contrast of axis which was certainly deliberate, the core of Archer's interior space and a feature common to his and Hawksmoor's churches.

[100] W. A. EDEN, "Rebuilding a masterpiece", *Country Life*, CXXXI, 1962, pp. 445–7. The scheme is to be carried out.

St Paul, Deptford (1713–30) is in boldly rusticated Doric and stands on a plinth which is approached by concentric steps on the west and balustraded flights at the sides; the interior galleries and aisles are contained by staircase vestibules at each end, and the theatre-box effect of their appearance is increased by the small box-like galleries at the corners of the church. The feeling of the interior is strongly that of a central rectangle with subsidiary spaces. Archer's influence may be inferred in two unexecuted plans in Lambeth Palace Library (Fig. 49); one has apsidal side entrances and aisle ends and niches in the sides of the tower, the other is oval with long transeptal sides and doors not only on the north and south but also on the diagonals. The Commission also had a model for a circular church by Archer to stand in Lincoln's Inn Fields. The triangular parsonage at Deptford was also designed by Archer (Fig. 46). Its picturesque plan and silhouette are contemporary with Vanbrugh's experiments in small turreted houses (Pl. 552); as a result of initial arguments about the expense of its design it took from 1717 to 1724 to erect. It was demolished about 1885.

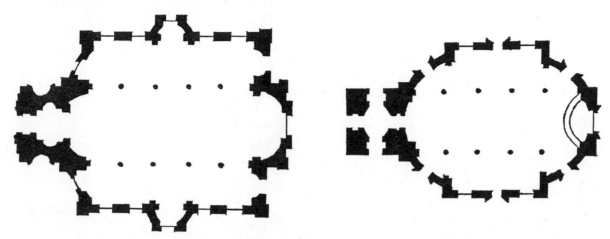

Fig. 49.   Unexecuted plans for two of the Fifty New Churches.

Hawksmoor's six churches are all designed round intersecting axes. St Alfege, Greenwich (1712–18) was appropriately the first church to be begun, a rectangular box with transeptal projections containing entrances and the gallery stairs (Fig. 50a, Pls 417–20). There are no internal supports or divisions except the side and western galleries and their pillars; the chancel is merely a shallow apse which is emphasized by wooden columns grouped under concave triangular entablatures, for the detail of which Grinling Gibbons was paid, and illusionist perspective coffering painted by Thornhill.[101] This device was necessary because the east end of the church faces the street and has an eastern portico of the same giant Doric order which encompasses the whole exterior.

The three Stepney churches were all begun in 1714: St Anne, Limehouse (finished 1730, gutted 1850 and restored), St George-in-the-East (finished 1729, gutted 1941 and the exterior restored 1964) and Christ Church, Spitalfields (finished 1729). The first two were planned on the Wren formula of a Greek cross within a square; St George had intersecting vaults like Archer's St John but of extremely low pitch (Pl. 416) and comparison with that church is further invited by the provision of four lateral stair turrets (Pl. 414) and the use of a split pediment on the west façade. Hawksmoor's plan was more complex, however, as it had no central north and south doors and had transept-like bays east and west of the central square (Fig. 50f). St Anne (Pls 400–1, 403, Fig. 50e) has a flat ceiling with a heavy circular band in the centre; there is an extra western bay over a gallery, and although side entrances were planned they were discarded in favour of eastern ones. Nevertheless, and in spite of the imposing circular porch set into the west front (Pl. 410), the centralized

[101] DOWNES, *Hawksmoor*, p. 170.

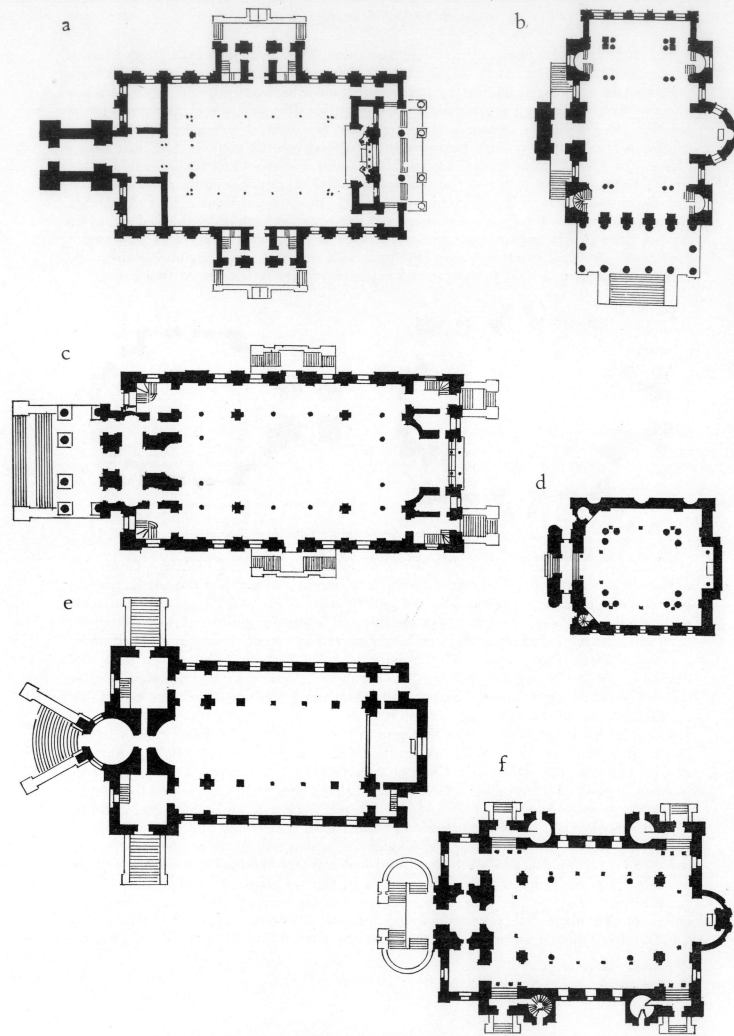

Fig. 50. Plans of (a) St Alfege, Greenwich. (b) St George, Bloomsbury.
(c) Christ Church, Spitalfields. (d) St Mary Woolnoth. (e) St Anne, Limehouse.
(f) St George-in-the-East.

feeling remains strong. Christ Church, which at the time of writing has been closed for seven years and is still awaiting major repairs, originally had side entrances as well as eastern ones (Fig. 50c); the steps, like the side galleries, were removed without trace in the nineteenth century, and the side doorcases were mangled into meaningless aedicules. The cross axis was originally emphasized by these entrances, by division of the pews, by the wider arches of the centre bays, and by the screens of columns at each end of the "nave"; it is no longer sufficiently marked to balance the long shape of the ground plan and the ceiling compartment (Pls 429–30).

St George, Bloomsbury (1716–31) is the most complex of the churches, and in the course of a succession of alterations its original interior arrangement with north and south galleries and the altar in the eastern apse has completely vanished, and with it has gone the effect of entering through the south portico and finding oneself facing a cavernous northern recess but not the altar. Hawksmoor here had to contend with a deep narrow site, the Commission's demand for an eastern altar, and the need for entrances both from the south and through the tower door from the Bloomsbury estates on the north. The clerestoried centre of St George (Pls 426–8) is square, and small differences in ceiling panels and wall articulation preserve its ambiguity of direction between the two main axes. At St Mary Woolnoth (1716–27), the smallest of the "Fifty" churches and also one with a restricted site, there was no room for ambiguity. The chancel is a shallow recess with a flat baldacchino, and the square-in-a-square geometry is asserted by the overpowering tripled columns at the corners of the central square; the side galleries, removed in 1875, stood behind the columns and can have taken little from the effect (Pls 411, 421). Apart from the west front the north wall was the only one originally visible, and its sculptural niches make it an impressive one; it is windowless in order to keep out street noise. The southern wall, which was revealed by the construction of King William Street and covered again by the outworks of Bank Underground station, could be seen only in sharp foreshortening, and its articulation is therefore

Fig. 51.   St John, Smith Square. One of the four towers as designed
Fig. 52.   St Alfege, Greenwich. Reconstruction of Hawksmoor's tower design.

plain but very bold: tall deep round-headed upper windows, and strongly projecting sills (which survive and are visible in Pl. 406) to the lower ones.

The preoccupation with axial entrances is largely peculiar to Archer and Hawksmoor; it is not entirely so, and Wren's paragon, St James, Piccadilly, originally had a door in the south side facing down Duke of York Street. Hawksmoor's spatial schemes are both more complex and vaguer than Archer's, and their element of vagueness can only be explained (since it is not common to all his buildings) as one of deliberate confusion or ambiguity. It is the nearest approach, in the architecture of a religion little given to mystical expression, to emotional spatial effects of the same order as the swinging arches and ovals of Catholic Baroque churches, but achieved by different means.[102]

The Commission's terms of reference included porticoes and steeples, the former to impress at close quarters and the latter to advertise at a distance. Two porticoes were originally considered at Greenwich and there was a question at Deptford of two porticoes and two steeples. Shaftesbury seems to have learned of the Commission's proposals at once (p. 11) and the steeples of Deptford, Greenwich and Stepney still ride over London's dockland as boldly as he feared they would. Gibbs's graceful little steeple at St Mary-le-Strand owes more to Wren than to Rome; so does the one nearby with which he completed Wren's church of St Clement Danes (Pls 404, 407). Archer's steeples also owe a good deal to Wren's St Paul's and St Vedast. James's lantern at Hanover Square (Pl. 405) is based on Chelsea and Queen's College, Oxford (Pls 13, 521); his hexastyle portico is contemporary with Hawksmoor's at St George, Bloomsbury and Gibbs's at St Martin-in-the-Fields. The steeple James added at Greenwich in 1730–2 is a failure because it is too small in scale for the church.

Hawksmoor's steeples are all individual and all striking. His design for Greenwich (Fig. 52) was a buttressed octagonal lantern; when the building of Greenwich tower was deferred he modified the design and added it to St George-in-the-East, even incorporating on the top the Roman altars from the base of the Greenwich portico (Pls 414, 419). At St George the tower bursts from the west front and is echoed in form by the staircase turrets; like the doors into the turrets (Pl. 415), which are composed from basically ordinary elements to produce an extraordinary whole, they evoke rather than state, with a romantic force more common in music than in architecture. The emotional element of Baroque is seldom so powerful, seldom projected with such economy of means. The steeple of St Anne, Limehouse, is hardly less remarkable: its Gothic look is a fairy-tale one, which preliminary drawings show to have been arrived at by way of forms as classical as the Doric piers of which it is composed. The spire of Christ Church has lost during nineteenth-century restoration the three dormer windows on each face, the flame-like "crockets" running up the corners, and the large stone finial; it was thus originally more a suggestion than a copy of a Gothic broach spire. The breadth of the belfry across the west front is even greater than in St George and St Anne, being increased by what are in effect single giant buttresses with hollowed-out sides (Pl. 425). The front of Christ Church is a unique and colossal experiment in patterning with niches, arches and roundels and even with the Venetian window motif transmuted into a giant portico. The monolithic twin-towered front of St Mary Woolnoth was the logical conclusion of the development in breadth (Pl. 406); formally it has associations not only with the rusticated doorways of the Kensington Orangery, the court gates of Blenheim and the entrance front of Seaton Delaval (Pls 84, 250, 275) but with the broad elevation of medieval cathedrals.

At St George, Bloomsbury and the two churches designed jointly with James, Hawksmoor went as far as actual quotation of classical forms out of their normal context. The steeple of

---

[102] For a more detailed examination of Hawksmoor's church interiors see DOWNES, *op. cit.*, ch. X–XII.

St George is a miniature reconstruction, based on a theoretical one by Wren, of the tomb of Mausolus, King of Caria, described by Pliny; this is the source both for the stepped pyramid and for the porticoes below it which also stand in formal relation to the big portico down below. To this erudite motif Hawksmoor added George I's statue on the top and a large animated hatchment in the form of stone lions and unicorns at the base of the pyramid (removed as ruinous in 1871), as bold and literal a Baroque gesture as any contemporary carved keystone. At St Luke, Old Street, he (for James can hardly have invented such a piece of extravagance) used a fluted ashlar obelisk (Pl. 434) and St John, Horselydown formerly carried proudly and incongruously a tapered Ionic column (Pl. 432). Parallels can be found in unexecuted Hawksmoor projects; study of these and the circumstances of the building of these two churches suggests that, had the Commission allowed its architects as much time, money and freedom in 1730 as in 1714, second thoughts would have produced more complex and more successful results.

Had the Commission agreed on the "general design or form" for all its churches debated in 1712, had each of its churches been built for the £10,000 to which the Surveyors were limited for St Luke and St John, Horselydown, the money would have gone much further: as with the "Waterloo" churches a century later we should have had more buildings but fewer masterpieces. In an age in which to build hopefully was often better than to complete, genius and economy were not naturally coupled, and subsequent generations found themselves saddled with palaces and churches they could maintain with difficulty, if at all. Nevertheless, if the past is of any value to us, we should be thankful that in a fair number of cases genius had the upper hand. The pilgrimage to Stepney ought to be as rewarding aesthetically – and as popular – as that to the Asamkirche in Munich.

OTHER CHURCHES IN TOWN AND COUNTRY

Some hundreds of English churches were built or rebuilt during the eighteenth century; the majority are decent and plain, sometimes handsome, structures of brick or, where the material was cheap or money plentiful, of stone. Eighteenth-century established religion was a comfortable, decent, rather dull affair, and it is not surprising that eighteenth-century churches, and alterations to earlier buildings, were characterized by the same qualities. There are not many which can be called Baroque. The exceptions are of three varieties. There are those by the major architects of the period, those by lesser men which are clearly attempts in the same spirit, and those in which, as in some of the more peculiar houses of the period, an imperfect understanding produced results which are singular and sometimes bizarre.

Wren designed little of consequence in the field and nothing of relevance outside London. Vanbrugh and Talman designed no churches, although Vanbrugh almost certainly designed the Duke of Newcastle's theatrical pew in the south aisle of old Esher church, Surrey, for which a faculty was obtained in 1724 (Pl. 286). Hawksmoor may have designed the church at Thirkleby, Yorks, which was built about 1722 by Sir Thomas Frankland but does not survive: his sale catalogue included drawings "for Sir Thomas Franklands". He may also have designed the former Archbishop's Throne at Canterbury (c.1704, Pl. 436) and the monumental little King mausoleum in Ockham church, Surrey (1735, Pl. 435).[103]

One of the finest churches of the period is Archer's St Philip, Birmingham (now, and with the addition of a nineteenth-century chancel, the Cathedral). It was designed to serve a new and growing area and was built in 1710–15, but the tower was not finished until 1725

[103] CLARKE, p. 81; DOWNES, *Hawksmoor*, pp. 213–14, 277.

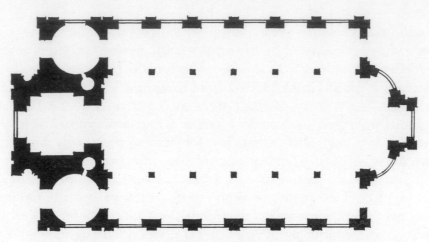

Fig. 53.   St Philip, Birmingham. Original plan.

(Pls 439–44). Archer was no doubt chosen as the architect as a native of Umberslade, a few miles south-east of Birmingham. The plan (Fig. 53) is simple, much simpler than Archer's London churches, being a nave with galleried aisles. The galleries come halfway up the arcade piers and halfway up the single row of large round-headed windows. An early nineteenth-century print (Pl. 440) shows the original interior arrangement, with the tall box pews, common to nearly all churches of the time, hiding the pedestals of the piers, a carved wooden reredos and a "three-decker" pulpit centrally placed in front of the Communion table. The original squat Corinthian capitals survive at the west end (Pl. 441) but the interior retains little of its original logic. The exterior has fared better, although it has been refaced entirely at least once, and probably all the detail is nineteenth-century. The Birmingham sculptor, Peter Hollins, began the refacing in memory of his father, William, but while of the east doorways (Pl. 443) not even the original stones remain,[104] the west ones with splayed jambs and the grotesque windows over them (Pls 442, 444) are – as far as can be determined on style and from the engraved elevation in *Vitruvius Britannicus* – faithful copies.

John James designed Twickenham Church, Middlesex, 1713–15 (Pls 451–2). The giant Doric order and pedimented side projections owe something to Vanbrugh and Hawksmoor and the interior owes more to Hawksmoor's St Alfege, but there is little feeling of a cross axis and the gallery fronts, decorated with Doric triglyphs, assert the longitudinal character of the church. St George, Tiverton, 1714–33, is in James's plain style (Pl. 449). Henry Aldrich, Dean of Christ Church, Oxford, not only designed university buildings (p. 115) but rebuilt the Oxford parish church of All Saints, of which he was a trustee, in 1706–9 (Pls 437–8). This is a grandiose version of Wren's St Lawrence Jewry (Pl. 27) in which the coupled pilasters outside and fasciated ones inside give the walls an undulating movement which is more Baroque than anything else by Aldrich. His first, engraved, design had a door in the centre of the street wall instead of at the west end. The steeple was completed in 1718–20 after Aldrich's death by the masons Townesend and Peisley, combining the original design with the round peristyle lantern taken from a design by Hawksmoor.

Gibbs's St Martin-in-the-Fields, 1721–6, illustrates the extent to which, while continuing to take Wren as a model, he modified his Baroque training to suit his patrons. St Martin was a fashionable – and therefore a prestige – church, and it is rich in plaster decoration and external stone relief. Gibbs's first designs (Pls 459, 461) were for a round church with twelve columns within a concentric gallery and a long apsed chancel. This is Roman in plan, but the elevations are restrained in detail. The final design (Pls 460, 462) is rectangular with galleries, and while the concave splayed walls facing the chancel are Baroque in feeling the

---

[104] They are in a private garden at Selly Park, Birmingham.

chancel itself is rather plain, shallow, and dominated by the clear east window. The interior giant Corinthian order is repeated outside, with "Gibbs" rusticated windows, and the piers and columns at the ends make the side elevations symmetrical. The steeple with its concave-faced spire derives from Wren rather than directly from Italy. Except for the solecism by which the steeple rises behind the portico with no logical relation to the ground, St Martin is as distinguished and professional as any work of Gibbs, but it breaks little new ground. The steeple was imitated not only in England and Scotland but in North America, while at Gainsborough, Lincs, Francis Smith (p. 95) reproduced the exterior articulation. Smith's elder brothers, William (1661–1724) and Richard (1658–1726) continued to live and practise in Tettenhall. William and Francis were joint contractors for St Mary, Warwick (p. 122) and for Gibbs's All Saints, Derby (1723–5), and there is little doubt that William designed a number of churches himself, for some of which he contracted jointly with Richard, such as Burton-on-Trent (1719–26, Pls 446, 448). Whitchurch, Salop (1712–13) for which William Smith made an estimate and John Barker, the carpenter, a design,[105] is so like Burton inside and outside (Pl. 447) that it must be its prototype. Smith built similar churches, now destroyed, at Lichfield (St Mary, 1717–21) and Newcastle, Staffs (1720–1). St Peter-at-Arches, Lincoln (c.1720–4, rebuilt 1936 at Lincoln St Giles in brick instead of stone but with the old dressings and lengthened by one bay) is still very similar on the outside (Pl. 445), and it seems likely that the pattern for all these was invented by Smith rather than by Barker. The tall nave windows with plain aprons above them, the chancel apse, the coved nave ceiling and the juxtaposition of gallery and arcades, as well as the impressive scale of these flat-topped churches, suggest inspiration from Archer's Birmingham church rather than from Wren. The old St Peter-at-Arches was decorated inside with wall paintings by Vincenzo Damini; he was an inferior Venetian artist, but such decoration is uncommon and the only surviving church completely painted is now Chandos's parish church at Little Stanmore, where the structure was designed by John James, retaining as at Twickenham the medieval tower (p. 87, Pls 115–17).

John Price, variously described as of London, Richmond, Wandsworth (p. 89), and York Buildings, may have been one or more people of unequal talent, and in one capacity laid improbable claim to being the architect of Cannons and of Chandos's projected London house (pp. 87, 97). It is, however, quite likely that all were the same man and that the quality of the designs known to be by "Mr. Price" varied proportionately with the location and with the amount of money available. St Mary-at-the-Walls, Colchester (1713–14, demolished 1871) was a plain brick church based on the type of Wren's St Bride, but with only a western gallery,[106] but St George's Chapel, Yarmouth (1714–16, disused since 1960, Pls 453–6) is altogether more elaborate and in a rather unsophisticated way one of the most handsome town churches of the period. The interior is again based on Wren prototypes, with high galleries, cross-vaulted aisles and a somewhat depressed barrel-vaulted nave. Price's exterior is ambitious to the point of indiscretion. The side elevations are articulated with giant Doric pilasters and isolated sections of entablature, while at the ends smaller pilasters support pediments containing arches; the order at the east end is Corinthian. The four corners of the church are lobed; Wren had designed a lobed east end for St Clement Danes to fit an irregular site and to frame the Communion table inside. Price imitated this formula, and made the plan symmetrical by repeating it at the west end to house the gallery staircases. He accepted the implications of his curved walls, giving the entrances to these staircases a curvature worthy of Borromini's Oratory (Pl. 455). The wooden steeple is also indebted to either Baroque Italy or the west towers of St Paul's.

---

[105] CLARKE, p. 35.
[106] *Essex Archaeological Soc.*, n.s. XXIII, 1942–5, pp. 311 ff.

The same hand would seem to be responsible for the tower of Laleham, Middlesex, 1731, which has heavy Vanbrughian pilaster strips in brick. The Borough Church, St George the Martyr, Southwark, 1734–6, which was paid for by the Fifty Churches Commission (p. 98) is more urbane but less interesting, and was probably intended to conform with anti-Baroque taste (Pls 457–8).

Edward Wing, a mason of Aynho, Northants, rebuilt the body of Aynho church in 1723–5. Aynho is Baroque in scale and in the choice of big motifs such as the unmoulded window architraves, the segmental headed upper windows, the broken-based side pediments and the giant pilaster strips, and from these and the symmetrical side elevations with central doors Wing appears to have been familiar with recent London church building and perhaps with the works at Oxford and Blenheim (Pl. 463). Nevertheless these motifs are deployed decoratively rather than growing organically as though they were part of the life of the walls as in, for example, Hawksmoor's Greenwich (Pl. 418). Other motifs, owing nothing to Vanbrugh or Hawksmoor, could be applied in the same way at Gayhurst, Bucks (1728, Pl. 464): as Wing worked at Fenny Stratford in the same county Gayhurst was within his orbit and may have been his work. Aynho was remodelled inside in 1863; Gayhurst remains unspoilt and complete (Pls 465, 482) and has an unusually large and elaborate chancel. The monument balancing the pulpit is to Sir Nathan Wrighte and his son, George, the principal benefactors of the church. Another chancel of some size and distinction is at Bruton, Somerset, rebuilt in 1743 by Nathaniel Ireson (Pl. 481). Of Ireson's rebuilding of his own town church at Wincanton (1748) only the south aisle door remains.

The authorship of a group of churches in Worcestershire and neighbouring counties is still rather confused. Nash's *Worcestershire* (1781) attributes to Thomas White, the Worcester mason-sculptor who built the Guildhall there, several churches in the city. St Swithin, however, bears a tablet over the west door giving the date 1736 and Edward and Thomas Woodward as the architects. These competent brothers owned a workshop and quarry at Chipping Campden; they are known to have built and no doubt designed St John the Baptist, Gloucester (1732–4), while St Anne, Bewdley (1745–8) is also attributable to them. These churches have similar, though not identical, east end compositions, of which the Worcester church is the most impressive (Pl. 468). It is based on a Wren formula but the plain attic, the combination of pilasters and fluted pilaster strips and the breaks in the pediment have some Baroque feeling. The interior is more remarkable than the others which are simple aisled naves: St Swithin has a shallow vault with applied ribs and bosses, and the fluted order reappears in two columns at the front corners of the screens which separate the chancel from the corner vestries (Pl. 466). The east end of All Saints (1738–42) is based on a similar formula – the round aisle windows occur in the Woodwards' Gloucester east end – but the centre part of All Saints projects strongly beyond the aisles (Pl. 467). The builder of All Saints was Richard Squire, another Worcester mason. St Nicholas was rebuilt 1730–5 by Humphry Hollins. The façade (Pls 469–70) shows an attempt at Baroque movement in the use of single and coupled pilasters, as if it were the lower half of a seventeenth-century Italian façade, but both the main pediment and that of the doorcase break back in the centre whereas in true Baroque they would break forward. The severe bell-shaped steeple derives from one of Gibbs's rejected designs for St Mary-le-Strand, published in his *Book of Architecture* (1728). There is no evidence beyond Nash's statement (and much of his account of White is demonstrably false) that White designed either All Saints or St Nicholas, and they do not show enough links with the Guildhall to be attributed by comparison. He was, however, concerned with the rebuilding of the church at Castle Bromwich, Warwicks, 1726–31. The contract of Thomas Clear *alias* Smith, a local mason, to rebuild the tower shows White at least to have been consulted.[107] The prevalence at Castle Bromwich

[107] *Country Life*, cx, 1951, pp. 204, 207.

of segmental-headed windows and the decorative preference for patterning the walls with panels, compartments and surface relief and with aprons under the windows (Pl. 471) are much closer to the Worcester Guildhall (Pl. 493) than anything in the Worcester churches.

There is insufficient evidence for crediting White with the sophistication of St Thomas, Stourbridge, begun in 1726 (Pls 472–3). It has been altered by the addition of a chancel and other projections and the raising of the tower, but it retains its galleries and original ceiling. The latter is based on St James, Piccadilly, but the lines of the Stourbridge ceiling run independently of structural forms with a freedom and delicacy worthy of a German Baroque church.

John Bastard's church at Blandford (1735–9, Pls 474–5) is also much above average, and the Doric severity of the exterior and the near-Rococo lightness of the interior accompany an appreciation in the plan of the Baroque London churches. The pedimented porches on the north and south sides form transepts inside, and these and a wider central inter-columniation establish a north-south cross axis which the galleries – added later in the eighteenth century[108] – to some extent destroy. As at Stourbridge and most of the grander churches a chancel was added to suit Victorian religious taste; the old apse was reconstructed on the end of the chancel, but the original appearance can best be seen in a westward view.

The freaks and sports of the period belong to something like a tradition of architectural dissent which runs through the seventeenth and eighteenth centuries. Thomas Platt of Rotherham's St Paul, Sheffield (1720–40) remained almost in its original state until its demolition in 1938 (Pl. 450, Fig. 54). It was modelled on the churches of William Smith (Pl. 448) with an eastern apse, but the exterior had certain unusual features such as the serpentine pediments at the east end which became reversed over the west door like a neo-Classical sofa. In the industrial north as in London the toll of churches has been heavy. The destroyed churches of St Mary, Manchester (1750) and St Peter, Liverpool (consecrated 1704) had octagonal lanterns; the latter building's "chief merit lies in the woodwork"[109] of which the unusually elaborate carved reredos and other panels, now at North Meols, Southport, show, in the illusion of flow and chiaroscuro rather than in dexterity with the chisel, a very competent imitation of the Gibbons style (Pls 476–7, 479).

Holy Trinity, Sunderland, a plain brick church of 1719 with stone pilasters and dressings, has a dramatic addition of 1735, apparently unaltered but unattributed: the chancel is circular, lit by a Venetian window and separated from the body of the church by an unsophisticated triumphal arch (Fig. 55). The tiny church at Honiley, Warwicks, dated 1723, is a country mason's attempt at eclectic creation. It has obvious faults of proportion and placing – the belfry windows, for example, rise too high – but some of the evocative and picturesque qualities of Hawksmoor and Archer have filtered down to its single pilaster order and the scrolls and round windows and pyramids of the steeple (Pl. 483).

In some cases only decorative details are singular. The doorway of Stoke Doyle, Northants, 1722–5 (Pl. 485) has a segmental pediment which breaks back in the centre and also has an interrupted base, and the keystone projects both downwards and forwards from the rest of the door arch. The tower window at Adderley, Salop, 1712, has a hood broken by a large and rustic keystone which is nevertheless in the same spirit as the shells and triglyphs of Hawksmoor (Pls 484, 248). Archer's church on his estate at Hale, Hants, has been considerably altered, but the doorways survive to show both the lettered and, in the roughly cut scrolls,

[108] WHIFFEN, p. 38.
[109] V.C.H., *Lancs.* IV, 1911, p. 45. The carver was Richard Prescot of Liverpool (P. FLEETWOOD-HESKETH, *Murray's Lancashire Architectural Guide*, London, 1955, p. 45).

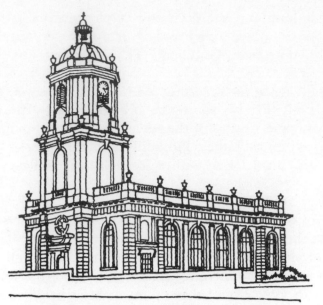

Fig. 54. St Paul, Sheffield (destroyed).

Fig. 55. Holy Trinity, Sunderland. (a) Interior looking east. (b) Exterior from east.

the unlettered approach to Baroque vocabulary (Pls 486–7). The sensitive detail of Gay-hurst includes also capitals which have all the confectioner's delight but none of the architect-sculptor's feeling of contemporary European work (Pl. 482).

The churches of Archer and Hawksmoor and Gibbs's St Mary-le-Strand are each unique and their remarkable qualities were not susceptible of imitation either by lesser men or where money was limited. Money was in fact limited almost everywhere except in the grander London churches; the sheer masonry of a St George-in-the-East is expensive. The provincial churches of the eighteenth century are more rewarding than is sometimes suggested, but a proper study of their typology would undoubtedly confirm the extent of their dependence on Wren. They have a definite place among the marginalia of English Baroque.

MINOR PUBLIC BUILDINGS

From the Whitehall schemes onwards, the ambition held by every eighteenth-century English architect and fulfilled by few was to build a great palace or public building. The efforts of Shaftesbury, Campbell and Burlington to reform public taste were even more successful – if to a considerable extent negative – in the field of public architecture than in the houses of noblemen, and, just as Jerman's Royal Exchange, built after the Great Fire of London, represented a middle-class taste noticeably and almost archaically conservative in its time, so the relatively small body of Baroque public buildings preserves the style of Greenwich Hospital at dates when enlightened taste had moved on. Examples of town rebuilding have already been mentioned (p. 97), but the town hall (Pl. 491) which John and William Bastard built for Blandford in 1734 reflects Palladian taste rather than the Baroque of the church and the inns across the market place; Francis Smith's Court House at Warwick (1725–8, Pl. 350) also has an Italian Cinquecento air. Elsewhere, the advanced style of Abingdon in 1680 (Pl. 489) became the old fashion of the market halls of York (1705–6, Fig. 56) and Milborne Port (Fig. 57) or the town halls of Worcester in 1721–4 (Pl. 493, Thomas White), of Monmouth (Pl. 492) and of Morpeth, Northumberland in 1714 (Pl. 494, now a basically faithful Victorian rebuilding of a Vanbrugh original). Morpeth is more imaginative than the others, but it is as closely related to Vanbrugh's designs for little houses as the others are to the houses of lesser men. There is thus little to add to the account of domestic buildings already given, although some other unusual buildings deserve mention.

Fig. 56.   York. Butter Market (destroyed).   Fig. 57.   Milborne Port. Market.

The commodious Prison at York, 1709 (Pl. 498), now part of the Castle Museum, is a robust building which certainly owes something to Castle Howard in its scale and mass and in the central cupola; it stands at the same remove architecturally from Vanbrugh as the elevations of Duncombe (Pl. 322) and may be by the same architect, William Wakefield. There are further similarities with Fountaine's Hospital, Linton-in-Craven, Yorks, 1720, the most heroically detailed alms-house in England, which displays such Wakefield features as "Gibbs" windows and a central niche derived from a modified Venetian window like the features in the hall at Gilling (Pl. 499).

The Charity School at Kensington, 1711–12, was designed by Hawksmoor, one of its trustees (Pl. 504). It anticipates in certain obvious respects the front of St George-in-the-East, and, like his earlier Writing School at Christ's Hospital (1692–5, Pl. 502), is on a higher plane than other schools such as the Bluecoat School, Westminster of 1709 (Pl. 501) or, for a later example which is basically a town house with giant Doric angle pilasters, the Old Grammar School at Dedham, Essex, of 1732. On the other hand the large brick and stone building erected in 1709 at Kirkleatham, Yorks, by Cholmley Turner to house the school founded by his uncle, Sir William Turner, has great distinction and boldness (Pl. 500); it has since been converted into dwellings and the entrance loggias filled in.

Of Vanbrugh's Opera House in the Haymarket, London, nothing survives. It was designed and partly financed by him in a premature and unsuccessful attempt to domesticate Italian opera in London. It was begun in 1704 and opened the following April with Greber's *Loves of Ergasto*; Vanbrugh lost heavily on the venture and disposed of his interest. The building was not of great architectural importance, and the only part visible from the street, the vestibule façade, was a simple three-bay affair of brick with rusticated stone windows (Pl. 497).

That Baroque survived in official building after 1715 was due to the presence of Vanbrugh in the Office of Works. One of the later acts of the 1710–14 Tory government was to deprive him in April 1713 of the Comptrollership, but although Archer engaged Shrewsbury to gain him the post, no successor was appointed and Vanbrugh, first knighted by the returning Whigs, was reinstated in January 1715 and six months later received a new post made for him, of Surveyor of Gardens and Waters. Either he as Comptroller or Hawksmoor, who between 1715 and 1718 was Secretary to the Board of Works and Clerk of Works at St James's Palace, was responsible for two additions there in 1716–17, both still extant: the cavernous new kitchen (shown in J. B. Pyne's view, Pl. 506) and the arcade in Stable Yard (Pl. 507) in which the bare "back front" utility style of Queen Anne Base Block at Greenwich (Pl. 100) contrasts with charming pyramidal leaded roofs on the end pavilions.

A curious domestic example of this style is to be found in Biddesden House on the Hampshire border of Wiltshire, which was begun in 1711 for John Webb, one of Marlborough's generals.[110] The two main storeys have gauged brick round-headed window arches all round the house and the attic has similar segmental headed windows. The three-bay frontispiece has round windows on the first floor lighting the upper part of the two-storey hall. The conception is close to the St James's Stable Yard and the frontispiece recalls the St James's kitchen or Vanbrugh's Opera House. There is no ornament except small trophies over the segmental brick pediment of the frontispiece.

Vanbrugh's reinstatement after 1714 was only one of several, including that of Marlborough as Master of Ordnance. A new Surveyor-General of Ordnance was also appointed, Brigadier-General Michael Richards, one of Marlborough's officers, who became nominally responsible for the design of any new military buildings. England's strengthened European position at the conclusion of the French wars might have seemed in any case a suitable occasion for reorganizing dockyards and military buildings, but in the light of the Old Pretender's invasion of 1715 it was a necessity. The new barracks at Berwick-on-Tweed were a direct product of this event, the new marine buildings at Plymouth, Portsmouth and Chatham indirect ones. At the same time the Royal Foundry was transferred from Moorfields to the Warren at Woolwich, a move which led to the development of Woolwich Arsenal, now the Royal Ordnance Factory. Mr Laurence Whistler was the first to point out the stylistic likeness connecting all these centres and to deduce from it the activity of a single guiding hand and that one from the Office of Works, which had no formal connection with the Board of Ordnance.[111] The style is the Works' utility style but Vanbrugh's on the whole rather than Hawksmoor's, round arched, castellated, and big in conception.

The Foundry building at Woolwich, 1716–17, now a garage, was extensively remodelled in 1771–2,[112] and while the doorway and the general shape of the entrance pavilion are

[110] *Country Life*, LXXXIII, 1938, pp. 352 ff., 376 ff.
[111] WHISTLER, *Vanbrugh*, 1954, ch. IX.
[112] O. F. G. HOGG, *The Royal Arsenal*, London, 1963, pp. 431 ff.

Fig. 58.   Woolwich Arsenal. Dial Square. South range.

Fig. 59.   Kensington Water Tower (destroyed).

original the veracity of the rest is uncertain (Pl. 512). The south gateway to the Grand Square (Dial Square) opposite (1717) survives though without the pyramids of cannon-balls which originally topped the piers (Pl. 515, Fig. 58). The north gate, which no longer exists, had piers of more complex plan and carried a big trophy (Pl. 514); this and the Landport Gate at Portsmouth (Pl. 513) may owe something to Hawksmoor, while decoratively they derive from a tradition of fortified and heraldic town gates which must have been one of the roots of Vanbrugh's style. The latter's hand is unmistakable in the gateway of Chatham Dockyard (1720, Pl. 517) and the Great Storehouse there, 350 feet long (Pl. 516); it is recognizable at one remove at Berwick (1717–after 1725), and directly, in the finest of all the Ordnance buildings, the old Military Academy at Woolwich (Pls 508–11). This was built in 1718–20 as the board room and saloon of the Board of Ordnance, the two tall rooms separated by a central vestibule. The board room on the right, towards the Thames, is now used as a mess. It rises the full height of the building and has a coved ceiling; at the end a depressed pro-scenium arch frames a bow window looking out over the river. This room retains its original stone fireplace, very large with leafy scrolls at the ends but not specifically Vanbrughian. The exterior, of yellow brick with red brick voussoirs, has become a uniform brown with age, but its portholes and massive central arch retain the grandeur of scale and motif of its con-temporary, Eastbury (p. 84). With the modern reorganization of the Arsenal some of the unsightly surroundings of this block have been removed and the view to the river is once again open.

Looking back at the Vanbrugh period across the works of the engineer-builders of the nineteenth century, one is tempted to regret that Vanbrugh did not live in the great age of steam. Many nineteenth-century industrial buildings, especially those connected with the supply of water such as the big halls housing stationary steam engines, show a similarity to the earlier style which may in some cases be deliberate, and it is interesting to note that Vanbrugh's Office of Works did design and erect similar buildings though on a smaller pre-industrial scale. The great water engine designed by Aldersea to pump water up to

Blenheim was housed under the Blenheim bridge but with no special building; on the other hand the older part of the pump-house on the Thames bank below Windsor Castle is early eighteenth century and in the Office of Works style (Pl. 505). The water tower on Kensington Palace Green, long demolished, was built in 1722–4 and must have been by Vanbrugh or Hawksmoor or their follower, Henry Joynes, who came from Blenheim to succeed Hawksmoor as Clerk of Works at Kensington in 1715 (Fig. 59). Its towers recall the Belvedere at Claremont, but that Joynes was sympathetic to the style is confirmed by the attribution to him of the water tower by the river Wandle in the grounds of Carshalton House, Surrey, of about the same date (Pl. 503). Besides the pumping room this contains a bathroom, a plaster vaulted saloon and an orangery, and the top of the tower holds, like the east gateway at Blenheim, the big cistern for supplying the house. On a much smaller scale is the Vanbrughian well-head on the Great North Road near Skelbrooke, Yorks (Pl. 496) which bears a scratched date of 1711.

THE UNIVERSITIES

That Oxford is remarkable for its Baroque buildings and Cambridge is not could be taken as sufficient illustration of the dependence of the style on the influence of individual persons and source-buildings and its failure in their absence. To some extent the difference between the two universities is geological: Oxford stone, bad though it is, has always been abundant, and its very tendency to decay has preserved not so much the buildings as a succession of masons engaged on repairing them. Cambridge, on the other hand, has always had to import stone, and a building like Wren's Trinity Library was only possible when money was free enough to pay for its carriage – in this case from Ketton in Rutland.[113] From Wren's time onwards large imports of good stone were quite common and a considerable amount of building was undertaken, but stone-masonry, like the stone, was still an importation. The Cambridge mason of the period, Robert Grumbold (1639–1720) was a Northamptonshire man who only came to the city at the age of 30, and while he built Trinity Library his thoroughly provincial training produced from his own resources the artisan mannerist elevations of the river front of Clare and the Westmorland Building at Emmanuel (Pl. 528).

Cambridge can boast the fine reredos in Trinity College chapel (Pl. 529) and two buildings in which an architect of national standing was brought in. Hawksmoor's grand design of 1712 for King's College was never begun, but he was succeeded by Gibbs who designed the Fellows' Building, 1724–9 (Pl. 526). This looks the importation it is, being made of white Portland stone against the yellow Northamptonshire stone of the chapel. Its façade is that of Wanstead but the central archways are not Palladian although their components derive from Palladio and Wren; they are Mannerist rather than Baroque in their complexity. Gibbs's other building, the Senate House, 1722–30 (Pl. 525) is a single great room and the counterpart of Oxford's Sheldonian. It occupies the same position between Baroque and Palladian as St Martin-in-the-Fields. Its flat-ceiled interior is ornate but without Baroque feeling, but its giant order stands firmly and directly on the ground with some of the assurance as well as the richness of Blenheim, in particular the transition from plain pilasters to fluted three-quarter columns and the decisive and dramatic doubling of the end pilasters. The Senate House was planned as one of three sides of a rectangular court, but the middle and opposite sides were abandoned. Its general lines were suggested by Sir James Burrough of Gonville and Caius College (1691–1764), amateur architect, but what appears to be his

113 R.C.H.M., *Cambridge*, 1959, I, pp. xcviii ff.

design[114] lacks both the energy and the distinction of the final one; Gibbs claimed the latter as his own in his *Book of Architecture* and on quality alone this claim would have to be upheld.

Oxfordshire masonry was much stronger in numbers and experience, so strong in fact that the Kempsters and the Strongs worked on St Paul's Cathedral and elsewhere outside their own county, and they were capable both of labour to meet new and increased contracts and of the skill and experience necessary to interpret the designs of the Office of Works and its Oxford imitators.

The proximity of Blenheim influenced both patrons and masons in Oxford (for instance Vanbrugh House, Pl. 349) and facilitated direct contact with Vanbrugh and Hawksmoor in the city. Oxford also had the fortune to be the home of two dons with a penchant for architecture, Henry Aldrich, Dean of Christ Church (1648–1710) and Dr George Clarke of All Souls (1661–1736). Aldrich was a collector and dilettante and an amateur architect of considerable learning and the author of an academic treatise on architecture which was only published long after his death. His will directed that all his personal papers be destroyed, and attributions therefore rest mainly on style and the somewhat nebulous evidence of unsigned drawings and proof engravings in his collection in Christ Church Library and in Clarke's collection at Worcester College. A coherent group of Oxford buildings can be formed from All Saints church (p. 106), the chapel of Trinity College, 1691–4 (Pls 530, 532), the library of the Queen's College, 1693–4 (Pl. 531); all these depend on Wren's works of the 1670's and '80's and all share the same attitude to wall surfaces. Both inside and outside walls are broken up into panels which make a repetitive surface pattern rather than either exploring and varying the depth and solidity of the wall or bringing it to life: the contrast should be evident between the exterior of Trinity Chapel or Queen's Library and Hawksmoor's Clarendon Building (Pls 518–19). His drawing-board conception of architecture is equally apparent in the only building certainly designed by Aldrich, the three sides of the Peckwater Quadrangle of his own college, built by William Townesend 1706–13 (Pl. 523); its Palladian formula and its Palladian sobriety antedate by some twenty years John Wood's elevations of Queen Square at Bath, and although it is lacking in depth it is, like All Saints, striking and successful in scale.

Peckwater marks the meeting of the two Oxford amateurs, for the free-standing library building on the south side, originally planned by Aldrich, was considerably altered by Clarke before it was begun in 1717. The giant half-columns were Aldrich's idea, but Clarke discarded the ground floor rustication Aldrich intended to lie behind them, altered the elevation from three storeys (as on the rest of the quadrangle) to two at the same height, and inserted a small pilaster order between the half-columns (Pl. 524). This scheme is based on Michelangelo's side palaces on the Capitol, but Clarke, like Aldrich, depended on size and scale rather than on the movement and tension of the Italian.

Clarke was in effect Aldrich's successor and was the more important figure. From 1685 to 1714 he led an active public life in a number of Government posts; on the death of Queen Anne he retired to All Souls of which he had been elected a Fellow in 1680, continuing nevertheless to represent the University in Parliament. His influence on Oxford building was felt both before and after his retirement, and embraced both patronage and designing. Clarke is also remembered with gratitude for the collections he formed of books and prints and of drawings by Inigo Jones and Webb and by his own contemporaries, in particular Hawksmoor; as the result of a dispute with his college he left all these to the new Worcester College which he had been instrumental in founding, together with many sketches and notes of his own. His connection with Hawksmoor probably dates as far back as 1702–5 when Clarke, as Joint Secretary to the Admiralty, met Hawksmoor over Greenwich Hospital.

---

[114] In the British Museum, King's Maps (SUMMERSON, *Architecture in Britain*, 1955 ed., pl. 115B).

Fig. 60. Dr George Clarke's design for the Queen's College, Oxford. Street front.

From a study of the Clarke collection it appears that he advised on the Clarendon Building and work at All Souls, University, Brasenose (his old college, unexecuted), Magdalen, Worcester and the Queen's Colleges and had a considerable share in the design of the last named; he was also concerned with schemes for a monument to Dr John Radcliffe and for the planning of the Radcliffe Camera.[115]

The rebuilding of the Queen's College which had begun with the library was continued in 1710 with the commencement of a new front quadrangle facing the High Street. Hawksmoor made a number of schemes, and designs were also made by William Townesend, the contracting mason. From drawings in the Clarke Collection it appears that Clarke planned the arrangement of hall and chapel with a central vestibule, on the pattern of Chelsea (Pl. 14) but ultimately deriving from Wren's old Oxford college, the Jacobean Wadham. One of Clarke's schemes placed the hall and chapel on the street front with a full portico; from drawings and proof engravings of this scheme (Fig. 60) it is clear that the executed elevation begun in 1714 (Pl. 521) owes more to Clarke than anyone else, though how far Hawksmoor and Townesend were consulted will probably never be known. The ends of the hall (Pl. 535) seem to be by Townesend (*cf.* Fig. 61) and the sculptured pediment below the cupola (Pl. 521) was designed by Thornhill, no doubt at Clarke's invitation.[116] The high plinths under the hall and chapel windows resemble those outside Aldrich's Trinity College Chapel, but also occur under the west front windows of St Paul's (Pl. 50). The door to the chapel (Pl. 522) suggests a Roman Baroque source. The only part of the college for which Hawksmoor was directly responsible is the front screen and gateway, 1733–6 (Pl. 536). It has been suggested that Townesend altered Hawksmoor's design, but both drawn and written contemporary evidence confirms its authenticity.[117]

Townesend was capable of a rough and vigorous Vanbrughian, as his designs for the Clarendon Press, Queen's and All Souls show, and he may be presumed to have designed certain works which he built such as the range north of the chapel at Trinity, 1728 (Pl. 520),

[115] For Clarke and his collection see COLVIN, *Worcester College*, where many drawings are reproduced.
[116] COLVIN, *op. cit.*, p. xix.
[117] DOWNES, *Hawksmoor*, p. 107, n. 14.

the east and south gates to the college (Pl. 534), the cloister at Corpus Christi, 1712, an arcade with large keystones and Doric pilasters, and the very reserved Fellows' Building there which has Ionic pilasters.

Clarke was also responsible for the library block at Worcester College (begun 1720); he consulted Hawksmoor and received drawings from him, of which the executed design is a watered-down version (Pl. 533). His most important contributions to Oxford architecture, however, were the opportunities he secured for Hawksmoor in the Clarendon Building and All Souls. The University Press had been housed in the attic and basement of the Sheldonian Theatre, a situation which did no good even to a roof as scientifically constructed as Wren's was supposed to be. The profits from Clarendon's *History of the Great Revolution* (1702–4) suggested to the University the plan of building a separate home for the Press, but by 1711–12 when work started this money had been otherwise used and new funds were tapped. The co-existence of two "firms", the learned press and that authorized to print at a profit the King James Bible and the Prayer Book, dictated the form of the building, and Clarke received designs for a structure in two halves joined by a central vestibule and staircases from William Townesend (Fig. 61), John James[118] and Hawksmoor. The latter probably got the commission, which was carried out by Townesend, through his persistence and his usual practice of sending several designs, his reputation at Blenheim and in the last resort through Clarke's recommendation, and it is evident from the Queen's College buildings and Christ Church Library that Clarke liked Hawksmoor's giant Doric building – enough, perhaps, to imitate it: as all known designs used that order it may have been Clarke's stipulation for the Press. Hawksmoor's building (Pls 518–19) with an applied portico on the south and a projecting one towards Broad Street on the north, with its exuberantly thick walls cut back in layers and relieved into flat architraves, with its heavy keystones and window aprons, brings the language of Blenheim into Oxford as Wren's Trinity Library had brought the language of St Paul's into Cambridge a generation earlier.

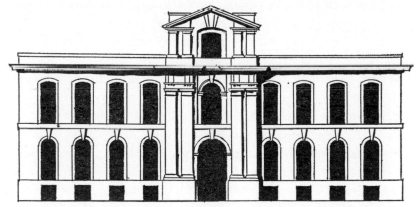

Fig. 61.   William Townesend's design for the Clarendon Building, Oxford.

At All Souls, Clarke acted as intermediary between the college and architects, who included John Talman, William Townesend, John James and Edward(?) Wilcox as well as Hawksmoor (Fig. 62).[119] All made designs in 1708–9 for a block of lodgings on the north of what was then the college garden and is now the north quadrangle, on the site now occupied by Hawksmoor's Codrington Library (Fig. 63). Talman, who on occasion carried messages between his father, William – who perhaps hoped for a commission[120] – and Clarke, produced a design with a decided French – or Austro-Italian – oval staircase vestibule projecting from the centre of the block, and also a Gothic design for the hall and chapel (p. 122). Christopher

[118] COLVIN, *op. cit.*, pl. 104; Hawksmoor's preliminary designs are on pls 105–8.
[119] *Ibid.*, pls 45–86.
[120] Letters from John to William Talman, 1 April and 7 July 1708; Bodleian MS. Engl. Letters e. 34.

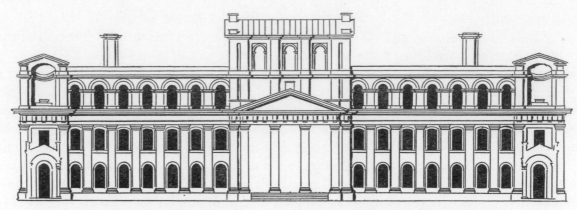

Fig. 62.   Hawksmoor's design for the north lodgings, All Souls, Oxford.

Codrington's death early in 1710 and the bequest of his books and a sum for building a home for them put speculation on a firmer footing and also changed the function of the proposed north building, and after many designs and much deliberation Hawksmoor's library was begun in 1716. At the same time the lodgings and Common Room were begun on the east of the quadrangle; the cloister on the west side, replacing an earlier covered walk, was begun in 1728 and two years later a new hall was started, forming with the medieval chapel a southern block facing the library. The exteriors of Hawksmoor's quadrangle are, unlike the interiors, all "Gothic" and must be described later (p. 121); the quadrangle was not complete until shortly before his death, and the library was only finished some years after, the squared ceiling he intended not being carried out.

By designing a ground floor library Hawksmoor broke with a long tradition of academic building on the upper floor over arches or columns, examples of which are Wren's Trinity Library, that of Queen's College, Oxford, and his own building for Christ's Hospital. He also rejected the usual arrangement of bookcases running out from the side walls to form bays, and kept all the shelves on the walls; the long gallery-like plan is thereby fully revealed, and seen to be related to the earlier gallery at Easton Neston and the later fitting up of the Long Library at Blenheim (Pls 213, 251). Like them, the All Souls Library was intended to be entered in the centre – by the door in the long wall facing the quadrangle – with the interior extended dramatically to left and right. Hawksmoor's spatial manipulation elsewhere in the college is richer. The stone-vaulted Buttery is one of the few oval rooms in English Baroque (Pl. 538). The plaster-vaulted hall (1730–3, Pl. 537) is also related to the Continent; the closest parallel to the extraordinary freedom of section and compartmenting of the balloon-like ceiling is the sacristy of Borromini's San Carlino in Rome, and it also recalls the free vault shapes of Central European Baroque of the same date, of which Hawksmoor is not likely to have known directly. The plastic treatment of the ceiling is intensified by the opposing curve of the screen seen in silhouette below it.

The chapel screen at All Souls also owes its present form to Clarke and Thornhill, who in 1715–16 refurbished the structure of 1664 and added a pedimented attic over the centre, raising the arch into it (Pl. 527).

The 150 surviving drawings by Hawksmoor for university buildings – a quarter of all his known drawings – reflect in their variety, comprehensiveness and grandeur of thought the recurrent conflict between architect and colleges. The latter thought nearly always in terms of piecemeal additions, dependent on benefactions as they were made and needs as they were realized. Even Worcester College, a new foundation, and the Queen's College, virtually a new one architecturally, were affected by this attitude, and Aldrich's uniform Peckwater Quadrangle is an exception and a part of an exceptionally large college. Traditions remain powerful in academic building to this day, and architects ignore them at some risk. In

many parts of Redbrick the staircase system survives, in which lodgings are arranged verti-
cally, one or two to each landing of a common staircase which is entirely separated from
neighbouring ones. The alternative, the corridor system, is one of the innovations Hawksmoor
attempted and failed to make in one of his Queen's College designs which has lodgings
entered from either side of a central corridor on each floor (Fig. 64). This arrangement,
which is a commonplace of modern life, probably derived from the plan of the ward blocks
at Chelsea and Greenwich which had set new standards of convenience in communal
accommodation; it was not acceptable.

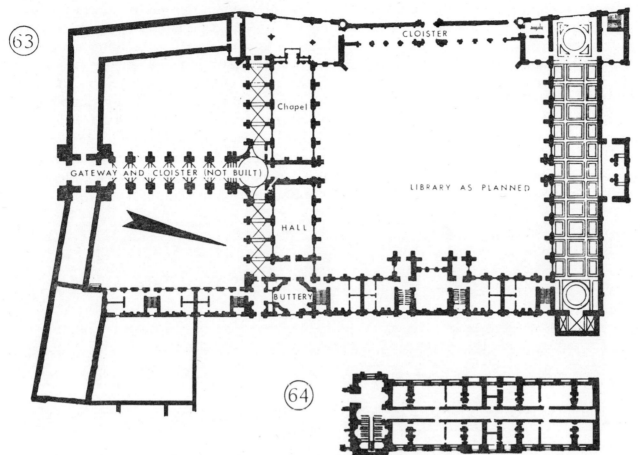

Fig. 63.   All Souls, Oxford. Hawksmoor's plan.
Fig. 64.   Hawksmoor's corridor-block for the Queen's College, Oxford.

The same process of fertile invention, piecemeal effort and extreme procrastination
produced at Oxford the last Baroque building in England and its unique setting. Dr John
Radcliffe, Queen Anne's physician, decided in 1712 to pay part of the cost of a new library
building for the University and two years later his will directed it to be built adjacent to the
south side of the Schools Quadrangle of the Bodleian. Hawksmoor, no doubt through the
agency of Clarke, produced several designs first for a square and then for a round building,
and in 1717 Radcliffe's trustees began to buy houses on the site, which is now Radcliffe
Square. In 1720 they considered inviting designs from Wren, Vanbrugh, Thornhill, Archer,
Hawksmoor, James and Gibbs, but negotiations for the site were resumed only after a
further lapse of thirteen years. In 1734–5 Hawksmoor and Gibbs made further designs and
a model of Hawksmoor's, now in the Bodleian, was made. Gibbs, however, was appointed
architect before Hawksmoor's death in March, 1736, and it was to his design that the
library was begun in 1737, being finished in 1749 (Pls 539–40). Gibbs's decisive contribution
was to detach the building from the Schools and move it into the centre of the square; other
features of his building, the open basement arcade (now glazed in), the internal arcades,

the circular form itself and the exceptional richness of articulation, seem to derive from Gibbs's undoubted knowledge of Hawksmoor's designs. The Radcliffe Camera is one of the noblest buildings in Oxford and much finer than Gibbs's original rectangular design. Although the triangular pediments and rusticated arches of the ground floor and the windows of the main storey have a Palladian origin and a Palladian dryness their combination with giant coupled three-quarter columns gives the great cylinder a Baroque animation of surface and a complexity of bay rhythm between the storeys. This is continued above the entablature in the buttresses and ribs of the lead and timber dome, which stand over the bay centres and not over the columns. Above all, the Camera dominates and seems to fill the irregular square in which it stands, because it is very large and tall; yet because the entrances to the square are at the corners, which are unobstructed, the building can be seen from an adequate distance. The view is sudden and dramatic as you enter the square, and this spatial surprise is the creation of both Gibbs and Hawksmoor. In 1712–13 the latter made plans for rebuilding the centres of both Oxford and Cambridge as a series of nearly closed spaces of varied shape, set between college quadrangles and linked by axial siting towards university and public buildings and other extraneous focal monuments such as obelisks.[121] He conceived Radcliffe Square as part of his Oxford scheme at the time of the early designs for the library, and the only parts of his conception ever realized are the square and the contrasting Gothic quadrangle of All Souls immediately east of it.

[121] See DOWNES, *Hawksmoor*, ch. VIII.

V

Tailpieces

GOTHIC

In no part of the seventeenth century was there no Gothic building at all, and the survival of Gothic traditions and the conscious revival of medieval forms overlap and are sometimes indistinguishable. The vaulting ribs of the crypt of Hawksmoor's Mausoleum at Castle Howard are almost pure Gothic although they were built after 1729 in a structure the rest of which is based obviously and avowedly on classical and Renaissance forms. These particular moulding profiles appear therefore to have been used because the local masons were familiar with them, or because the architect thought them particularly suited to the construction. Wren's use of flying buttresses at St Paul's (Fig. 11a) was solely structural, and they were so alien to his artistic intentions that he concealed them and few people know of their existence. Wren's approval of Gothic was grudging, even shamefaced. He was called upon to advise on several medieval structures, and in a report on Westminster Abbey he admitted that he had used Gothic forms "where I was oblig'd to deviate from a better Style". Such were the octagonal stone belfry of Tom Tower at Christ Church, Oxford, with an ogee stone cap, the repairs to the north transept end of Westminster Abbey and the re-creation at St Dunstan-in-the-East of the original steeple form of old St Mary-le-Bow, in which a central pinnacle rested on four converging flying buttresses (Pl. 541). Wren's eclecticism, and still more the wider eclecticism of Hawksmoor and Vanbrugh, meant in fact that no architectural source was necessarily ruled out. Style became, although not to the same extent as in the Romantic era, something like a suit of clothes which could be chosen according to the circumstances. Tom Tower was a matter of complementing an existing scheme, but the imitation Tudor of Wren's St Mary Aldermary (Pl. 542) was one of deliberate archaism and so was Hawksmoor's later completion of the tower of St Michael, Cornhill, 1718–24 (Pl. 543) where the church is in no way Gothic. Either the formal or the historical qualities of the style appealed – or perhaps both. Hawksmoor projected a recasing of Westminster Abbey in a Gothic version of a giant Tuscan order, which would have ruined the building: fortunately he was only allowed at the end of his life to design the existing west towers, which fit the building extremely well (Pl. 551). They suggest the verticals of Gothic when in fact their predominant lines are horizontal, and it is the measure of their success that they so frequently pass unnoticed. Hawksmoor's aim was perhaps above all iconographical, for he defended his design with a dissertation on twin-towered cathedral west fronts; there seems, however, to be a connection, of which there are other examples, between his successful creation of an illusion of a Gothic front and the general Baroque tendency towards illusionism.

The same feeling for the effect of Gothic forms and for the play of light on them is evident in Hawksmoor's project for the High Street front of All Souls, Oxford (Pl. 545) and in the fairy-tale atmosphere of the executed north quadrangle (Pl. 544), whose inspiration seems to be the towers of Beverley Minster (which he knew) but by way of the un-Gothic towers of Blenheim and Limehouse; in each case Hawksmoor's liberties with the classic vocabulary of the style in which he worked are considerable. His letters appear to make him desirous of retaining as much as possible of the old work at All Souls, but he intended to regularize the old south quadrangle and add another storey to it. His wish, which may have been prompted by the fellows' attitude, was to preserve useful masonry rather than an old building. Sketches show that, like any architect, he hoped to rebuild it all. It should not be forgotten that although he appealed for funds to repair St Albans Abbey and Beverley Minster, the restoration of the latter, for part of which at least he was responsible, and of all of which he approved, included Doric galleries in the nave. A much more literal antiquarian display was offered by John Talman in 1708 for encasing the chapel and a new hall at All Souls in Venetian Gothic; Talman was the first secretary of the Society of Antiquaries of London, but his unmodulated pen style suggests that the relief crust would have been dense and even and devoid of monumental feeling (Fig. 65).

Fig. 65.   John Talman's design for All Souls' hall and chapel, north side.

The rebuilding of the nave and tower of St Mary, Warwick, after the town fire of 1694, presents historical problems which have not yet been entirely solved. In this case Gothic seems to have been chosen because of the survival of the chancel and the Beauchamp chapel and a desire to preserve the historical continuity of the building. Payments were made by the Warwick Commissioners both to Wren and to his "man" who can be identified as Hawksmoor[122] and by whom designs for a new nave and tower, made soon after the fire (Pl. 549), exist at All Souls. The architect finally chosen, however, was Sir William Wilson, the mason-sculptor of Sutton Coldfield, and the contractors were Francis and William Smith (p. 107). The interior (Pl. 548) is a remarkable piece of vaulted construction and appears superficially medieval, although neither the mouldings (Pl. 550) nor the pier plans are in the least Gothic. The window tracery and the whole exterior are a scramble of medieval and Renaissance ideas.

The tower (Pl. 547) differs from the church in being both richer in surface decoration and more plastic in relief, and it is known from documents not to be Wilson's original design. Wilson's tower, which stood over the western bay of the nave, was begun and was taken up 29 feet above the nave roof, but the eastern piers then failed and work stopped; these piers may be seen inside the church. A new tower was begun standing west of the church on open arches; it shares this position with Hawksmoor's design which is otherwise quite different.

[122] *Ibid.*, pp. 54–5.

Fig. 66. St Mary, Warwick. Conjectural reconstruction of tower design of 1700.

Fig. 67. Somersby, Lincs, c.1722.

According to *Parentalia* a design was provided by Wren at this stage, and was used. The problem here is that the general aspect of the tower is unlike either Wren's or Hawksmoor's other Gothic work: both depended on a multiplicity of bold mouldings to give the plasticity and shadow of real Gothic to their re-creations. On the other hand, prolonged acquaintance with the tower in many lights and from many angles shows both how remarkable it is and of what disparate elements it is composed. Both in distant silhouette (Pl. 546) and in the deep slightly pointed arches that fill the middle of each face it gives the illusion of a great Gothic tower, with the same force and the same inaccuracy though not the same vocabulary as Hawksmoor's towers of Westminster Abbey and All Souls. The other components of the design, the colonnettes and strings and the shallow, round-headed niches in the corners, belong to a different conception of surface decoration. Taking all the known facts, historical and visual, into consideration, it is worth suggesting that *Parentalia* was basically correct, that the Commissioners, returning to Wren, received a new design something like Fig. 66; further that they found this in turn too bold, and that as a result the surface decorative modifications which we now see, and which weaken the effect, were introduced locally.

The early eighteenth century made no distinction between Gothic and Romanesque. The corbel-table between the towers of All Souls is Romanesque in origin, and Vanbrugh in particular is indebted to the earlier medieval period: examples are the gates of Eastbury (Pl. 270) and Chatham (Pl. 517), the Pyramid Gate at Castle Howard, the kitchen court arcade at Blenheim (Pl. 252) and above all his smaller buildings (Fig. 67). The Carrmire

Gate at Castle Howard seems so late as to be by Hawksmoor after Vanbrugh's death, but its inspiration is no different from that of the other bastions and walls of the estate (Pls 557–8). Vanbrugh's "Castle air" (p. 17) is nowhere more evident than in his own house, Vanbrugh Castle at Blackheath, where with the minimum of true medieval forms and the maximum of medieval solidity he created the first sham castle of the picturesque movement, indulging his taste for the apparatus at once of war, of the stage and of building (Pl. 552). There is no illusion here, rather the more literary aim of association of ideas, of deliberate make-believe. The rest of Vanbrugh's little colony of houses on the hill has gone; two were for his brothers, and one of these he typically nicknamed "the Nunnery". The scenery at least was ready for the Gothic novel.

GARDENS AND GARDEN BUILDINGS

In his small works as in his large ones Vanbrugh anticipated the Picturesque, and on Greenwich Hill he created the first garden village, placing both houses and grouping with the effect of random accretion. The unique landscape round Castle Howard, too, is dotted with his and Hawksmoor's buildings which appear over the crest of hills as if they had grown there and are as natural to the landscape as trees. In the hands of William Kent and then of Lancelot "Capability" Brown this planned casualness was to be applied to English landscape and was gradually to sweep all before it until "*le jardin anglais*" was known and imitated on the continent of Europe. The history of garden design is beyond the scope of this book, but buildings cannot be understood without the ground they are built upon, and surroundings were particularly important when they carried on the order and geometry of the house – so important that vast sums were spent on the gardens of the great Baroque houses while they were still rising from foundations. Today the lawn rolls up to the doors of Blenheim and Castle Howard and to the terraced walls of Chatsworth; the great parterres laid out in regimented rectangles of clipped shrubs, have gone. Many of the great avenues survive, although in some inevitable decay has decimated the trees and replanting has not always been done in time. The landscapists preferred adding trees to destroying them, but the effect of clump planting and asymmetrical addition to avenues was analogous to the grassing and rounding of the formal gardens and the elision of terraces as at Burley-on-the-Hill: the park became a picture instead of the frame, or a series of pictures, and the house became part of it.

Today the original setting of Baroque buildings can be visualized from old views, from the radiating avenues and the long canal which survive at Hampton Court (Pl. 553), from the reconstructed west garden at Blenheim (Pl. 240) and the surviving series of hedge- and tree-walks at Melbourne (Derbys) and Bramham (Pls 554–5). The formal parterre was inherited and accepted as the immediate environment of the Baroque house, but the great avenues and alleys aligned towards buildings or monuments were the creation of the age which first appreciated what Celia Fiennes called, at the time, the "visto". The long straight streets ploughed through medieval Rome by Pope Sixtus V before 1600 were perhaps their prototype, and the new gardens originated in France during the reign of Louis XIII; the greatest example remains the park of Versailles laid out for Louis XIV by André Le Nôtre (1613–1700). Charles II's artistic importations from France, which were later largely a matter of personal imitation and rivalry of his cousin (p. 33), probably grew initially from pure aesthetic enthusiasm for the possibilities of the new type of garden. He attempted to borrow the French king's chief gardener in June 1662, and that Le Nôtre actually visited England is implied by an authorization of 25 October 1662 to "Le nostre, the King's architect [i.e. Louis's] to transport six horses to France, Custome free"; the export of horses as gifts was fairly common.[123] Le Nôtre made a design for Greenwich Park, and Hawksmoor writing in 1723 credited him with the executed design,[124] but the evidence is not conclusive; his assistant, André Mollet, was in England from 1660 to 1665 and is more likely to have laid out the radiating avenues of Hampton Court and St James as well as supervising those of Greenwich. A further attempt to obtain Le Nôtre's services was made by Portland for William III in 1698 for the design of a new garden at Windsor, but this came to nothing.[125] The need for his services could be disputed, for England could then boast George London, Henry Wise and Charles Bridgeman. London planned Castle Howard, Bridgeman was to plan Stowe and Wise to work among other places at Kensington and Blenheim and to lay out Melbourne; Bramham was laid out in the 1720's by John Wood the elder.

John Nost's great vase of the Four Seasons at Melbourne (Pl. 554) is one of the richest but one of the smaller objects to which alleys were directed; the "historical pillar" at Blenheim was intended by Hawksmoor to mark on its original site a junction of avenues and to carry inscriptions both guiding and instructing the visitor, and the great obelisk at Castle Howard (Pl. 560) actually occupies a similar position and function; it marks the crossing of two straight roads which traverse the estate, one leading south to York and north towards Helmsley and the other forming the main approach to the house.

It is on the north to south Castle Howard road that the Pyramid and Carrmire Gates (Pls 557, 559) stand, and the hilly approach from York brings into view in turn the rough Carrmire, the Pyramid and finally the obelisk. Each brings in succession perception and surprise and then attainment, and each thus typifies the whole Castle Howard landscape. The other buildings are sited more freely, according to the lie of the land: the great pyramid roughly south of the house which is a memorial to Carlisle's Elizabethan ancestor and the founder of the estate, Lord William Howard (Pl. 563), Vanbrugh's Belvedere Temple east of the house and Hawksmoor's Mausoleum beyond it, and the objects designed by the latter far to the south-east in Pretty Wood (Pl. 556). There is there a small rusticated pyramid set, with Hawksmoor's feeling for the separateness of forms, on a pedestal. There is also the Four Faces, a monument of the same kind as those at Melbourne and Bramham (Pls 554–5) for which the same function must have been intended. The Four Faces must always have been mysterious, so far from the house and so unexpected in shape; the mystery is enhanced by the fact that no roads are now aligned on it, if they ever were, and the fascination of the object remains even when we realize that its upper section, part urn and part flaming pinnacle, is a big vase left over from the skyline of the house. Hawksmoor must also have been responsible earlier for many of the pedestals for lead garden figures, some of which (Pl. 561) are large and in themselves sculptural.

The Temple, for which Hawksmoor had made a Borrominesque design full of concave curves, was carried out by him to Vanbrugh's design after the latter's death in 1726 (Pls 562, 564). Iconographically it derives its four porticoes and its domed central cube boldly from one of the sacred monuments of Palladianism and the prototype of Chiswick and Mereworth – the Villa Rotonda. But the proportions are different, and if the Temple seen on a summer day in the clear air of Yorkshire stands out with a Virgilian clarity and purity seldom equalled north of the Alps, the massive bareness of the cube shows all the more clearly the stamp of Vanbrugh. The decoration of the interior, in black, white, grey and

[123] Cal. Treas. Books, 1660–7, p. 443. Cf. for example Luttrell on 18 June 1695: "The king has sent a present of 20 fine English horses to the King of Sweden".

[124] Le Nôtre's plan was published by E. DE GANAY, André Le Nostre, Paris, 1962, pl. CLVI; Hawksmoor's notes on a Greenwich plan of 1723 at Wilton refer to "The Grand Esplanade by Mons. Le Notre 1666".

[125] N. JAPIKSE (ed.), Correspondentie van Willem III en Hans Willem Bentinck, i.ii, The Hague, 1928, pp. 289–91; Desgots, Le Nôtre's nephew, figures in the correspondence. For Mollet see Country Life, CXIX, 1956, pp. 272–3.

gold stucco and scagliola, one of the first uses of the latter, was carried out in 1737–9 by
Francesco Vassali.[126]

The Mausoleum, the burial place of Lord Carlisle and his family, was often called "the
church" by contemporaries; in fact it is the most splendid garden building of all (Pls 565, 569).
It is also one of the greatest Baroque buildings and one very well documented by the series
of letters written by the architect from London to the patron on the spot during its construction. It was begun in 1729 and finished after both men were dead, in about 1741–2, but the
only departures from the design were the steps and the outer podium. Carlisle's son-in-law,
the Palladian amateur Sir Thomas Robinson and a minor architect, Daniel Garrett, were
responsible for these with some advice from Lord Burlington, and Garrett's steps are
modelled on those of Burlington's Chiswick. The Mausoleum grew gradually in the architect's mind, stimulated by Carlisle, to be a building of extraordinary emotional power. On
its hill-top site it is visible from many angles and great distances and has, like the Temple,
an air of the Roman Campagna; comparisons with antiquity were never far from the
architect's mind in his letters about the building. The columns of its Doric peristyle were set
extremely close, only a diameter and a half apart, partly because the local quarry did not
yield stones big enough for a wider span of the entablature, partly because Hawksmoor
liked the effect. The Mausoleum appears dark and forbidding outside, its columns like a
palisade, and the wrongness of Garrett's steps lies in their broad open invitation to enter.
By contrast the interior seems lighter, from the tall windows in the inner cylinder and those
above immediately under the dome, but the lightness, more imagined than real, is offset by
the emotional disquiet of the extremely even illumination, the claustrophobic smallness of
the single door and the partial enclosure of the interior columns in the wall so that the latter
is felt as pressing in on all sides. From the evolution of the design and the singleness of the
effect it is clear that the charged atmosphere of this house of the dead was intentional.
The Mausoleum differs from St George-in-the-East or the spatial sequences of Easton Neston
only in the greater intensity and greater clarity of its emotional effect and the greater
simplicity of the formal means used to achieve it. Such buildings as the temple at Duncombe (Pl. 568) derive from it formally but totally lack its particular force and drama.

Most garden buildings were light-hearted; the Castle Howard Temple was intended as
a summer-house where Carlisle could read, drink and contemplate the landscape of which it
was itself an animating feature. Gibbs designed in 1720 James Johnston's octagon room at
Twickenham, brick outside and stucco inside (Pl. 570). In intention the frivolity survived
changes of taste until social changes made the erection of such buildings impossible and
their upkeep scarcely practical; in form, however, many English attempts at lightness
degenerated into self-conscious pomposity or mere poverty of invention, but there is no
definite break between Baroque and post-Baroque in garden buildings. Among the many
existing and destroyed temples at Stowe, Bucks some were by Vanbrugh, some by Kent and
some by Gibbs.[127] Kent's temples are unmistakably Palladian, but that Vanbrugh was
capable of pseudo-Palladianism is shown by the temple and bagnio he designed for Eastbury
(*Vitruvius Britannicus* (III), 18–19). At Stowe Vanbrugh's Rotundo survives, though with a
new entablature and lower dome given it about 1760 by the obscure Signor Borra; originally
it was closer (Fig. 68) to the open temple at Duncombe (Pl. 567). Borra added domes to
Gibbs's twin Boycott Pavilions, originally designed about 1730 with pyramidal roofs; as
altered they still pass for Baroque buildings (Pl. 574).

Some of the finest garden buildings of any date in England were designed by Archer.
The Cascade House above Chatsworth, 1702, has already been mentioned (p. 63, Pls

[126] G. W. BEARD, "Italian stuccoists in England", *Apollo*, LXXX, 1964, pp. 48–56.
[127] L. WHISTLER, "The authorship of the Stowe temples", *Country Life*, CVIII, 1950, pp. 1002–6.

Fig. 68.   Stowe. The Rotundo before alteration.

154–5). About 1711 he designed two pavilions for the Duke of Kent at Wrest Park, Beds. The Hill House had four straight sides alternating with four concave ones and a flat roof; this no longer exists, but the more complex pavilion at the end of the canal survives (Pls 571–3). It has three round and three rectangular projections from a central domed cylinder, one of the rectangles being the entrance porch. The interior is painted in *grisaille* and gold and signed by Louis Hauduroy, 1712. The brick exterior is a text-book illustration of Baroque movement and diversity, presenting different silhouettes and volumes as distance and viewpoint change, and it is worth recalling that Archer alone of English Baroque architects had seen something at first hand of Central Europe (p. 3).

The cascade and fountains which survive at Chatsworth (Pls 154, 158) are but a token of those known from the accounts and from descriptions, and in general water-gardens suffered as badly in the Romantic era as did formal planting and bedding. The cascade terraces and channels at Bramham indeed survive, but they are dry. The biggest remaining fountain, the so-called Diana in Bushy Park at Hampton Court, is now a composite work (Pl. 72). The figure of Arethusa on top, the sirens spouting water from their breasts, the boys and the shell-basins were cast by Fanelli for Charles I. In 1699–1700 they were repaired and re-arranged on a newly made base carved with fishy emblems. The fountain so constituted remained in the Privy Garden until 1712–13, when it was moved to form the upper half of the present structure on a new base built for it in the great pond in Bushy Park; at this time the figures were further repaired and some were re-cast.[128]

CRAFTSMANSHIP AND DETAIL

The architect, unlike the painter and the sculptor, necessarily depends on a team of workers to carry out his design. These range from the excavators, bricklayers, stonemasons, carpenters, plumbers, glaziers and paviours to joiners, wood- and stone-carvers, smiths, plasterers, painters and gilders. Certain limits between trades and crafts were not defined, for example between stone-masonry and carving or between plain and decorative painting or plaster-work, and frequently the same men would be responsible for both. Craftsmen were often left to make their own designs for work to fill areas specified by the architect: drawings

[128] The casting was done by Richard Osgood, who also made in 1715 two large tritons and two large sea-horses for the Bushy Park pond. See LAW, *Hampton Court*, III, pp. 108, 139, 199, 202–3, 441; *Wren Soc.*, IV, p. 67.

exist for decoration at Blenheim and Hampton Court, in which Grinling Gibbons has elaborated panels within a framework drawn out by Vanbrugh's or Wren's office. On the other hand, an architect's detail derived its character not only from his preference for certain craftsmen (for example, Talman's team, p. 61) but also from his own knowledge of ornament; Wren, Hawksmoor and the Talmans were able to draw their own detail and also, undoubtedly, to invent it.

It would be rash to argue that craftsmen were more important in one age than in another, but the preceding pages contain many names and the plates illustrate many of their products, and anyone seeking a slick formula might characterize the age as one of craftsmanship rather than of taste. What can be said is that Baroque art depended on illusion, dexterity, exuberance and wit. Evelyn admired above all the ability of Gibbons to simulate the texture of fruits and fabrics and the fragility of flowers, lace and plumage; he admired hardly less the ability of Verrio to produce a half-credible extension of the real world into painted illusion. It is significant that the greatest illusion of all, scene-painting, was part of the decorative mural painter's job, and the Baroque had no scruples about painting flat surfaces to look like relief, wood to look like plaster or stone, plaster to look like bronze, or wood, stone or plaster to look like marble. The richness of the Guard Chamber at Kensington Palace came from wood-graining and marble-veining (p. 43). The interiors of churches were commonly finished in what the accounts call "stone colour", and this sometimes included the application of the colour to what was already stone.

Dexterity was largely a matter of training, and during the building of St Paul's Wren built up a tradition and a body of highly skilled craftsmen, who were supplemented in the years after 1685 by Huguenot refugee craftsmen from France. Gibbons was hardly superior in skill to Watson, the Chatsworth carver, or to William Emmett. Moreover, extreme naturalistic detail was not used where it would not show, and the works for which Gibbons's own shop was responsible included a number like the panels now in Windsor Parish Church which, as far as is known, came from the May-Gibbons-Verrio chapel in the Castle (Pl. 478). They were perhaps painted or gilded; they are in any case competent but not exceptional, and they deserve comparison with Gibbons's stonework outside the apse of St Paul's (Pl. 32), his wooden reredos in St James, Piccadilly, and that made by an imitator for St Peter, Liverpool (Pl. 479).

The qualities of exuberance and wit are sometimes distinct and sometimes overlapping. The lead pots and boys of Nost and the stone reliefs below them on the Flower Pot Gates of Hampton Court (Pl. 70), the trophies over the palace itself or those of Blenheim, the emblems of William and Mary and Queen Anne in the hall vestibule at Greenwich (Pl. 92) and the satyr masks outside under the buttresses of the dome – as hard on the naked eye as the roof bosses of Gothic (Pl. 94) – all these are exuberant. There is also wit at Greenwich, in the swags of shellfish on King William Block (Pl. 95) where one would normally expect garlands, a substitution similar to those of the 1660's in the galleries of the Amsterdam Town Hall.[129] Greenwich also bears, on the outside of the Painted Hall, that superb conceit composed entirely of marine emblems, the four winds blowing, a sea lion and unicorn with fishy tails, seaweed, dolphins of a species unknown to science, and trophies with ropes and anchors (Pl. 93). At Chelsea the corbels under the hall-chapel colonnade have animal head forms which grimace and give under the weight they carry (Pl. 577); at Hampton Court there are Emmett's lion-skin and orange windows (Pl. 68); at Wren's St Bride, Fleet Street the stock flaming urns of seventeenth-century tomb imagery, symbolizing life after death, are enlivened with gargoyle-like demons (Pl. 575); at Blenheim there are the pinnacles whose form summarizes the whole Blenheim epic (p. 80, Pl. 237).

[129] K. FREMANTLE, *The Baroque Town Hall of Amsterdam*, Utrecht, 1959, pls 41, 44, 57.

One of the commonest occasions for witty decoration was the mask combined with a keystone, scroll or other architectural projection. The combination amounts to a pun in that the projection has not only its expected formal meaning but a facial one as well; the latter is more obvious in some cases than in others, but the principle is the same as that of the aedicules on the outside of St Paul's (Pl. 56) and the doorways of St George-in-the-East (Pl. 415) – elements overlap and hold double or ambiguous functions. In the Greenwich dome the mask is unambiguous (Pl. 94), but over the round windows of Hampton Court and the doorways of the Kensington Orangery (Pls 64, 102) the face begins to be confused with foliage and shell-forms. At St Philip, Birmingham and the pavilion at Wrest the faces are broken up into the same ambiguous forms as the surrounding carvings, but eyes, nose, mouth, ears and hair are still identifiable (Pls 442, 578), just as they are in the folds draped over the urns of Drayton (Pl. 178). Others are still more broken, and while the face is certainly present in the shell-niche at the bottom of the stairs at Easton Neston (Pl. 290) although one may not realize it for some time, the keystone and scrolls of the door in the middle of the Long Library at Blenheim (Pl. 249) are completely ambiguous. The elements are familiar: the leaf like a forelock, the two flowers like popping eyes, the underside of the crown like a gaping mouth, the cartouche like a beard. The whole face seems on analysis not to be there at all, yet it is unmistakable. The evidence is there in the building, directly perceived though it may escape definition. The same might be said of the whole English Baroque style.

INDEX

Names of writers and authorities after 1800 are in italic
* Denotes a reference in the Bibliography. Plate numbers are in italic
Text figures are not noted separately

I PERSONS

Albemarle, 2nd Duke of, 57
Alberti, 2, 4
Aldersea, Mr, 112
Aldrich, Henry (1648–1710), 14, 46, 106, 115, 116, 118, *437–8, 523, 530–2*
Ammanati, 73
Ancaster, Robert Bertie, 1st Duke of, 84, 86; Peregrine Bertie, 2nd Duke of, 86
Anne, Queen, 13, 33, 42, 43, 57, 77, 80, 81, 96, 119, 128
Archer, Thomas (?1668–1743), 3, 7, 9, 12, 13, 14, 62–3, 69–72, 84, 90, 93, 94, 95, 97, 99, 100–1, 104, 105–6, 109, 110, 112, 119, 126–7, *151, 154–5, 167, 169–70, 191, 196–202, 205, 207–8, 368, 399, 402, 412–13, 422, 439–44, 486–7, 571–3, 578*
Argyll, John Campbell, 2nd Duke of, 11, 94
Artari, Alberto (1660-after 1725), 95, *390*; Giuseppe (1697–1769), 93
Arthur, 82
Atherton, Robert Vernon, 92
Aubrey, John, 6
Badeslade, T. (engraver), *147*
Bagutti, Giovanni (*fl.*1710–31), 77, 87, *126*
Baker, C. H. Collins,* 18 n, 87 n, 98 n
Baratta, Giovanni (1670–1747), 87
Barker, John (*fl.*1712), 107, *447*
Barry, Sir Charles, 68
Bastard family, 13, 14, 89, 90, 94 n, 98; John (*c.*1688–1770), 98, 109, 111, *319, 474–5, 491*
Beard, G. W., 71 n, 92 n, 126 n
Bell, Henry (*c.*1653–1717), 5, 97, *488*
Bellucci, Antonio (1654–1726), 87, 88
Benson, Benjamin, 7; Robert, *see* Bingley; William (1682–1754), 2, 7, 10, 11, 13, 43, 47, 49
Bernini, 10, 25, 36, 37, 44, 61, 72
Bess of Hardwick, 60
Bickham, George, 19 n, 21 n
Bingley, Robert Benson, Lord, 71, 72
Bird, Francis (1667–1731), 32, *53*
Blathwayt, William, 65
Blount, Sir Edward, 96
Bodt, Jean (1670–1745), 46, 72, *205–9*
Booth, A., 71 n
Borra (*fl.*1750–63), 126, *574*
Borromini, 10, 25, 80, 107, 118
Bott, *see* Bodt
Boujet, 58 n
Bourchier, 71
Bowles, J. (engraver), *133*
Boynton, L., 67 n
Bramante, 2, 4
Bridgeman, Charles, (d. 1738) 125
Bridges, George Rodney, 94 n; John, 73
Brown, Lancelot, 81, 124
Bruant, Libéral, 51
Brunetti, Gaetano (d.1758), 88, *114*
Buckingham, George Villiers, 2nd Duke of, 6, 64, 69, 92
Buckingham, John Sheffield, 1st Duke of, 10, 68–9

Burghclere, Winifred Lady, 69 n
Burlington, Richard Boyle, 3rd Earl of (1694–1753), 2, 8, 11, 111, 126
Burrough, Sir James (1691–1764), 114
Campbell, Colin (d.1729),* 2, 7, 8, 10, 11, 12, 13, 46, 58, 67, 83, 90, 99, 111, *221, 297*
see also Vitruvius Britannicus
Campen, Jacob van, 18
Capon, William (draughtsman), *497*
Carlisle, Charles Howard, 3rd Earl of, 13, 41, 75, 76, 77; Frederick, 5th Earl of, 76
Carpenter, Samuel (1660–1713), 76 77, *243*
Cartwright, Francis (*c.*1695–1758), 90, 94 n
Cary, Thomas 71
Catharine of Braganza, 19
Chafin, George, 90
Chandos, James Brydges, Duke of, 12, 87, 92, 94 n, 98, 107
Charleton, Walter, 10 n
Charles I, 35, 44
Charles II, 1, 4, 16, 18, 19, 21, 27, 28, 33–4, 36, 43, 49, 69, 124
Chéron, Louis (1660–1725), 56
Chester, Sir John, 95
Cibber, Caius Gabriel (1630–1700), 33, 35, 54 n, 56, 60, *17, 52, 54, 63*
Clarendon, Edward Hyde, 1st Earl of, 57, 59, 117; Henry Hyde, 2nd Earl of, 36, 57, 59
Clarke, B. F. L.,* 105 n, 107 n
Clarke, George (1661–1736), 93, 115–19, *521, 524, 527, 533*
Claude, 3, 15
Clear, Thomas, 108
Clive, Robert Clive, Baron, 84
Clutterbuck, R., 25 n
Cobb, Gerald*
Cobham, Sir Richard Temple, Baron and Viscount, 13, 84
Codrington, Christopher, 118
Colbert, 13, 33
Coleman, William (*fl.*1707), 81
Colvin, H. M.,* 46 n, 52 n, 67 n, 90 n, 116 n, 117 n
Conway, Edward, Earl of, 58, 64
Cornforth, John, 66 n, 68 n
Cousin, René (*fl.*1675–94), 17
Craven, William, Earl of, 68
Croft-Murray, Edward,* 55, 56
Damini, Vincenzo (*fl.*1720–41), 107
De Beer, E. S.*
Defoe, Daniel,* 41, 47, 87, 88
Delaval, Francis, 84; George, 84, 85
Denham, Sir John (1615–69), 4
Desgots, Claude, 41 n, 125 n
Devonshire, William Cavendish, 1st Duke of, 12, 41, 60–3, 75; William, 6th Duke of, 61
Dickinson, William (*c.*1671–1725), 43, 67, 99
Dodington, Bubb, 84; George, 84
Dormer, Henry, 64
Downes, K.,* 26 n, 43 n, 76 n, 101 n, 104 n, 105 n, 116 n, 120 n

Draper, M. P. G., 71 n
Draper, William, 52
Du Cerceau, Jacques Androuet, 44, 92
Duchêne, Achille, 81
Duncombe, Charles, 92; Thomas, 92
Dunlop, Ian, 87 n
Eboral, Thomas, 95
Eden, W. A., 100 n
Elsheimer, 3
Elsworth, John (*fl.*1703–15), 76
Emmett, William (*c.*1641–*c.*1700), 35, 40, 128, *68*; William (1671–1736), 46–7
Emmott, Christopher, 94
Enthoven, E. J.*
Etty family, 14; William (d.1734), 84, 92
Evelyn, John,* 3, 18 n, 21, 22, 50, 52, 57, 69, 128
Exeter, John Cecil, 5th Earl of, 55
Fairfax, Brian, 69
Falconieri, Paolo, 46, 70
Falda, Giovanni Battista, 30
Fanelli, Franceso (*fl.*1608–65), 127, *72*
Faulkner, T. (engraver), *504*
Fermor, *see* Lempster
Field, John*
Fiennes, Celia,* 62, 124
Fitch, John (*fl.*1663–1700), 62–3
Fleetwood-Hesketh, P., 109 n
Flitcroft, Henry, 92, 95
Fontana, Carlo, 10, 15, 99
Frankland, Sir Thomas, 105
Fréart, Roland, 52, 94
Frederick I of Brandenburg, 46
Frederik Hendrik, Prince of Orange, 18
Fremantle, K., 18 n, 128 n
Fuller, Isaac II (*fl.*1678–1709), 23
Galilei, Alessandro (1691–1737), 46–7, 82, *255*
Ganay, Ernest de, 125 n
Gandon, James, 10 n, 69
Garrett, Daniel, (*fl.*1736–50), 126
George I, 7, 10, 47, 54, 98, 105
Gerbier, Sir Balthasar (1591–1667), 68
Germain, Sir John, 66
Gibbons, Grinling (1648–1720), 18, 21, 22, 24, 30, 40, 44, 77, 80, 81, 88, 101, 109, 128, *4, 8, 11–12, 32, 41, 120, 244, 248, 436*
Gibbs, James (1682–1754), 11, 13, 14, 15, 22, 59, 87, 93, 99, 104, 106–7, 108, 110, 114–15, 119–20, 126, *298–300, 364, 404, 407–9, 423, 459–62, 525–6, 539–40, 570, 574*
Girouard, Mark, 65 n
Giulio Romano, 2
Goodhart-Rendel, H. S., 51
Gotch, C., 82 n
Gotch, J. A., 8 n
Goudge, Edward, 55
Grange, Richard, 90
Greber, Jacob, 112
Green, David,* 77 n, 97 n

II PLACES

III OTHER NAMES, TITLES AND TOPICS

1.   May. Windsor Castle. St George's Hall (1682–4, destroyed).

2.   Windsor Castle. Queen's Drawing Room (*c.*1676, destroyed).

3. Windsor Castle from the north, *c*.1770.

4. Windsor Castle. Charles II Dining Room (*c*.1676).

5. Windsor Castle. Upper Ward, looking west, *c.*1770.

6. Windsor Castle. Window in Henry III's Tower.

7. Windsor Castle. Queen's Presence Chamber (*c.*1678).

8. Windsor Castle. King's Chapel (1680–4, destroyed).

9. Antonio Verrio. Catherine of Braganza as Britannia (c.1678). Queen's Audience Chamber, Windsor.

10. May. Windsor Castle. Queen's Guard Chamber (1679–80, destroyed).

11–12. Grinling Gibbons and Arnold Quellin. Angels from Whitehall (1686). Burnham, Somerset.

13. Wren. Chelsea Hospital. Portico.

14. Chelsea Hospital. Figure Court (1682–9).

15. Wren. Winchester Palace (1682–5, destroyed).

16. Wren. Chelsea Hospital. West outer
frontispiece.

17. Caius Gabriel Cibber. The Monument: Charles II
succouring the City of London (1674).

20. Wren. St Mary Abchurch (1681-6, painted after 1708).

19. Wren. St James, Garlickhythe. Lantern (after 1708).

18. Wren. St Stephen, Walbrook. Steeple (1672–after 1708).

22. Wren. St Antholin (1678–82, destroyed).

21. Wren. St James, Garlickhythe (1676–83).

23. Wren. St Mary-le-Bow. Steeple (1680).   24. Wren. St Vedast. Steeple (1694–7).

25. Wren. The Great Model for St Paul's (1673–4).

26. Wren. St Andrew, Holborn. Tower (1703).

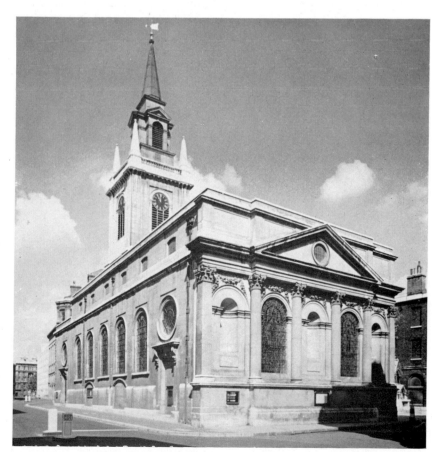

27. Wren. St Laurence Jewry from east (1671–7).

28. Wren. St Paul's from south-east (1675–1710).

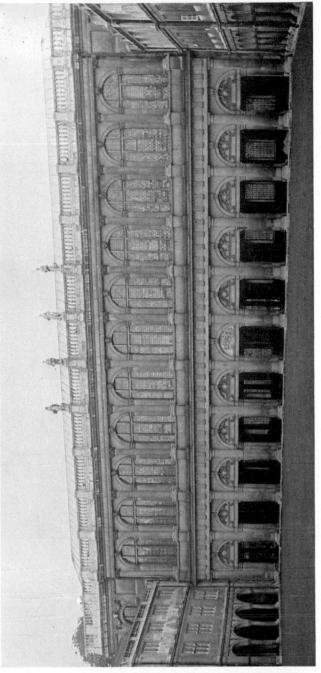

32. St Paul's. Relief on apse exterior.

29. Inigo Jones. Whitehall Banqueting House (1619–22).

30. Wren. Cambridge, Trinity College Library (1676–84).

31. Wren. St Paul's. Nave capitals.

33. St Paul's. Interior looking west.

34. St Paul's. Dome and west towers (1704–10).

36. St Paul's. South transept.

35. St Paul's. South-west tower.

37.   Wren. St Stephen, Walbrook. Dome.

38.   Wren. St Paul's. Crossing soon after completion.

39. St Paul's. Dome.

40. St Paul's. Crossing from north-west gallery.

41.   Grinling Gibbons. St Paul's. Choir Stalls (1696–8).

42.   Wren. St Paul's. Choir in 1706.

43. St Paul's. Interior looking east.

44. St Paul's. View towards north transept.

45. St Paul's. Impost of north transept window.

46. St Paul's. Detail of west nave bay.

47. St Paul's. West bay of nave.

48. St Paul's. Niche in crossing pier.

49. Wren. Trinity college Library, Cambridge. Door on river front.

50. St Paul's. Window on west front.

51 St Paul's. Dean's Door.

52   St. Paul's. Gable of south transept.

53.   Francis Bird. The Conversion of St Paul (1706). St Paul's. West front.

54. Caius Gabriel Cibber. Triumph of Hercules (1694). Hampton Court.

55. Wren. St Michael Royal. Steeple (1713).

56. Wren. St Paul's. Detail of nave screen-wall.

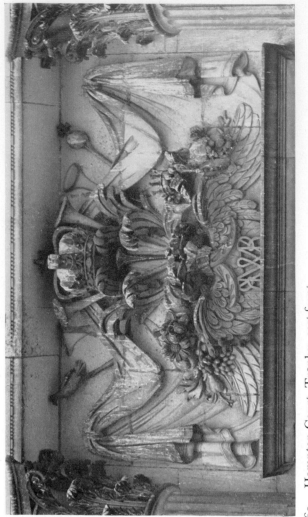

58. Hampton Court. Keystone, east front.

57. Wren. Hampton Court. East front (1689–95).

60. Hampton Court. Trophy, east front.

59. Hampton Court. Door hood relief, east front.

62. Wren. Hampton Court. South front.

64. Hampton Court. False window, south front.

61. Hampton Court. Trophy, south front.

63. Cibber. Arms on south front, Hampton Court (1692).

65.   Hampton Court. Exedra, Fountain Court.

66.   Hampton Court. Fountain Court.

67. Hampton Court. Colonnade in Clock Court.

68 William Emmett. Window in Fountain Court.

69. Hampton Court. Urn in Clock Court.

73. Edward Pierce. Urn from Hampton Court. Windsor, East terrace.

72. Hampton Court. Diana Fountain, Bushy Park (before 1640–1713).

74. Wren. Sketch for Whitehall Palace (1698).

75. Wren. Whitehall project. Elevation D (reconstruction of worn drawing).

77. Wren office. Whitehall project. Banqueting House (A) and block C.

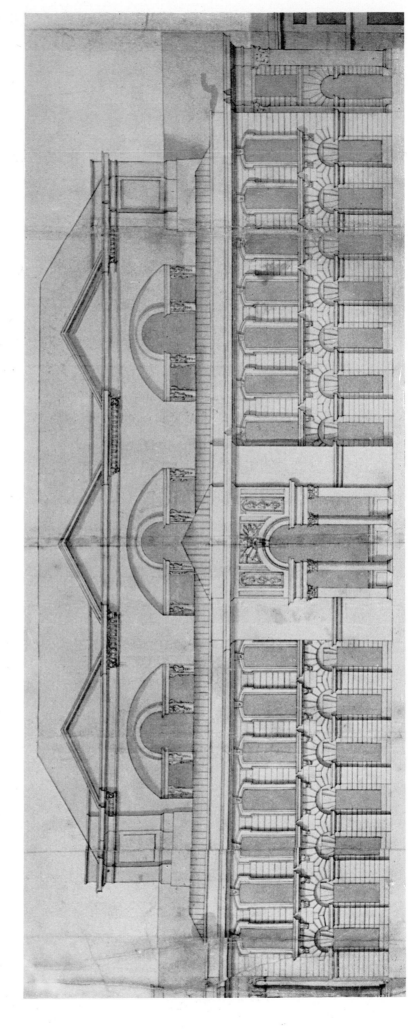

78. Wren office. Whitehall project. Parliament block (F).

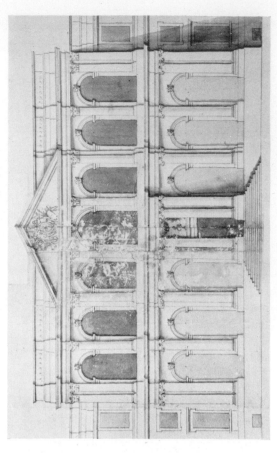

80. Wren. Smaller Whitehall project. Block H.

82. Wren. Smaller Whitehall project. Block G.

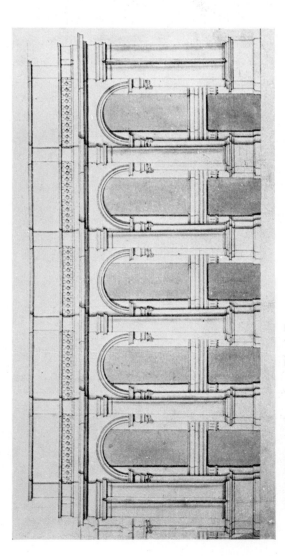

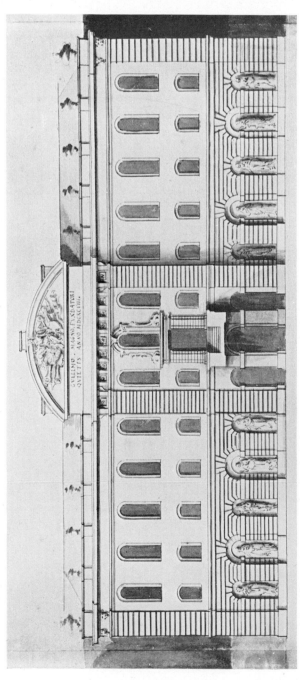

79. Wren. Whitehall project. Block E.

81. Hawksmoor. Project for south front, Windsor Castle (1698).

85. Kensington Palace. Orangery. Interior.

83. Wren and Hawksmoor. Kensington Palace. King's Gallery (1695–6).

84. Hawksmoor. Kensington Palace. Orangery (1704–5).

86.   Webb. Greenwich Hospital. King Charles Block (1663–9).

87.   Wren and Hawksmoor. Greenwich. King William Block. West side (1698–1707).

88.   Greenwich Hospital. King William Block. East side.

89. Greenwich Hospital. Queen Anne Block. West side (1725–8).

90. Greenwich Hospital from river terrace.

91. Greenwich Hospital from the Isle of Dogs.

92.　Wren and Thornhill. Greenwich. Vestibule of Painted Hall (1698–1705 and 1726–7).

93. Robert Jones. Sea creatures, winds and trophies. Greenwich (1701).

95. Robert Jones. Capitals in King William Court (1702).

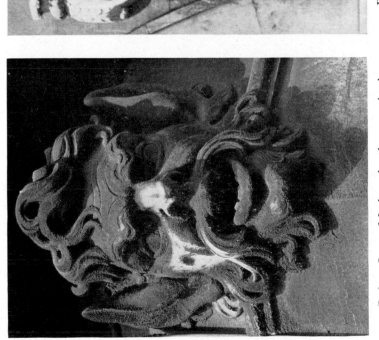

94. Robert Jones. Mask under dome peristyle. Greenwich (1701).

96.   Wren and Hawksmoor. Greenwich. Queen Anne Block. Court (1700–17).

97.   Greenwich Hospital. Queen Anne Block. Overdoor in court.

98.   Greenwich Hospital. Door under Painted Hall.

99.   Greenwich. King William Block. South front window.

100.   Hawksmoor. Greenwich. Queen Anne Block. East side (1700–3).

101.   Greenwich Hospital. Door to Painted Hall.

102.   Benjamin Jackson? Mask. Kensington Orangery.

103. Thornhill. Greenwich Hospital. Painted Hall (1708–12).

104. Samuel Watson. Chatsworth. Detail of Chapel gallery.

105 Wren and Robert Streater. Oxford. Sheldonian Theatre (1663–9).

107. Louis Laguerre. Christ in Glory (1689–93). Chatsworth, chapel.

106. William Talman. Chatsworth. Chapel (1687–93).

109. Antonio Verrio. King's Staircase, Hampton Court (1700–2).

108. Burghley. State Dressing Room (c. 1689).

110. Verrio. Burghley. Heaven Room (1694–5).

111. Verrio. Detail of cove. Burghley, Dining Room and Drawing Room (1690–3).

112. Verrio. Detail of cove. Burghley, Dining Room and Drawing Room (1690–3).

113. Louis Laguerre. Apollo and Phaeton (1689–94). Chatsworth, Music Room.

114. Little Stanmore. Chandos Mausoleum. Tomb by Grinling Gibbons (1717), paintings by Gaetano Brunetti (1736).

115.   John James. Little Stanmore Church from south (1714–5).

116.   Louis Laguerre. Little Stanmore Church. Interior looking north-west.

117.   Little Stanmore Church. Interior looking north-east.

119. Blenheim. Caryatids on west front.

120. Grinling Gibbons (restored). Blenheim. Trophy on east colonnade.

118. Laguerre. Blenheim. Saloon (c.1720).

122.   Thornhill. Glorification of Marlborough (1716). Blenheim, Hall.

121.   Thornhill. Sabine Room, Chatsworth (1706–7).

124. Lanscroon. The story of Perseus (c.1698). Burley-on-the-Hill.

123. Gerard Lanscroon. Hercules and Justice striking Envy, Hatred and Malice (1712). Drayton.

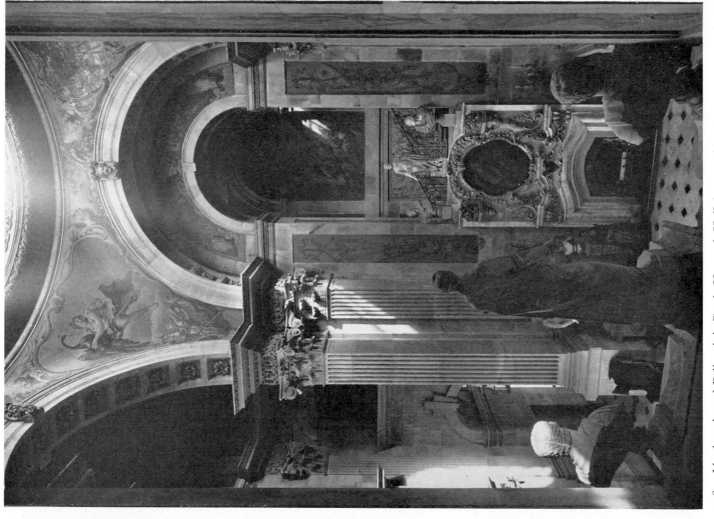

126.   Vanbrugh and Pellegrini. Castle Howard. Hall (1702–12).

125.   G. A. Pellegrini. A Roman triumph (1708). Kimbolton.

127. Sir Roger Pratt. Clarendon House, Piccadilly (1664–7, destroyed).

128. Ashdown House (c.1664).

129. William Winde (?) and William Stanton. Belton (1685–8).

130. Robert Hooke. Bedlam (1674–6, destroyed).

131. William Rudhall. Hanbury Hall (1701).

132. May. Eltham Lodge (1663–4).

133.   Montagu House, Bloomsbury. The second house (1686–8, destroyed).

134.   Boughton. North wing (*c*.1690–4).

135.   Petworth. West front (*c*.1688–90).

136.

137.

136–8.   Petworth. Details of west front.

139.   John Selden. Petworth. Trophy in Carved Room.

140. Talman. Chatsworth. South front (1687–9).

141. Chatsworth. Terrace (1696) and west front (1700–2).

142. Talman. Chatsworth. Detail of south front.

143. Chatsworth. Terrace. Frosted bust

144. Chatsworth. Terrace. Mask.

145. Talman. Trianon project for William III. Perspective.

146. Talman. Trianon project for William III. Entrance front.

147. Talman. Kiveton (1694–1704, destroyed).

148. Burley-on-the-Hill. North front (1696–8).

149. Talman. Dyrham. East front (1700–3).

150. Talman. Dyrham. Orangery.

153. Samuel Watson. Panel from east front, Chatsworth (1696).

152. Samuel Watson. Setting for anonymous relief (1693). Chatsworth, Grotto.

151. Nadauld. Dolphins. Chatsworth, Cascade House (1702).

155. Chatsworth. Cascade House. Interior.

154. Archer. Chatsworth. Cascade House (1702).

156.   Talman. Chatsworth. East wall of court (1688–92).

157.   Chatsworth. Panelling in chapel.

158.   Chatsworth. Sea-horse fountain in south garden.

159.   Chatsworth. Trophy panel on west garden wall.

160.   Talman. Dyrham. Detail of east front.

161.   John Harvey. Eagle (1703). Dyrham, east front.

162.   Cound Hall. East front (1704).

163.   Edward Strong? Addiscombe House (1702–3, destroyed).

164.   Cound. West doorhead.

165.   Cound. Panel on west front.

166.   Cound. Capital on west front.

167. Archer. Roehampton House (1710–12). Steps. The upper wings are modern.

168. Herriard Park (1704, destroyed). West front.

169. Roehampton House. West front.

170. Archer. Cliveden (after 1706, destroyed).

171. Anonymous project for a house, c. 1700.

172. Talman and Benjamin Jackson. Drayton. South gate.

173. Talman and Jackson. Drayton. Hall front and north side of court (1702–3)

174. Drayton. Trophy over Hall door.

175. Drayton. South front.

176. Drayton. South side of court (before 1676) and colonnade (after 1706).

178. Drayton. Urn on Hall front.

182. Drayton. Detail of Hall front.

177. Drayton. Frieze over Hall door.

179–81. Drayton. Details of south gate piers.

185. Benham Park. Pier from east gate, Hampstead Marshall.

183. Hampstead Marshall. South gate piers.

184. Edward Pierce? Hampstead Marshall. North-east gate piers.

186.   Newby Hall. West front (*c.*1700).

187.   Wotton House, Wotton Underwood. North front and east wing (1704).

188.   John James. Appuldurcombe House (1701–10).

189.   Bramham Park. North-east front (before 1715).

190.   Beningbrough Hall. North front (before 1716).

191.   Archer. Heythrop House (begun *c*.1705). State before 1870.

192. Beningbrough. The Hall.

193. Beningbrough. Door at stair-foot.

194. Beningbrough, Chamfered corridor arch.

195. Beningbrough. Centre window of north front.

196.   Archer. Heythrop. Capital.

197.   Archer. Aynho. Detail of west wing (1707–11).

198.   Archer. Heythrop. Window on north-west front.

199.   Heythrop. Window on south-west front.

200. Heythrop. North-west front after reconstruction.

201. Heythrop. South-east front. Photograph before 1870.

202. Heythrop. Entrance door-head.

203. Hawksmoor. Easton Neston. East front (1702).

204. Easton Neston. West front.

205.   Bodt and Archer. Wentworth Castle. South front (1710–14).

206.   Wentworth Castle. Relief on south front.

207. Wentworth Castle. South front. Upper window.

208. Wentworth Castle. South front. Lower window.

209. Wentworth Castle. South front. Overdoor relief.

211. Easton Neston. Staircase.

210. Hawksmoor. Easton Neston. North front.

213. Easton Neston. Niche in Gallery.

212. Easton Neston. Staircase.

214. Vanbrugh and Hawksmoor. Castle Howard. South elevation (1699).

215. Vanbrugh. Castle Howard. South front (1702–10).

216. Vanbrugh. Blenheim. Trophy on south front (c.1710).

217. Vanbrugh and Hawksmoor. Blenheim. South elevation (1704–5).

218. Vanbrugh. Blenheim. South front (1705–16).

219. Blenheim. Project for south front (published 1715).

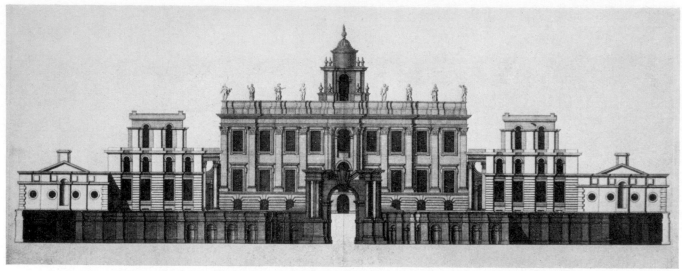

220. Hawksmoor. Easton Neston. Project for west front (published 1715).

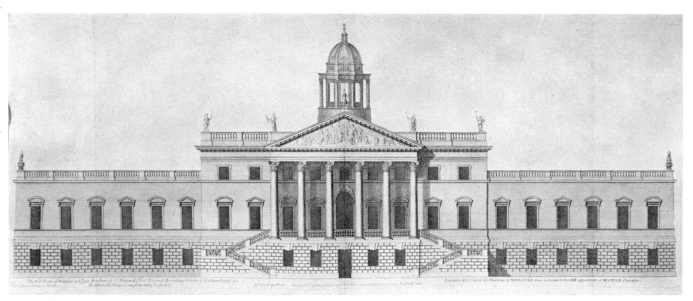

221. Campbell. Wanstead (1715) with proposed lantern (published 1717).

222. Vanbrugh. Castle Howard. Kitchen wing from north.

223.　Hawksmoor. Easton Neston. Hall, before alteration.

224.　Easton Neston. Door in Gallery.

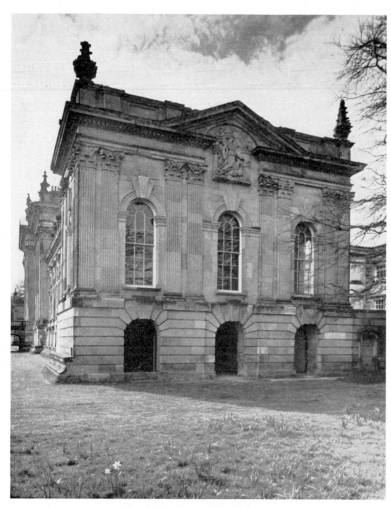

225.　Vanbrugh. Castle Howard. South-east end (before 1706).

226.　Castle Howard. North corridor.

227. Castle Howard. North front (begun 1702) and north-east wing (begun 1700).

228. Vanbrugh. Blenheim. North front.

229.   Chatsworth. West pediment.

230.   Castle Howard. South pediment.

231. Blenheim. North pediment.

232. Woolton. North-west pediment.

233. Chicheley church. East pediment (1709).

234. Petworth. Gate-pier trophy.

236. Hawksmoor. Blenheim. Hensington Gate, formerly in east garden.

238. Hawksmoor. Blenheim. Ceiling of Green Drawing Room (1723-4).

235. Hawksmoor. Blenheim. Woodstock Gate (1723).

237. Blenheim. Corner tower.

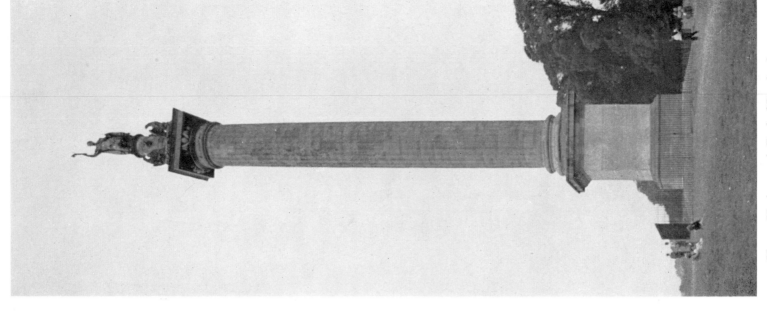

241. Henry Herbert, 9th Earl of Pembroke. Blenheim. The Column (1730).

239. Vanbrugh. Blenheim. South front of Kitchen block.

240. Vanbrugh. Blenheim. West front.

242.   Vanbrugh. Blenheim. The Bridge.

243.   Samuel Carpenter. Castle Howard. Capital in Hall.   244.   Grinling Gibbons. Blenheim. Capital in Hall.

245.   Vanbrugh and Hawksmoor. Blenheim. Hall.

247. Vanbrugh and Hawksmoor. Blenheim. Kitchen court tower.

246. Vanbrugh. Blenheim. East Gate.

249. Hawksmoor and William Townesend. Blenheim. Long Library doorcase.

248. Hawksmoor and Gibbons. Blenheim. Saloon doorcase (1712).

250.   Vanbrugh. Blenheim. East side of north court.

251.   Hawksmoor. Blenheim. Long Library (1722–5).

252.   Vanbrugh. Blenheim. Kitchen court.

253.   Hawksmoor and Isaac Mansfield. South dome of Long Library.

254. Vanbrugh. Kimbolton. West front (1707–9).

255. Vanbrugh and Alessandro Galilei. Kimbolton. East front (c.1719).

256. Vanbrugh. Kimbolton.
Detail of north front.

257. Blenheim. Internal
court.

258.   Vanbrugh. Claremont. Belvedere (*c*.1720).

259.   Vanbrugh. Swinstead. Belvedere (*c*.1720).

260.   Vanbrugh. Claremont (1715–20, destroyed). View *c*.1750.

261. Vanbrugh. Kings Weston. Garden (east) front (1711–14).

262. Kings Weston. Entrance (south) front.

263. Kings Weston. Niche on staircase.

264. Thomas Sumsion. Kings Weston. Urn (1717).

265. Kings Weston. Brewhouse.

266. Kings Weston. Staircase.

267. Kings Weston. West loggia (*c.*1718).

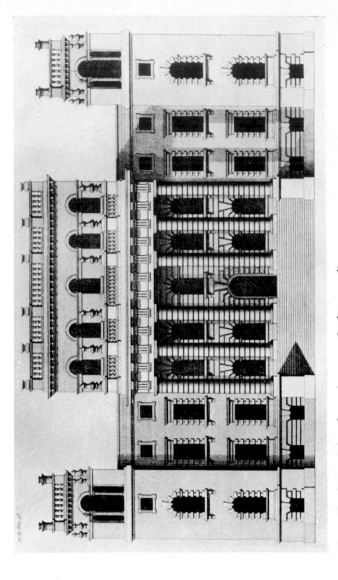

269. Eastbury. West front (c.1724–38, destroyed).

268. Vanbrugh. Eastbury. First project (c.1715).

271. Eastbury. North wing.

270. Eastbury. West arch of north court.

272. Vanbrugh. Seaton Delaval. From north (1718–29).

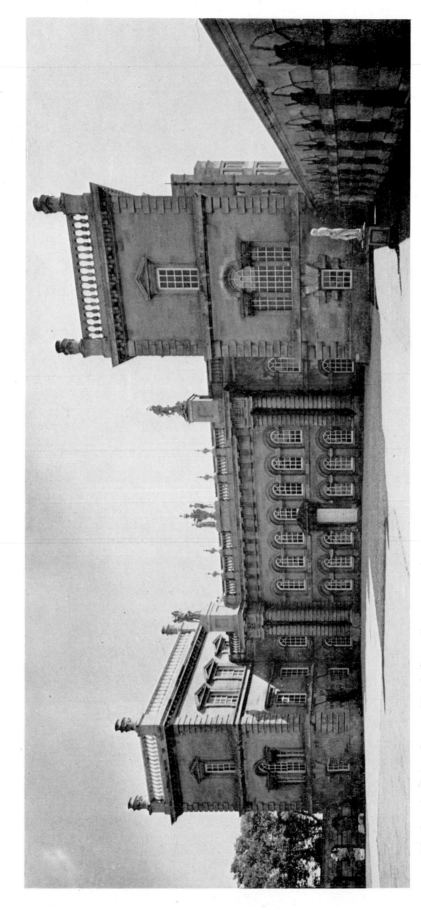

273. Vanbrugh. Grimsthorpe. North front (begun 1723).

274.   Seaton Delaval. South front.

275.   Seaton Delaval. North front.

276.   Seaton Delaval. Hall (gutted 1822).

277.   Seaton Delaval. Stable.

278.   Vanbrugh. Grimsthorpe. Hall.

279.   Grimsthorpe. Hall fireplace.

280.   Hampton Court. Fireplace in Prince of Wales's Bedroom.

281–2.   Hampton Court. Fireplaces in Prince of Wales's Drawing Room and Presence Chamber.

284. Vanbrugh. Audley End. Staircase and screen (c.1708).

283. Vanbrugh and Hawksmoor. Grimsthorpe. Chapel (after 1726).

286. Vanbrugh. Esher Old Church. Newcastle pew (1724).

285. Vanbrugh (and Hawksmoor?). Grimsthorpe. Door in hall gallery.

288. Castle Howard. Door in Saloon (destroyed).

287. Stowe. Vanbrugh's north portico (c.1720).

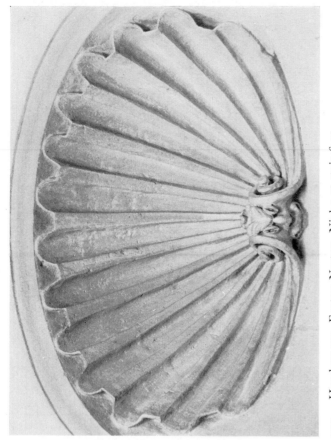

290. Hawksmoor. Easton Neston. Niche at stair-foot.

291. Vanbrugh. Grimsthorpe. Panel in hall.

289. Vanbrugh. Seaton Delaval. Kitchen.

292   Vanbrugh and Pellegrini. The *Fall of Phaeton* and the *Four Elements* (1709–12). Castle Howard.

293.   Vanbrugh. Seaton Delaval. Detail of north front.

294. Moor Park. Hall ceiling (after 1730).

295.   Moor Park. Hall.

296. Thornhill. Wimpole. Chapel (1721–4).

297. Colin Campbell and Francesco Sleter. Mereworth. Gallery (*c*.1720–5).

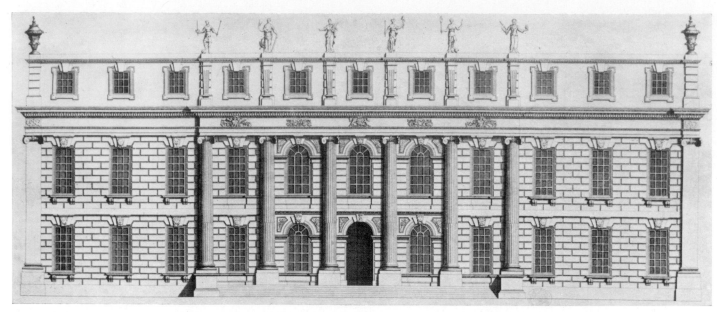

298. Gibbs. Cannons. South front (1719–20, destroyed).

299. Cannons. East front (destroyed).

300. Gibbs. Ditchley. North front (1720–5).

301.   John Price. Project for Chandos House, Cavendish Square (1720).

302.   Bridgwater. Castle Street. North side (1723–5).

303.   John Nost. George I (bronze, 1717–22). Birmingham.

304.   Bridgwater. Castle Street. Doorway.

305. Nathaniel Ireson. Crowcombe. South front (begun 1734).

306. Chettle House (c.1720).

307. Crowcombe. North front.

308. Ven House. South front (c.1730).

311. Crowcombe. Capital.

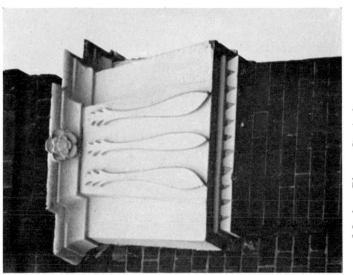

314. Chettle. Capital.

310. Marlow Place. Capital.

313. Marlow Place. Capital.

309. Crowcombe. West front.

312. Marlow Place. East side.

315. Bishopsworth Manor.

316. Benjamin Holloway. The Lions, Bridgwater (c.1725).

317. Widcombe Manor, Bath. South front (c.1727).

318. Weymouth House, Bath (destroyed). 319. John Bastard. Poole. Thompson House (1746–9).

320. The Ivy, Chippenham (c.1728).

321. William Wakefield. Duncombe Park (begun 1713). Original east front.

322. Duncombe Park. West front.

323. Duncombe Park. Hall as reconstructed.

324. Gilling Castle. Hall.

325–6.   William Wakefield. Atherton Hall (begun 1723, destroyed) and surviving wing.

327.   Duncombe Park. Detail of west front.

328.   Kettlethorpe Hall, Wakefield (1727).

329.   William Wakefield. Gilling Castle. Court.

330.   Farfield Hall (1728).

331. Wentworth Woodhouse. West front (1725–8).

332–3. Wentworth Woodhouse. Detail of west front.

334. Wentworth Woodhouse. Relief on west front.

335. Thomas White. Worcester. Guildhall. Relief (1721–4).

336. Wentworth Woodhouse. West doorhead.

337. Aldby Park. East pediment (1726).

338. Compton Verney. South front (1714).

339. Richmond, Surrey. Trumpeter's House (*c.*1709).

340. Netherhampton House.

341. Hale Manor, Lancs. (*c.*1705).

342. Emmott Hall (1737).

343. Brizlincote Hall (1714).

344. House near Bredgar, Kent (1719).

345. Woodnewton Hall.

346. Burford. House in High Street.

347. Salisbury. No. 68 The Close.

348. Woodstock. Hope House.

349. Oxford. Vanbrugh House.

350. Warwick. Church Street and Jury Street. Post-1694 houses and Court House (1725–8).

351. Schomberg House, Pall Mall (1698, reconstructed).

352. Lichfield. House in Bore Street.

353-4. Blandford. Detail of Red Lion Inn; House in Salisbury Road.

355-6. Blandford. Greyhound Inn; capital in Market Place.

357. King's Lynn. Duke's Head (begun 1683).

358. Wincanton. White Horse Inn (1733).

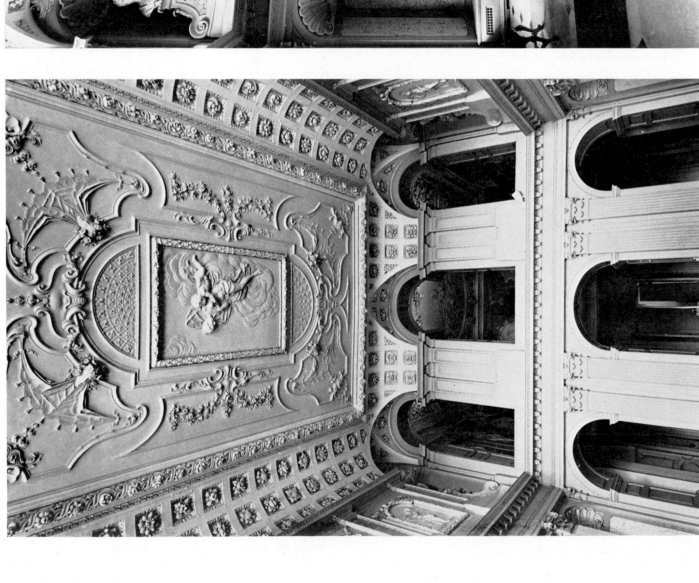

359–60. Barnsley Park (c.1720). Hall.

365. Marlow Place. Hall.

364. Ditchley. Detail of garden room.

361–2. Barnsley Park. West and south fronts.

363. Barnsley Park. Doorcase at stair-foot.

366.   Finchcocks, Goudhurst (1725).

367.   Moor Park. West front (1721).

368.   Archer. Harcourt (Bingley) House (1722).

369. John James. Warbrook, Eversley (1724).

370. Thornhill Park (c.1720).

371. Portico from Wricklemarsh (1721). Beckenham.

372. Iver Grove (1722–4).

373. Avington Park. Portico.

374.   Francis Smith Stoneleigh Abbey. West front (begun 1714).

375.   Francis Smith. Chicheley Hall. Detail of west front (1720–5).

376. Chicheley. West front.

377. Chicheley. South front.

379. Chicheley. East front.

378. Stoneleigh. Window, west front.

380. Chicheley. West door.

381. Chillington Hall. South front (1724).

382. Elford Hall (destroyed). South front.

383. Calke Abbey. South front, c. 1734. From a painting.

384. Mawley Hall from south-east (1730).

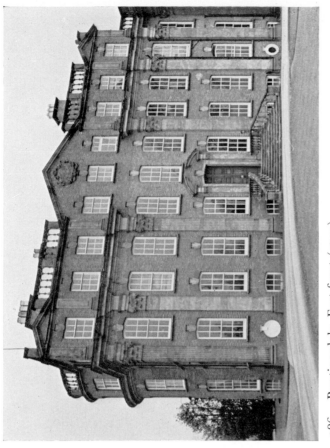

385. Kinlet Hall. West front (1727–9).

386. Buntingsdale. East front (1721).

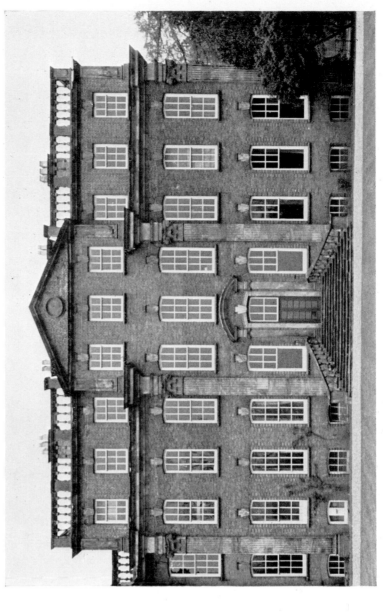

388. Buntingsdale. West front.

387. Swynnerton. South front (after 1714).

390. Sutton Scarsdale. Detail of upper room.

392-3. Mawley. Capitals in south-west bedroom and hall.

389. Francis Smith. Sutton Scarsdale (begun 1724, gutted). East front.

391. Mawley. Niche in hall.

395. Mawley. Hall chimney-piece.

396. Mawley. Marquetry room.

394. Mawley. Staircase.

399.   Archer. St Paul, Deptford (1712–30). Interior.

397.   Great Witley. Church (1747) looking west.

398.   Great Witley. Church. Detail of ceiling.

401. St Anne, Limehouse. Interior.

400. Hawksmoor. St Anne, Limehouse from east (1714–30).

404. Gibbs. St Mary-le-Strand from west (1714–17).

403. St Anne, Limehouse from west.

402. St Paul, Deptford from west.

407. Gibbs. Steeple for St Clement Danes (1720).

406. Hawksmoor. St Mary Woolnoth from west (1716–27).

405. James. St George, Hanover Square from north-west (1720–5).

408-9. Gibbs. St Mary-le-Strand. Exterior from south-east and interior.

411. St Mary Woolnoth. Interior.

410. St Anne, Limehouse. West porch.

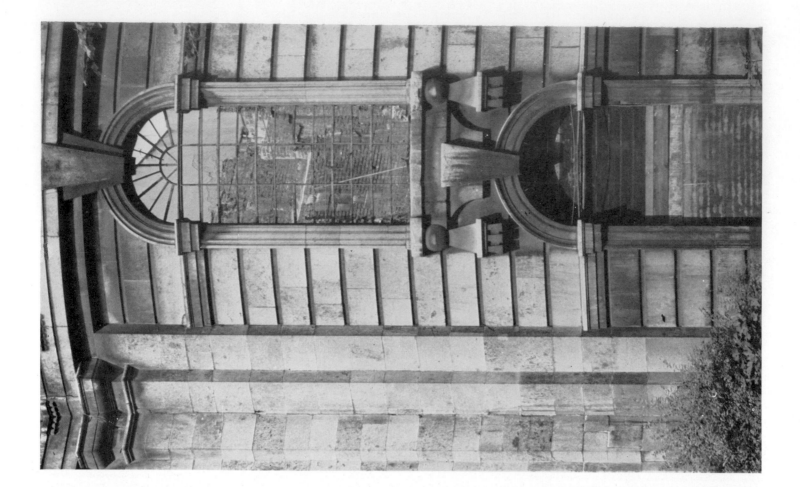

412–13. Archer. St John, Smith Square. Exterior and corner detail (1713–29).

414-15. Hawksmoor St George-in-the-East. Exterior from south and gallery door (1714-29).

416. St George-in-the-East. Interior (destroyed).

417. Hawksmoor. St Alfege, Greenwich. Interior (1712–18).

418. St Alfege, Greenwich from south-east. Steeple by James (1730).

419–20. St Alfege, Greenwich. East end.

421. St Mary Woolnoth. North wall.

422. Archer. St Paul, Deptford. Ceiling detail.

423. Gibbs. St Mary-le-Strand. Apse detail

424. Hawksmoor. St Anne, Limehouse. East door.

425. Hawksmoor. Christ Church, Spitalfields (1714–29). Spire.

426. Hawksmoor. St George, Bloomsbury. Apse ceiling.

428. St George, Bloomsbury. Interior looking north-east.

427. St George, Bloomsbury (1716—31). South front.

430. Christ Church, Spitalfields. Interior.

429. Christ Church, Spitalfields. West front.

432. James and Hawksmoor. St John, Horselydown (1727–33, destroyed).

431. James. St George, Hanover Square. North wall.

433-4. James and Hawksmoor. St Luke, Old Street (1727–33). Interior (destroyed) and exterior.

436. Grinling Gibbons and Hawksmoor? Canterbury. Former
archbishop's throne (c.1704).

435. Hawksmoor? Ockham. King mausoleum (1735).

437–8. Henry Aldrich. All Saints, Oxford (1706–9, steeple 1717–20).

440. St Philip, Birmingham. Interior c.1825.

439. Archer. St Philip, Birmingham from south-west (1710–25).

441–2.   St Philip, Birmingham. Interior capitals and west lobby window.

443–4.   St Philip, Birmingham. East and west doors.

445. Lincoln St Giles. Former St Peter-at-Arches (c.1720–4), rebuilt 1935–6.

446. St Modwen, Burton-on-Trent (1719–26).

447. St Alkmund, Whitchurch (Salop) (1712–13).

448. Burton-on-Trent. Interior

450. John Platt. St Paul, Sheffield (1720–40, destroyed).

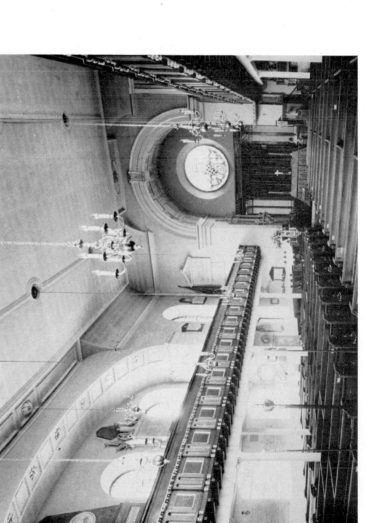

449. James. St George, Tiverton (1714–33).

451–2. James. St Mary, Twickenham (1713–15).

453. John Price. St George, Great Yarmouth from north-east (1714–16).

454–5. St George, Great Yarmouth. Exterior from south-west and corner door.

456. St George, Great Yarmouth. Interior.

457. Price. St George, Southwark (1734–6).

458. Price. Laleham. Tower (1731).

459. Gibbs. St Martin-in-the-Fields. Project elevation.

460. Gibbs. St Martin-in-the-Fields. Exterior (1722–6).

461. St Martin-in-the-Fields. Project section.

462. St Martin-in-the-Fields. Interior.

463.   Aynho. Church from south-east (1723–5).

464–5.   Gayhurst. Church (1728).

466. Edward and Thomas Woodward. St Swithin, Worcester (1736).

467. All Saints, Worcester (1738–42).

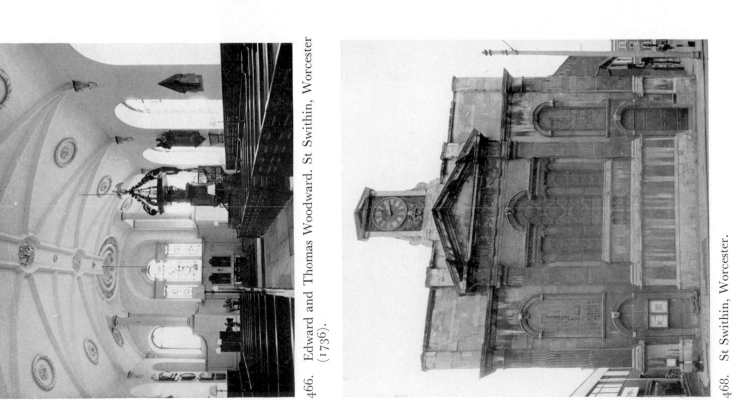

468. St Swithin, Worcester.

469–70. St Nicholas, Worcester (1730–5).

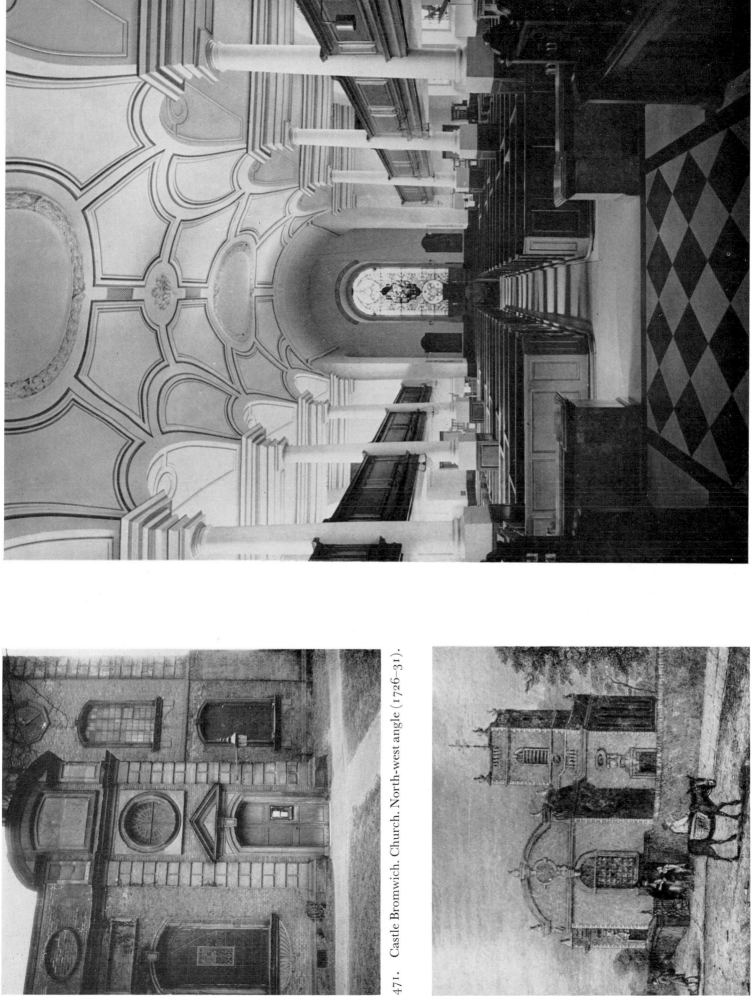

471. Castle Bromwich. Church. North-west angle (1726-31).

472. St Thomas, Stourbridge (begun 1726). Before alteration.

473. St Thomas, Stourbridge. Interior looking west.

475. Blandford. Interior looking west.

476. Richard Prescot. Reredos from St Peter, Liverpool (c.1704). North Meols.

474. John Bastard. SS. Peter and Paul, Blandford (1735–9).

478. Windsor Church. Panel from Royal Chapel in Castle.

479. Detail of reredos. North Meols.

477. Chancel panel. North Meols.

480–1. Nathaniel Ireson. Bruton. Chancel (1743).

481.

482. Gayhurst. Capital.

483. Honiley. Church (1723).

485. Stoke Doyle. South door (1722–5).

484. Adderley. West window (1712).

486–7. Hale (Hants.). Doors.

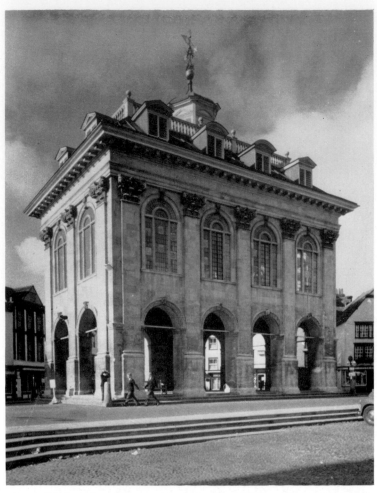

488. Henry Bell. King's Lynn. Custom House (1683).

489. Christopher Kempster. Abingdon. Town House (1680).

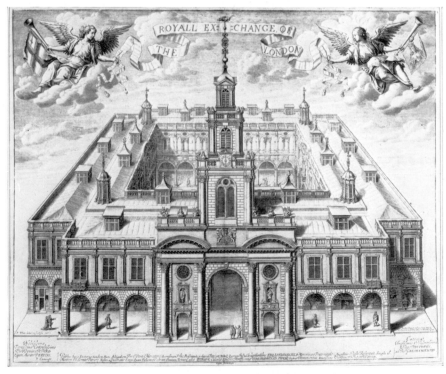

490. Edward Jerman. Royal Exchange (1671, destroyed).

491. John Bastard. Blandford. Town Hall (1734).

492. Monmouth. Shire Hall (1724).

493. Thomas White. Worcester. Guildhall (1721–4).

494. Vanbrugh. Morpeth. Town Hall (1714, reconstructed).

495. Edward Strong. St Bartholomew's Hospital. Gateway (1702–3).

496. Vanbrugh? Skelbrooke. Robin Hood's Well (c.1711).

497. Vanbrugh. Haymarket Opera House. Entrance (1704–5, destroyed).

498.   William Wakefield? York. Debtors' Prison (1709).

499.   Linton-in-Craven. Almshouses (1720).

500.   Kirkleatham. Sir John Turner's School (1709).

501. Blue Coat School, Westminster (1709).

502. Hawksmoor. Writing School, Christ's Hospital (1692–5, destroyed).

503. Henry Joynes. Carshalton. Water Pavilion (c.1725).

504. Hawksmoor. Kensington Charity School (1711–12, destroyed).

505. Windsor. Pump House on the Thames.

506. Vanbrugh? St James's Palace. Kitchen (1716–17).

507. Hawksmoor. St James's Palace. Stable Yard (1716–17).

508. Vanbrugh. Woolwich Arsenal. Old Board of Ordnance (1718–20).

509. Berwick-on-Tweed. Barracks. Main gate (1717).

510. Woolwich. Old Board of Ordnance. North end.

511. Berwick. Barracks. Courtyard block (after 1725).

512.   Woolwich. Old foundry (1716–17).

513.   Portsmouth. Landport gate.

514–15.   Woolwich. North and south gates of Dial Square (1717).

516. Vanbrugh. Chatham Dockyard. Great Store.

517. Chatham Dockyard. Gateway (1720).

518. Hawksmoor. Oxford. Old Clarendon Building. North side (1712–13).

519. Oxford. Old Clarendon Building. South side.

520.   William Townesend. Oxford. Trinity College. North range (1728).

521.   George Clarke and William Townesend. Oxford. The Queen's College. Hall and chapel front (begun 1714).

522.   Oxford. The Queen's College. Chapel doorhead.

523. Henry Aldrich. Oxford. Christ Church. Peckwater Quadrangle (1706–13).

524. Clarke. Oxford. Christ Church. Library (begun 1717).

525. Gibbs. Cambridge. Senate House (1722–30).

527. Oxford. All Souls. Chapel screen (1715–16).

530. Aldrich. Oxford. Trinity College. Chapel (1691–4).

526. Gibbs. Cambridge. King's College. Fellows' Building from west (1724–9).

529. Cambridge. Trinity College. Reredos (after 1706).

528. Robert Grumbold. Cambridge. Emmanuel College. Westmorland Building (1719–22).

531. Aldrich. Oxford. The Queen's College. Library (1693–4).

532. Oxford. Trinity College Chapel.

533. Clarke and Townesend. Oxford. Worcester College. Library (begun 1720)

534. Oxford. Trinity College. South gateway.

536. Hawksmoor. Oxford. The Queen's College. Gateway (1733-36).

535. Townesend. Oxford. The Queen's College. Hall (begun 1714).

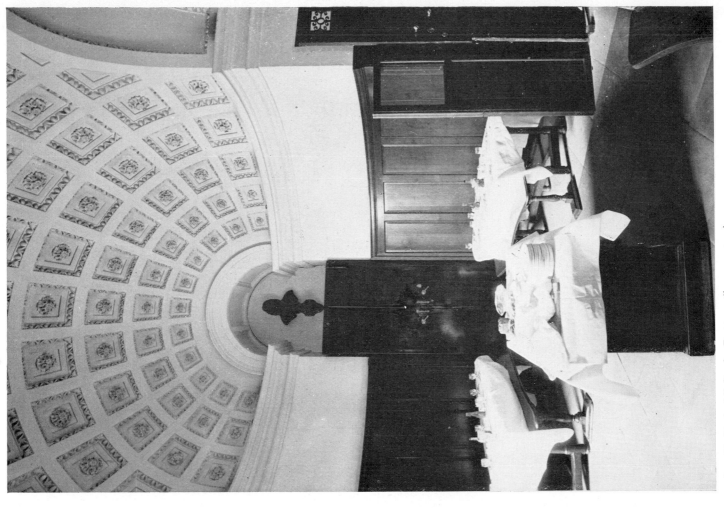

538. Oxford. All Souls. Buttery (begun 1730).

537. Hawksmoor. Oxford. All Souls. Hall (1730-3).

539-40. Gibbs. Oxford. Radcliffe Library (1737-49).

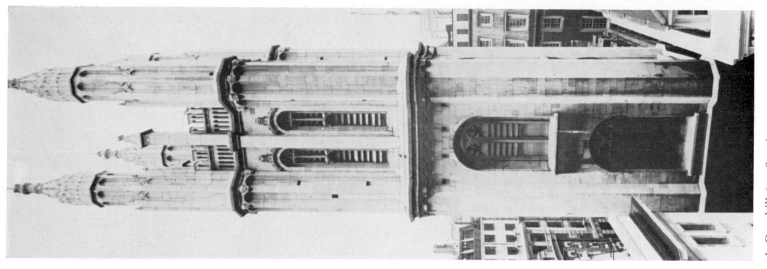

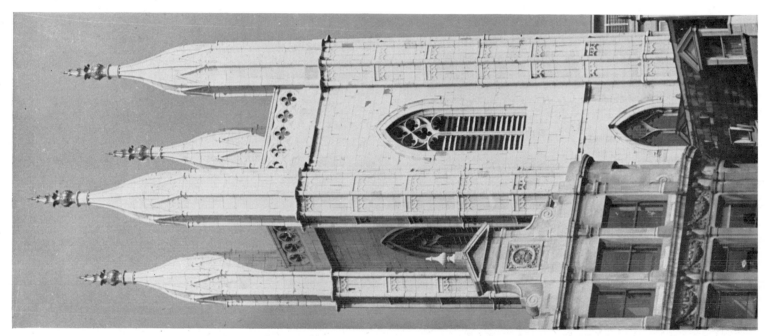

541–3. London Gothick towers. Wren. St Dunstan-in-the-East (1697–9). Wren. St Mary Aldermary (1702–4). Hawksmoor. St Michael, Cornhill (1718–24).

544.   Hawksmoor. Oxford. All Souls. North quadrangle (1716–35).

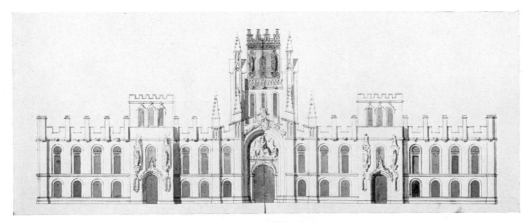

545.   Hawksmoor. Project for south front of All Souls (1708–9).

546.   St Mary, Warwick. From north.

547. St Mary, Warwick. Tower (1700–4).

549. Hawksmoor. Project for St Mary, Warwick (c.1694).

550. St Mary, Warwick. Nave capital.

548. Sir William Wilson. St Mary, Warwick (1698–1704).

552. Vanbrugh. Vanbrugh Castle, Greenwich (c.1718).

551. Westminster Abbey. Gable and west towers by Hawksmoor (1734-45).

THE ROYALL PALACE OF HAMPTON COURT
To the Right Honorable CHARLES SPENCER, Earle of SUNDERLAND, Baron of WORMLEIGHTON, one of her Majesty's Principal Secretary's of State &c.
This Plate is humbly Dedicated by your Lordships Most Obedient Servants

553. Hampton Court. View by Kip and Knyff (*c.*1710).

556. Four Faces. Castle Howard (*c.*1730).

555. Four Faces. Bramham (*c.*1725).

554. John Nost. Vase of the Seasons. Melbourne (1705).

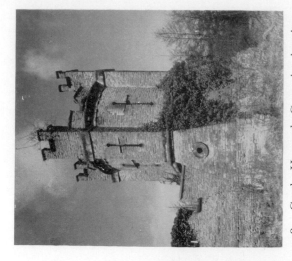

558. Castle Howard. Carrmire bastion.

561. Castle Howard. Garden pedestal.

560. Castle Howard. Obelisk (1714–15).

557. Castle Howard. Carrmire Gate (c. 1730).

559. Castle Howard. Pyramid Gate (1719).

564. Francesco Vassali. Castle Howard. Temple interior (1737–9).

562. Vanbrugh. Castle Howard. Temple (1726–39).

563. Castle Howard. Pyramid (1728).

565–6. Hawksmoor. Castle Howard. Mausoleum (1729–42).

567.   Duncombe. Open temple.

568.   Sir Thomas Robinson. Duncombe. Doric temple.

569.   Castle Howard. Mausoleum. Interior.

570.   Gibbs. Orleans House. Octagon (c.1720).

571–2. Archer. Wrest Park. Pavilion (1711–12).

573.   Wrest Park. Pavilion.

574.   Gibbs and Borra. Stowe. Boycott Pavilion (*c*.1730–60).

575. St Bride, Fleet Street. Urns.

576. The Monument. Finial.

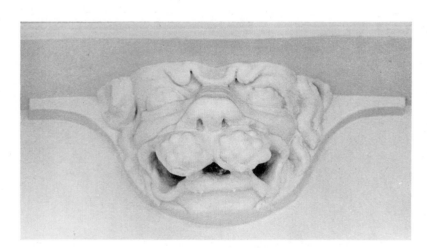

577. Chelsea Hospital. Corbel outside hall.

578. Wrest Park. Pavilion. Keystone.